THE ROAD TO
CIVITELLA
– 1944 –

THE ROAD TO
CIVITELLA
– 1944 –

The Captain, the Chaplain
and the Massacre

DEE LA VARDERA

FONTHILL

Fonthill Media Language Policy

Fonthill Media publishes in the international English language market. One language edition is published worldwide. As there are minor differences in spelling and presentation, especially with regard to American English and British English, a policy is necessary to define which form of English to use. The Fonthill Policy is to use the form of English native to the author. Dee La Vardera was born and educated in the United Kingdom; therefore British English has been adopted in this publication.

Fonthill Media Limited
Fonthill Media LLC
www.fonthillmedia.com
office@fonthillmedia.com

First published in the United Kingdom and the United States of America 2016

British Library Cataloguing in Publication Data:
A catalogue record for this book is available from the British Library

ISBN 978-1-78155-531-6

Typeset in 10pt on 13pt Sabon
Printed and bound in England

To my father, Warren Thomas Rawlins Richards (1900–1991)
Poet, soldier, priest and teacher

'INVICTUS'

Out of the night that covers me,
Black as the Pit from pole to pole,
I thank whatever gods may be
For my unconquerable soul.

In the fell clutch of circumstance
I have not winced nor cried aloud.
Under the bludgeonings of chance
My head is bloody, but unbowed.

Beyond this place of wrath and tears
Looms but the Horror of the shade,
And yet the menace of the years
Finds, and shall find, me unafraid.

It matters not how strait the gate,
How charged with punishments the scroll.
I am the master of my fate:
I am the captain of my soul.

William Ernest Henley (1875)

Prologue:
From Broken Stones

Sunday 6 May 2001
Church of Santa Maria Assunta
Piazza Don Alcide Lazzeri
Civitella in Val di Chiana
Italy

It had been raining hard that Sunday morning in Civitella, but now the warm Tuscan sun was back and the old flagstones in the square and the terracotta roof tiles were fast drying out. In the parish church of Santa Maria Assunta, the Holy Mass was drawing to a close. '*Vi benedica Dio onnipotente Padre, Figlio e Spirito Santo,*' intoned Don Tommaso Tonioni as he blessed the large congregation, who responded, '*Amen.*'

As Don Tommaso descended the altar steps, Keith Morgan turned to his mother, Barbara, who was sitting next to him. 'It's time to go, Mum.' They moved out of the pew and approached the altar. Barbara Morgan was carrying a small alabaster carving of the Last Supper, which she was giving to the church.

'Are you all right? Breathe deeply, smile, and imagine you are the Queen Mother,' Keith whispered. 'Don't worry, I'll do all the talking.' He had his speech folded safely in the inside pocket of his jacket. Two sheets—one in English, the other in phonetic Italian. 'I wish Dad was here,' he said.

'Your father would hate all this, you know, Keith. He really wouldn't have wanted a fuss made.' Barbara knew that her husband, Captain John Percival Morgan of the Royal Army Service Corps, was a quiet and modest man. He and his fellow officers and men of the British Eighth Army would never have expected that they would be remembered for their actions over fifty years ago. He would have been astonished to learn that a street had been named after him and a marble plaque erected in their honour in Civitella. He had simply done what any decent man would have done in his place; he helped women and children in need and brought relief to their suffering as much as he and his men were able to.

Like many soldiers who survived the war, once he was back home, John picked up from where he left off. He did not talk about where he had been, what he had seen, or what he had done; no one wanted to know anyway. Everyone just wanted to forget the horrors and privations of war, to get on with their lives and build a future for themselves and their families.

Although Barbara had seen the photographs John had taken while he was serving in the Army and had tracked his movements in North Africa and Italy, most of his time on active service was a mystery to her. She knew that he had been based near Arezzo, coordinating logistics for the Allied Forces (which were advancing north, towards Florence and the Gothic Line), but that was all. She also knew that he called Civitella in Val di Chiana his 'special village' and that he had seen terrible things that had upset him. John had told her that he and his friend Father Clement O'Shea, the Catholic chaplain (or 'Pop', as he called him), were in the area during the war and had spent time together in Civitella.

O'Shea had meant a lot to John Morgan. Friendships were precious back then; some lasted only briefly, others a lifetime. John and O'Shea had seen fellow officers blown up before their eyes and had escaped death themselves on a number of occasions. The bond formed in Italy between the two officers—the Welsh bank clerk and the Irish priest—was to last until O'Shea's death in 1965.

A few months before O'Shea's death, John and Barbara took their children, Keith and Alison, to visit him in his retirement home. Meeting O'Shea again must have awakened thoughts and memories in John, as when the family travelled to Italy on holiday that summer and made a special trip to Civitella. John was very quiet that day; he went off with Keith to visit the church and then walked slowly around the village, as if he was inspecting it. When he returned to the car, he said nothing and they drove off.

Barbara still missed her husband. He was just fifty-two years old when he died, in 1968. Today she felt particularly close to him and very proud. The people of Civitella had come to express their gratitude and love for him. She was not sure that John would have approved of the choice of gift; he had been brought up under the Church in Wales, but he had stopped going to church after the war. Pop, however, would have approved wholeheartedly. He would probably have made a joke about it— earning points in heaven. That was his way—always smiling, always joking, and making everyone feel at ease. They had been a good team, modest, softly spoken, upright John and loud, jolly, boisterous O'Shea.

Barbara had learned only recently what John and O'Shea (and the men under their command) had done to help the women and children of the village after the massacre of 29 June 1944, when the males in Civitella over the age of fifteen were rounded up and executed by the retreating Germans and Fascists. She could not bear to think about the suffering of all those people and how everyone gathered there that day had some connection to the horror; the legacy of war resonating down the generations.

As Barbara handed the gift to Don Tommaso, she bowed her head. Then she and Keith turned to face the side altar dedicated to *Caduti dell'eccidio di Civitella e di*

Cornia ('the fallen of the massacre of Civitella and Cornia) and bowed again. The seven-panelled marble wall plaque was inscribed with the names of 117 citizens of Civitella and fifty-eight of Cornia who died. An eternal flame shone above a framed photo of Don Alcide Lazzeri, the parish priest, who offered his life in exchange for those of his flock—but was the first one to be brutally murdered. There was so much to take in and to understand, so much to remember. Barbara returned to her seat.

Keith turned back to face the congregation, pausing while he prepared himself to deliver his speech from the lectern. He glanced around at the beauty and tranquillity of the church—the whitewashed walls, stained-glass windows, flickering candles, and polished oak pews. He remembered what his father had witnessed, recorded in photos taken just days after the village was liberated—the remains of charred bodies amongst the rubble of the nave. He took a deep breath and carefully enunciated the Italian version of his speech, thanking the inhabitants for their kindness to him and his family, saying how proud his father would have been at the way the people of Civitella had rebuilt their village and their lives.

After the applause from the congregation had died down, Keith returned to his seat and the Mayor of Civitella, Gilberto Dindalini, came forward to speak:

Ladies and gentlemen and friends, Mrs Morgan and her son Keith, welcome on this special occasion.

Captain Morgan, who during the period when the front line passed through here distinguished himself in the eyes of this community through his humanitarian acts and uncommon level of solidarity towards this community. That is to say that he has achieved not only what the Eighth Army accomplished in those years, that is, freeing our country from occupation by the Nazis and Fascists, but he also carried out substantial acts of love and solidarity towards the population stricken by war.

He did this in a deep, genuine and human manner, meaning putting at the disposal of the people not only what his Corps had available in terms of what was needed for survival, but also going without himself in order to obtain and bring toys to our children and allowing families and their children to have all the things they had a right to, not least hope, in that dreadful winter. For this, the community of Civitella is grateful to the family not only for being here, but also for those acts of humanity and great solidarity.

The *Santa Cecilia Filarmonica* band struck up the British national anthem. Everyone stood, and after a couple of verses, the music changed to '*Il Canto degli Italiani*', the Italian national anthem. The bells began tolling and the church doors were opened out into the square and the midday sun. Everyone streamed out and gathered in the square, smiling and chattering to each other. Many people wanted to have a word with the special visitors from England. Several women in their seventies and eighties came up to shake Barbara's hand and hug her. '*Grazie, mille. Mi ricordo il Capitano Morgan.*' ('Thank you very much. I remember Captain Morgan.')

One woman approached with a faded cotton handkerchief neatly ironed and folded, holding it out to Keith. She started to unfold it to show him. '*Questo era un regalo di Natale da vostro padre*,' ('This was a Christmas present from your father,') '*L'ho conservato da allora.*' ('I have kept it ever since.')

Another woman wiped a tear from her eye and said to Barbara in Italian and broken English, '*Un angelo nell'inferno* [An angel in hell]. I shall never forget Captain Morgan. He brought water. He brought life. He gave us hope.'

Barbara was overwhelmed by the kind words spoken by so many people, managing the occasional '*Grazie*', understanding the sentiments if not the meaning of every word.

'I'll tell you later, Mum,' Keith said, putting his hand on his mother's arm. He had picked up enough Italian to understand what was being said, and as he spoke French quite well, he made an intelligent guess at what he didn't know. The crowd was thinning out now as people moved away,

'Come on, Mum, let's get some pictures of the plaque.' Keith escorted his mother to the top of the steep cobbled steps leading down to Via di Mezzo, which led down towards the southern walls and Porta Aretina, the entrance to the village. This was now officially called '*Costa Capitano John Percival Morgan*'. British and Italian flags in sconces either side were unfurling in the light breeze. It was a wonderful partnership, Keith thought—a perfect union between Britain and Italy. He and his mother both looked closely at the inscription on the plaque on the wall, reading the words again:

COSTA
CAP. JOHN PERCIVAL MORGAN
COMUNE DI CIVITELLA

A ricordo di John Percival Morgan, di padre O'Shea e dei loro amici della 8th Armata Britannica, che offrirono preziosi aiuti ai sopravvissuti dell'eccidio del 29 giugno 1944

CIVITELLA, 6 MAGGIO 2001

8th BRITISH ARMY

In memory of John Percival Morgan, Father O'Shea and their friends of the 8th British Army, who gave precious aid to the survivors of 29th June 1944 Massacre

CIVITELLA, 6 MAY 2001

Keith put his arm round his mother and squeezed her close to him while someone took a photo. He could not help smiling; he was proud of the legacy of his father and his friend Father O'Shea. He was pleased that they had received recognition and that he was now part of it. His father had not said much to him except for recounting a few derring-do stories, such as escaping from France on a stolen motorbike and blowing up mines in the desert. Keith treasured those times he had shared with his father and regretted not spending more time with him. Now that he had learned so much about his father's past and what he did, he was able to see him in a different light.

Keith was proud that his father had made decisions at a difficult time; he had not walked away. He had taken charge of something he felt needed doing—actions that were not answerable to any commanding officer. It had been a group effort, of course, helping the villagers. Like any worthwhile enterprise, someone had to take the lead and do whatever it took to fulfil the task, even if it meant bending the rules and treading on a few toes. All this made Keith feel closer to his father. He had not always seen eye-to-eye with him, but then that was perfectly usual between fathers and teenage sons. If only John had lived to see him as an adult and father himself.

Keith moved away and turned to look again at the old buildings around the square, the *cisterna* (old well), the steps decorated with flowers, and the arches of the porticos leading towards Piazza Becattini, with more floral displays and flags. He remembered the photograph his father had taken of that view in July 1944, when he had jumped into a spare American truck in the depot and went to investigate the area. He came to a steep and inaccessible track leading up to what he could see was a fortified village, a ruined tower just visible atop the hill. He lit his pipe, put his foot down on the throttle, and kept going upwards, around bend after bend, until he reached the top and into the square. What he found there, he never forgot.

Acknowledgements

I would like to thank Keith Morgan for making his father's letters, photographs, and papers available and for his own research and memories of his father, mother, and grandparents. I would also like to thank his sister, Alison Newcombe, for her contributions and for lending me her father's diaries and photographs.

Grazie mille a: Dino Tiezzi and his wife, Gloria, for welcoming us into their home, for his willingness to talk to my husband and me about his life, and for sharing his vast knowledge of Civitella, showing us landmarks and places that Captain Morgan and Father O'Shea would have known well;

Monsignor Luciano Giovannetti, who talked to us during the torch-lit remembrance procession from Civitella Cemetery to Piazza Alcide Lazzeri on the evening of 28 June 2014, reliving the events of seventy years ago;

Ida Balò Valli, archivist and curator of 'Civitella Remembers', for her help and permission to use material from the commune archives, as well as quotations from survivors' memories, as collected in her book *Giugno 1944, Civitella Racconta* (1994);

Don Francesco Sensini for his insight into events from his own research for his book *Civitella 18 Giugno 1944 Eutanasia di una data*;

Terzilio Bozzi, for talking to us about members of his family who died in the massacre, and for showing us around the Remembrance Room;

and Maria Grazia Gualdani, owner of the beautiful *Antico Borgo*, for her hospitality, wonderful Tuscan cooking, encouragement, and help in contacting people.

Special thanks to: Giuseppe Lucarelli, for permission to use material from his website dedicated to his late mother, Lara Lammioni Lucarelli, including her *Memorie di un eccidio* (*Memories of a Massacre*) (1994);

Lt-Col. (Ret) Jonathan Powell for his help and military expertise;

Lt-Col. Vittorio Boccia, Officer of *Carabinieri*, Assigned to the Military Prosecutor of Rome, Doctor Marco De Paolis, for answering questions relating to the 'cupboard of shame' documents;

Alexander S. Grenfell, for the maps of Italy and Civitella;

Nicoletta Consales, for memories of her grandmother Enza Marsili, recorded as part of a school project;

to Richard Newman (who sadly passed away in 2014) for his memories of 'Cockie' O'Shea, and to his brother, Anthony Newman, for his help and permission to use photographs and extracts from the letters and diaries of his father, Major Philip Newman.

Thank you to: members of Merthyr Tydfil Historical Society for help with background information; Ceinwen Jones and Joe England (Cyfarthfa School); Mansell Richards (life in pre-war and post-war Merthyr); Jean Bevan, for inviting Keith and me to look around her home in The Parade; and John Meredith, for memories of working with John Morgan at Lloyds Bank, Cardiff.

Merci beaucoup à François and Bernadette Launay for hosting us and for organising a visit to *Musée Les Sanglots-Longs*, Réguiny, and to curator Françoise Le Breton for her guided tour and knowledge of the Resistance in Brittany.

Grateful thanks to: David Blake AMA, Curator, Museum of Army Chaplaincy; Father Godfrey Scott OSB and Alison Day at Douai Abbey Library and Archive; Father Patrick McKeowan CP of Our Lady of the Sacred Heart, Herne Bay, for drawing together archive material and also his kind gift of a 1937 Passionist prayer book; Father John Kearns CP, Provincial of the Congregation of the Passion of Jesus Christ in England and Wales, for his contacts and answering questions about the Order; Father Aidan Troy CP, Church of the English-speaking Community, Paris, for research in archives; Ms Elizabeth Teets, Special Collections Assistant, Passionist Historical Archives Collection at Weinberg Memorial Library of The University of Scranton, Pennsylvania; and Sylvia Gallotti, archivist, Lloyds Banking Group Archives.

Thanks to Eve Comper (who sadly passed away in 2015), Michael Baker, Tony Pozzetti and Patricia McMahan (*née* Jones) for their memories of Father O'Shea; and Mike Hedger for memories of the Herne Bay floods of 1953. Thanks also to Barbara Summerfield for reference to the diary of her father, Captain John 'Jack' Barrance MBE, Middlesex Yeomanry. Thanks to Norman Beale, Christine Cooper, David Hancock, Roy Quinton, Mary Rennie, Sue Richards, Adrian and Kate Scoyne, and David Shonfield for their help.

Thanks to the *Archivo della Memoria Civitella*; the IWM; the National Archives, Kew; the Second World War Experience Centre (SWWEC); the Royal Logistics Corps Museum; *Bundesarchiv*; the Lloyds Banking Group Archives; Herne Bay Historical Records Society; Cyfarthfa Castle Museum & Art Gallery; *The Catholic Herald*; and Telegraph Media Group Ltd for permission to use material. Thanks also to Pen and Sword for permission to quote from Philip Newman's memoir, which was reprinted as *Over the Wire* (2013).

Thank you to James Holland for answering queries about the war in Italy; to Victoria Belco for her advice on research and for reference to her splendid book, *War, Massacre and Recovery in Central Italy 1943–1948* (University of Toronto Press, 2010); and to Jay Slater and Joe Tranter at Fonthill Media, for their support.

Finally, special thanks to my husband, Alfred La Vardera, without whom this book could not have been written. He has been my translator, interpreter, fellow researcher, and critical friend. Also grateful appreciation is due for his translation of Lara Lammioni's memoir, *Memorie di un eccidio*.

CONTENTS

Maps

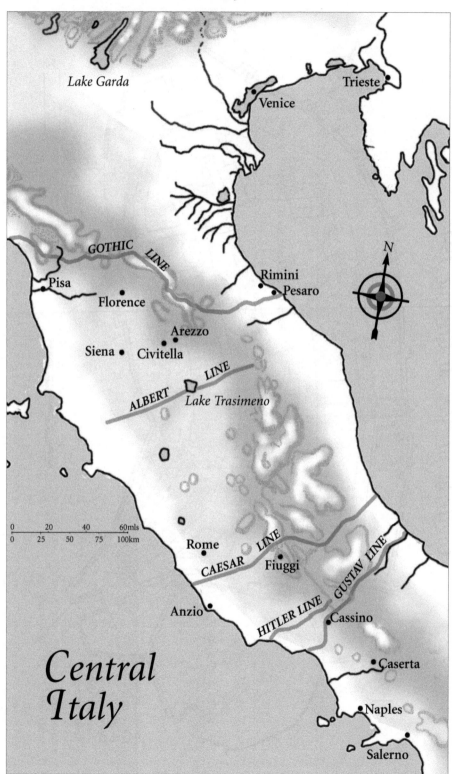

Central
Italy

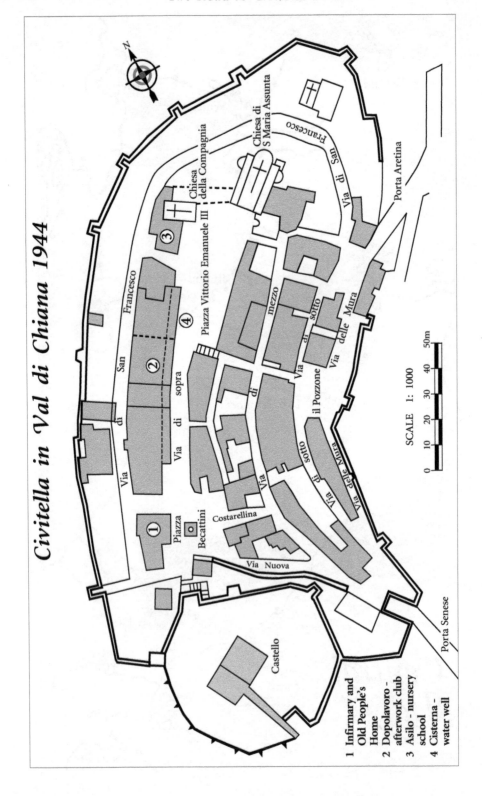

Civitella in Val di Chiana 1944

Porta Aretina

Chiesa di S Maria Assunta

Via di San Francesco

Chiesa della Compagnia

Piazza Vittorio Emanuele III

③

②

Via di sopra

Via di San Francesco

Via di mezzo

Via di sotto

Via delle Mura

④

il Pozzone

Via di sotto

Via delle Mura

Via delle Mura

④

①

Piazza Becattini

Costarellina

Via Nuova

Castello

Porta Senese

SCALE 1: 1000

0   10   20   30   40   50m

1 Infirmary and
   Old People's
   Home
2 Dopolavoro -
   afterwork club
3 Asilo - nursery
   school
4 Cisterna -
   water well

Author's Note and Glossary

Civitella

Civitella is both the name of a village and the collective name for the Commune of Civitella (*Il Comune di Civitella in Val di Chiana*). It is made up of Badia al Pino, the administrative centre since 1917, Ciggiano, Cornia, Oliveto, Pieve al Toppo, Pieve a Maiano, Tegoleto, Tuori, Viciomaggio, and other *frazioni* (hamlets). The village of Civitella is situated on the top of a hill, 530 m above sea level, overlooking the *Val di Chiana* (Valley of Chiana) in Arezzo province, Tuscany, in central Italy. In 2015, the Commune of Civitella has a population of 9,099; the population in 1944 was estimated at 9,400, which was about 1,000 more than before the war. This was due to the large influx of evacuees and refugees from other communes, the city of Arezzo, and other cities in Tuscany.

Italian Words

Il Podestà	The Mayor, not elected but appointed by the Fascist Party
L'Asilo	The nursery school
I Caduti	'The fallen' (in a battle or a war)
La Cisterna	The medieval well in the centre of the main square, Piazza Don Alcide Lazzeri (formerly Piazza Vittorio Emanuele III), where the village's rainwater supply was stored
Il Dopolavoro	Literally 'after-work', also known as *il Circolo* (*the Club*). The social and recreational clubs of the *Opera Nazionale Dopolavoro* (OND) were instituted during the Fascist regime to provide a meeting place for workers after work. They normally had a bar and a radio set and were run by locals trusted by the regime

Il massacro; l'eccidio; la strage	Italian words for 'massacre'
Il Podere	Farm
La Sala (stanza) della Memoria	The Civitella Remembrance Room, housed in the rooms formerly occupied by the *Dopolavoro*

Married Names

Italian women keep their own family name on marriage, but they sometimes combine both family names; the woman's family name comes first, followed by the husband's.

Memories of the Massacre

My retelling of the central events in this book—the 29 June 1944 massacre of Civitella, along with the important preliminary events of the shooting at the *Dopolavoro* on 18 June, is based on three main strands.

Firstly, of prime importance were the witness statements given to the Special Investigation Branch from November 1944 to March 1945, which were taken to record the events of that day and to help identify those responsible. These were written down in Italian and then translated into English and signed by the witnesses. There are about 230 statements available online at the Civitella Archives, digitised from original copies at The National Archives, Kew (see Bibliography). They were recorded soon after the events, but the questions asked were specific and limited. While many include personal feelings and reactions to what the interviewees had experienced, on the whole they are not like the victim statements that are presented in court today, which describe the impact and long-term effects.

Secondly, I have drawn on the memories recorded by Ida Balò Valli in 1994, fifty years after the massacre, published as *Giugno 1944: Civitella Racconta (June 1944: Civitella Remembers)*. These are more personal accounts, and they also include many of the young survivors who were not called to give statements in 1944. I also used the longer memoir of Lara Lammioni, which Ida encouraged her to write. This is a simple and heartfelt story of her life before the war, in her beloved Civitella, and the horrors of war and the suffering of her family that came afterwards. It is a valuable resource.

Lastly, I have used material from personal interviews in Civitella in 2013 and 2014.

I have weaved individual stories and accounts together to form one unified narrative, keeping to the original versions as much as possible and respecting each person's testimonies. There are undoubtedly inconsistencies and differences in perception in the recollection of such traumatic events—including, for example, ages, number of people present, location, and sequence of events. However, I have tried to take these into account and edit accordingly to avoid confusion.

Introduction

I first met Keith Morgan in May 2013. He thought I might be interested in hearing about his father's experiences during the Second World War in Italy—how he and his chaplain friend, Father Clement O'Shea, adopted a hilltop village in Tuscany in the aftermath of a terrible massacre on 29 June 1944.

Very little is known or has been written about the suffering of the residents of Civitella during this period of the war. The Italian civilians had been abandoned by their King to face the wrath of Germany, their betrayed ally, and a civil war that took place amidst the world war that was being fought around them. Similarly, the selfless help given by many British soldiers to the Italian civilians has gone largely unrecorded. Most of Italy suffered great loss of life and material destruction, but Tuscany was one of the regions most damaged by the war. As much as 10 per cent of the total destruction took place in this region, and over 13 per cent of the civilians who died in the war were Tuscan.

I felt that this was an important story to tell. Keith's own journey of discovery began as he followed in his father's wartime footsteps, which finally led Keith to Civitella in 1997. It was there that he discovered survivors who still remembered the British men from the Eighth Army who came to their aid in 1944. Through Keith's efforts, the memory of John Morgan and Clement O'Shea will be preserved in Civitella's collective memory; now, thanks to this book, the full story of the men's lives will be shared with a wider audience.

It has been a journey of discovery for me, too, in researching the lives of two very different men—a Welsh bank clerk and an Irish Passionist priest—examining material in archives and talking to people in the UK and in Italy who knew the men. I feel privileged to have met survivors of the massacre and members of their families in the beauty and tranquillity of their homes in present-day Civitella.

It has been difficult, at times, reading the many harrowing accounts by individuals who witnessed the massacre. Tragically, this was only one of many such atrocities that occurred in Italy during this period. Most of these killings were motivated by Hitler's efforts to eradicate any Italian partisan resistance by making the innocent civilian population viable targets. The order was to kill ten Italians for every German killed by partisans; it was eagerly acted upon by the Wehrmacht commanders and their troops.

I have learned a great deal while writing this book, and I have been greatly enriched by the experience. I hope that by relaying the narrative to the reader, I have done justice to everyone's contributions to this book and to the memory of those who gave their lives in the fight for freedom.

Dee La Vardera
Calne, Wiltshire
November 2015

PART I

PART I

Coal

Merthyr Tydfil—a stinking smog, foul, acrid air. The smell of Cyfarthfa Iron and Steelworks was in your nostrils from the moment you got up in the morning to the time your head hit the pillow at night. It was a place where the enamel on your bath, if you were lucky to have one, turned green from the acid in the air. There was a smell of rotten eggs—that rancid smell of sulphur released in plumes of smoke from the belly of the blast furnaces that forged the iron and steel to build a brave new world.

There was a huge appetite for materials in the developing world of technology and communications during the nineteenth and early twentieth century. Bridges and railways were hungry for girders and tracks across continents, serving new railway companies—many founded in the 1830s—from the Stockton & Darlington and New Orleans & Nashville to the Petersburg-Pauloffsky Railway. The enormous engines of war were fed by cannons for the Navy and munitions for the Army. Tall chimneys dominated the skyline of the Welsh valleys, their smoke a constant reminder of what kept thousands of men employed, putting food on the table and a roof overhead. Everything was fuelled by the need for coal.

Monday morning was washday, and the Morgan household at No. 9 The Parade, Merthyr Tydfil, was no different. Women at home everywhere were busy doing the washing and hanging it out to dry in back gardens or on lines across streets. A system of pulleys on either side of the road made it easy for women to collect in the dry clothes and then take them back indoors. If the furnaces at the steelworks at Dowlais had been opened that morning and were letting off smoke, a cry would go up: 'Washing in! Washing in!' Everyone rushed out to gather in the washing before the ash-laden fumes belching out from the open furnaces could cover their clean sheets and clothes in filth and smuts, undoing all their hard work of scrubbing, rinsing, and mangling.

All the sounds, smells and hustle and bustle of domestic life were familiar to young John Morgan. The pits and slag heaps and railway tracks were the backcloth to life; the iron and steel works were the beating heart of the town and district, casting a long shadow over every aspect of life in South Wales. Home was an immaculately kept semi-detached town house, at the centre of which was his mother, Louisa. The dining room was a sanctuary of polished wood, sparkling china and glasses, and white linen that was only disturbed for special occasions. John would never go in unless directed to do something: fetch a glass vase, put the cutlery out on the table.

The drawing room, on the other hand, was the family room. It was comfortable and well-used, although John and his father still tiptoed around and made sure that they put things back if they moved anything. Louisa's sharp eyes could spot a misplaced ornament, a bit of fluff, or a footprint on the parquet from a hundred paces. Even the leather-bound books stood to attention on Arthur's mahogany revolving bookcase, their bindings glossy from cleaning. The glass panes of the display cabinet sparkled—all the better to view the rows of butterflies and moths, pieces of amber, and fossils within. The hands of the grandfather clock in the corner were neither fast nor slow, always showing the correct time.

Everything ran like clockwork in the Morgan household, just like the trains that his father, Arthur, kept moving around the country for Stephenson Clarke Ltd. The company was part of the Powell Duffryn Steam and Coal Company, transporting coal from the collieries to the railways and the iron and steel works. Railways were in his blood, and coal was in his heart. His family had moved to Merthyr Tydfil from Hereford, where his widowed mother, Eliza Morgan, had been a licensed innkeeper of The Railway Inn, in Dinmore near Bodenham. She had a good head for business, and the inn prospered, conveniently placed as it was for the tired, hungry, and thirsty railway workers and engineers building the new line from Leominster to Hereford. The 1901 census for Merthyr lists a sixteen-year-old Arthur as 'Railway Traffic Manager'. By the time he married, he had advanced to the position of Agent for a wholesale coal company.

John Percival Morgan was born on 17 March 1916 to Arthur Percival Morgan and Louisa Nathina (*née* Evans), three years after their marriage at Cyfarthfa Parish Church on 6 January 1913. He was an only child and a sickly one in his early years, having survived an attack of peritonitis that made his mother ever more vigilant about her son's welfare. He was cosseted and protected and kept away from other children, not attending school until he was nearly twelve. Home was his whole world for much of his early childhood.

His mother tried to protect him from the outside world for as long as she could. She did not want him to speak Welsh, which she thought was a dead language; despite speaking it fluently herself, she saw it as an impediment rather than an asset. John would get a rap on the knuckles if he so much as said '*Bore da*' to anyone. His mother thought a good education was the key to success in life, and her son joining the ranks of the professional class would ensure that he did not end up going down the pits or working at the ironworks.

Arthur agreed with Louisa on most family matters; he would not have dreamed of airing his opinions or arguing against his wife's domestic decisions. They believed in leading a moral, upright life, working hard and doing the best they could. They wanted the same for their boy. They did not want their son exposed to the less salubrious aspects of an industrial town, or to be led astray by the common youths nearby; after all, the area known as 'Chinatown' was just down the road. It was a place once described as 'a den of drunkards, thieves, rogues and prostitutes, whose general behaviour was completely foreign to the normal hard working respectable Welsh Chapel way of life.'[1] It was a place best avoided due to its reputation, which acted as a warning to children—it was where they could end up if they did not behave themselves and keep out of trouble.

As a former teacher in the Rhondda Valley, it was an easy decision for Louisa to teach her son at home. She was fortunate to have her parents living next door at No. 7, along with her two sisters and two brothers (until they eventually married and moved away). They too had plenty of experience in education, and John's world expanded under their care.

Louisa's father, John Evans, was an inspector of schools in the Merthyr District, the family having moved to Merthyr in 1892. He was a brilliant teacher; on 22 July 1933, his obituary in the *Merthyr Express* described him as 'a burning and shining lamp' that had 'a profound knowledge of human nature, and [he] knew well how to deal with men'. He published numerous booklets on nature studies during his career, later being elected as Fellow of the Linnean Society, the world's oldest biological society. After he retired in 1923, he was awarded an MA from the University of Wales 'for services to his native country'.

Louisa's two sisters were distinguished teachers: Frances Juan Evans, a graduate of University College Aberystwyth, was the first headmistress of Cyfarthfa Castle Girls' Secondary School; Gwladys Evans became headmistress of Twynyrodyn Girls' School, Merthyr.

Family outings were popular. Everyone loved the busy, noisy fête and gala held at Cyfarthfa Park on bank holiday Monday in aid of the Merthyr Hospitals Fund. There were brass bands, sideshows, races, and prizes to win in the lucky dip. The family enjoyed going to film shows and entertainments at the Temperance Hall and Gilbert and Sullivan operettas performed by the local operatic group at their church. Louisa always wished she had learned to play the piano. When she inherited her mother's old upright, it took pride of place in the front room. She found John a music teacher so he could learn and kept an eye on his progress as he practised his scales every day.

John particularly liked the time he spent with his father. Arthur tried, unsuccessfully, to teach his son to swim at the Gwaunfarren Baths. He took John with him when he visited friends, especially when he dropped in on fellow lepidopterists to see what butterflies they had added to their collections, or to look at ammonites and insects captured in pieces of amber resin that had been found locally.

John was brought up to be curious and interested in the world around him. He loved reading and his mother and aunts read to him all the time. He bought *The Modern Boy* magazine each week with his pocket money. It was full of Biggles stories and free sets of cards to collect, or metal models of a train, a car, or a seaplane to send off for. He devoured his father's copies of *Wireless World* and used the knowledge he gained to good purpose, once building a crystal set in his bedroom.

His father was an avid reader and a keen naturalist, no doubt influenced by his father-in-law's interests. His bookcase was filled with volumes like *The Harmsworth Encyclopaedia*, *The Collected Works of Shakespeare*, copies of *The Astrological Year*, *Flora and Fauna of the British Isles*, Hume's *A Treatise on Human Nature*, Darwin's *On the Origin of the Species*, and Isaac Walton's *The Compleat Angler*. Even though he was a man of deep faith, a member of the Church of Wales, and a sidesman at Cyfarthfa Parish Church, he had an open mind and heart and a liberal outlook on life.

The time eventually came for Louisa and Arthur to decide on John's future schooling; satchels, uniforms, and homework beckoned. Arthur had attended Hereford Cathedral School and valued the traditions of such an esteemed educational institution. It was agreed that the best local school was Cyftharfa Castle Secondary School for Boys. Everything was founded on coal in the town, including the school, which was housed in a nineteenth-century turreted castle, the former home of the Crawshay family, whose wealth was made in the iron and steel industry and acquisition of collieries. Who could fail to be impressed by a school in a castle set in acres of parkland and gardens, and entering the grounds through wrought iron gates, up a long sweeping drive leading to the entrance? Education is a serious business.

The headmaster at the time was David John Davies. An inspection in 1929, two years after John Morgan joined the school, reported:

> The school is building up for itself sound traditions of culture, scholarship and athletics; the boys are cheerful, alert and well behaved, and should develop into worthy, thoughtful citizens.[2]

John was a popular boy and a good all-rounder, although not particularly sporty. He enjoyed working with his hands and making things at school. He gave his grandma a scissors rack he had made in woodwork. 'I had 8 out of 10 marks', he wrote in his diary. He also 'Made a table lamp for mother out of a ginger jar' and 'Made soap in Chemistry, brought some home'. He was very good at mathematics and science, and loved the time he spent in the science laboratory, peering into test tubes at sodium sizzling in water, or Petri dishes, checking on the progress of mould growing on some host substance.

The 1930 class photo shows fourteen-year-old John at the end of the middle row, arms firmly crossed, smiling confidently at the camera. He sits five places down from his Physics teacher and form master, Evan Davies. 'Dai Bump', as he was known to the boys, was an idiosyncratic character, famous, among other things, for being the owner of a motorcar—something rare in those days. John looked up to his form master and teacher; his own love of science and fast motor vehicles was firmly established at school.

There was obviously a bit of a rebellious streak in John's character. One day, he had stayed behind in the science laboratory after a lesson and decided to try an experiment of his own. He wanted to see what would happen if he detached the Bunsen burner from the rubber tube that connected to the gas tap and blew down the rubber tube into the hole leading to laboratory's main supply, which was provided by the Merthyr Gas and Lamp Company. Whatever he managed to prove scientifically is uncertain, except that a solitary schoolboy was capable of blowing the gas back along the pipe and extinguishing all the lights on the ground floor of the school. It could have resulted in a serious explosion, but the alarm was raised, the school evacuated, and no one came to any harm. This little adventure did not stop John from going on to complete his education and pass his Higher Certificate examination.

He still enjoyed spending time with his father. One of Arthur's great loves was fly-fishing, and John accompanied him on fishing trips to local rivers and reservoirs—although John did not take the sport up as an adult. He enjoyed being out in the fresh air, watching his father choosing and fitting the fly to the line and then waiting to see what fish would be fooled by the feathery lure. One diary entry in May 1930 records: 'Cycled up to the Beacons. Father up there. Caught 8 fish and gave 6 away.' Arthur was well-known in the area for his skill and expertise as a trout fisherman. In 1955, the headline of his obituary in the *Merthyr Express* proclaimed: 'Death of a fly fisherman'. The opening paragraph concentrated on this aspect of his life:

> Mr Morgan was a keen and noted fly fisherman, having taken an interest in the sport from an early age. He fished mainly in the Cardiff Corporation reservoirs and was a member of the Cardiff Fishing Club.

Arthur liked taking his son into town and particularly to his favourite high street retailer, Gay & Son, a saddler and fishing tackle merchant. On the way, he would point out landmarks and buildings that meant something special to him. Flooks, the jewellers, was one such place. Arthur would tell John again—for he knew the story well—how the shy young railway clerk won the heart of the pretty young schoolmistress. This story was passed down to John's son, Keith:

> My grandfather proposed to my grandmother Louisa on a bridge near the stream that flows from Pen y Fan. They were out on a Sunday ride and stopped to admire the view. They propped their bicycles against the stone bridge and he put his hand in his pocket and drew out a box. Inside was a selection of the engagement rings that Mr Flooks had entrusted my grandfather with on sale or return. My grandmother accepted the marriage proposal and picked her ring. They were married six months later.

His mother, Louisa, disliked anyone who disrupted her domestic harmony. Arthur had learned to keep out of the way when Louisa was 'on the warpath', as he put it—if something had been disturbed or misplaced, or if smuts had ruined her washing. However, he knew the importance of order and precision in thought and action, and also of attention to detail. His reputation at Stephenson Clarke depended on these qualities, so he respected and appreciated anyone else who displayed them at home or at work. John inherited this work ethic from his father.

Like many middle class men of his time, Arthur was fascinated by astrology. He used to prepare astrological charts for friends, spending hours poring over their information—dates and times of births, the position of the planets, the sun, and the moon at the moment of a person's birth. All they wanted to know was what the future held; Arthur began his son's chart on the day he was born.

In 1975, John's widow, Barbara, was sorting through her recently deceased mother-in-law's papers when she came across one of Arthur's astrological charts in a drawer. It caught her eye because of the heading: 'Chart for John Percival Morgan 17.07.1916'. It was her husband's future, mapped out in the positions of the planets and cosmic influences. She was so upset when she read the predictions that she destroyed it. According to Arthur's calculations, John was going to be away for a long time in difficult and dangerous circumstances, but he would come back safely. He would marry and have a good job, financial security and a happy life—but the chart stopped at 1968.

Even though John had been dead for nearly eight years, it was upsetting for Barbara to think that her husband's fate had not been in his own hands but sealed in the stars above. Ironically, during the last few months of his illness, when Barbara was nursing him at home, John found comfort in his favourite poem, 'Invictus'. He would keep repeating lines over and over again—'I am the master of my fate. I am the captain of my soul,'—as though he might be able to summon the power to conquer the deadly cancer within.

2

Money

John could not wait to leave school, but he had no idea what to do with the rest of his life. What any seventeen-year-old leaving school wants is money in his pocket and a degree of independence. He didn't know how he would achieve either; there was not a lot of choice in the current economic climate. His friend Geoff was going to university to study medicine, and Mervyn was joining the family grocery business. Neither of these careers was open to John.

There was not going to be any money for university, but if John found suitable employment then the burden would be eased at home. He may have been sheltered from the worst effects of unemployment, but his family was still feeling the pinch. He understood how tough life was. He had seen women queuing for parish relief and men hanging around street corners with nothing to do, nowhere to go, except up the reservoir to catch fish for their tea. There were others who went off to find fuel, scrabbling about in the shallow workings of the mines on the surrounding hills to dig up chips of coal for the fire or to sell on for a few shillings.

Life in South Wales in the 1930s was bleak; like other industrial areas, it had been affected by the decline in the reliance on heavy industries and the growing instability in Europe. What was young John equipped to do? Even though he was a dab hand at odd jobs around the house—painting and decorating, building a shed, repairing brickwork in the scullery, and even mending his grandma's vacuum cleaner—he did not see a future in this sort of work. Perhaps he would have to leave home to find work. Life was not going to be easy. He was comfortable at home, and he had always had the best of everything.

It was Uncle Emrys Evans who came to his nephew's rescue (and to Louisa and Arthur's relief). As the manager of Lloyds Bank in Rhymney, he knew when positions came up at local branches and told his sister that he would put in a good word for John and write him a reference if required. It was practically a *fait accompli* when a vacancy did arise. As there were no other opportunities open to him, John could not go against his parents' wishes.

The vacancy for a bank clerk came up at Lloyds Blackwood, about 14 miles from home, and John received a letter inviting him to an interview with the manager. His parents were delighted and Arthur set to preparing his son for the occasion, stressing the importance of making a good first impression; a firm handshake and a clear, confident voice were important, as were well-polished shoes.

Whether John followed his parents' advice or he was just his normal, charming self, Mr Mountjoy, the manager, offered him the position. Louisa was pleased to see her only child set on the path to a proper career, in a white-collar job with a pension—no black face or dirty overalls for him. It was a job with prospects—clean work, above ground, far away from the coalface and the burning heat of the furnaces and noisy and dangerous machinery. There were reminders everywhere of the dangers faced by working men. The man who served Louisa at Dickie's, the butchers, had lost both hands and forearms in an accident on the railways. Even though he could dextrously wrap the meat, take money, and give change using his stumps and mouth, it was a sad sight.

John's son, Keith, eventually went to work for Lloyds Bank as well. There, he witnessed the long-lasting effects of working down the mines:

> It's still vivid in my mind. I could identify the former miners as they came in by the sound of laboured, heavy breathing and rattling chests. I was shocked and fascinated by the gnarled and broken hands that reached across the counter to pay a bill or sign a receipt, marked with tattoos of coal dust in their veins.

John was grateful for the opportunity but not excited about going to work in an office. No sooner had he left one institution than he was joining another—although he would have no embroidered crest on his blazer. He left home each day in a three-piece suit, Van Heusen shirt, dark tie, and polished shoes, as befitted the position of a bank employee.

He started at Blackwood in May 1934, alongside two other clerks. It was a small branch, but it was a busy little place; the opening hours were 10 a.m.–3 p.m. weekdays and 9 a.m.–12 p.m. Saturdays. Of course, John had to be in earlier to set up the counter, check the post, and sort incoming letters and payments. He often did not get away until 5 p.m., and sometimes he was responsible for locking up, having control of the keys. Security was a serious matter at any bank, whatever the size, what with the responsibility for the safekeeping of cash and cheques overnight. He did not mind as it made him feel quite important as a junior. He started to enjoy the routine of work and was pleased to be doing something useful and bringing home a wage. More importantly, with any luck, he could keep some money to spend on himself. He knew what he would buy as soon as he had saved enough—a motorcycle.

John was bored with his bicycle and aspired to owning a motorcycle, having an eye on a Brough Superior like that of his hero, T. E. Lawrence. A fellow Welshman, Lawrence was also known as 'Lawrence of Arabia', the famous leader of the Arabs in the First World War. In the end, John could only afford a second-hand BSA 2.49-hp De Luxe, which he bought from the garage near where he worked. He spent any spare time he had riding the bike, polishing it, or just tinkering with it. He preferred staying in and cleaning spark plugs to going out to a football match or having a drink with colleagues.

After work and at weekends, John took off on his motorbike, heading out of town towards the lush greenness of the distant hills of the Brecon Beacons, racing along the main road, past the Cyfarthfa Park Lake, over the Taff, on up to the reservoir and the freedom of fields and dense woodland. One late afternoon, he left home, heading for the country out on the Brecon Road. Wrapped up in the speed and exhilaration of the moment, he misjudged a bend and veered off the road and onto the verge. He and the bike parted company. The bike ended up in a clump of brambles, while John went flying through the air, over the handlebars, landing on the other side of a dry-stone wall and knocking himself out. He lay there all night, waking up in the early hours of the morning to find himself still in one piece. He made his way back on to the road, retrieved his bike from the undergrowth, and pushed it all the way home. When he finally arrived home, his worried mother was waiting on the doorstep.

Taking risks was part of his nature, but not so at the bank. John was conscientious and meticulous with paperwork and friendly but not overfamiliar with customers. Mr Mountjoy recognised a good worker; pleased with his new clerk's manner and conduct, he sent John out to visit bigger branches to widen his experience. He also sent John on courses and entered him for the Institute of Bankers examinations, which John passed. After three years at the Blackwood branch, John moved to the slightly bigger branch at Dowlais in 1937, which was nearer to home. He remained there until he joined the Army.

He was a relatively independent young man now, gradually moving away from the loving tyranny of his mother's requests and routines. He had a work life and a social life separate from his parents, although he still attended church and visited his relatives. He had his own circle of friends, which had expanded to include girls from work and the sisters and cousins of friends he still knew from school. His friends were now young men and women who were working or studying, and he was even willing to leave his motorbike for other pursuits with them.

After work on Fridays, he met friends at Zanelli's in the High Street, where they talked for hours over tea and cake until someone said they felt like having fish and chips and they would go off find a place in town. On Saturday nights, if they felt flush and wanted to impress the girls, they would go to the Castle Cinema. There were proper usherettes and a lounge with wicker basket chairs and waitresses who served light refreshments before the show. Mostly, however, it was the smaller and cheaper Palace Cinema or a variety show at the Temperance Hall, near the railway station.

Marjorie Jenkins turned up one Saturday at Zanelli's, where a gang of his friends was meeting before going to the cinema. John recognised her instantly as the pretty girl he regularly saw at the tram stop near his office. So their friendship began. By the time the war came, John had bought his first car—a Ford Prefect—and acquired a fiancée.

It was only a matter of time until war was officially declared. Britain had been living with the possibility for over a year, since the Munich crisis in 1938 and the 'peace for our time' speech that Neville Chamberlain had given. The British people had been led to believe that Germany had no desire to go to war with Britain again; Hitler had signed the non-aggression pact despite having forced Czechoslovakia to hand over the Sudetenland to Germany.

Over the last few months, the prospective war had dominated the newspapers, the radio, and discussions at the dinner table. Headlines such as 'Germans Sweep On' and 'Hitler's Next Coups' added to the nation's fear and anxiety. Leaflets had already come through letterboxes—'War Emergency, Information and Instructions'—on such topics as lighting restrictions, closure of schools, and 'fire precautions and methods of dealing with incendiary bombs'. These leaflets ended with the supposedly cheery admonition: 'Keep a good heart: we are going to win through.'

For many people, even in these uncertain times, it meant carrying on as usual at home and work—'Keep Calm and Carry On', as another recently released Ministry of Information poster exhorted. Unanswerable questions hung in the air. How would work at the bank be affected? Who would be called up? Would jobs still be there to come home to? In spite of this, some were still shocked when the Prime Minister made the declaration of war.

At 11.15 a.m. precisely on Sunday 3 September 1939, Alvar Lidell announced that Prime Minister Neville Chamberlain was about to speak from the Cabinet Room of No. 10 Downing Street. Things would never be the same again. In spite of newspaper headlines declaring 'Britain at War' or 'War with Germany', people still hoped and prayed that Chamberlain might pull something out of the bag at the last minute, something that would prevent the country from going to war. However, they were to be disappointed:

> This morning the British Ambassador in Berlin handed the German Government a final note stating that, unless we heard from them—by 11 o'clock—that they were prepared at once to withdraw their troops from Poland, a state of war would exist between us. I have to tell you now that no such undertaking has been received and, consequently, this country is at war with Germany.

Despite the obviously negative connotations, war can offer opportunity; for example, it was potentially lucrative for some people in the Valleys. Coal, iron, and steel would be very valuable in Britain's war against Hitler, and what a shame so many works had closed and industries run into the ground. Of course, there were plenty of unemployed men who would now have employment of a completely different kind.

As he listened to that broadcast with his parents in the drawing room at No. 9 The Parade, John may have been most affected by the Prime Minister's final words:

> It is the evil things that we shall be fighting against—brute force, bad faith, injustice, oppression and persecution—and against them I am certain that the right will prevail.

Maybe it was the patriotic sentiments expressed:

> To serve your country and defend it from tyranny is one of the highest ideals of any society.

What would happen now to the Morgan family? Things had remained much the same for Arthur during the First World War. He had been in a reserved occupation, undertaking essential work at Stephenson Clarke, where his experience in coal transportation was vital. Things would be different now. Young men would leave the valleys and never return. Perhaps John's work at the bank would keep him safe. Indeed, his safety would have been assured if he had been two years older; under the National Service Act enacted at the outbreak of war, bank employees were deemed to be in a reserved occupation and exempt from military service if they were over the age of twenty-five.

At twenty-three years old, John must have felt ready to face what lay ahead and meet whatever challenges came his way. He wanted to be master of his own fate—captain of his soul. Like many young men, he may have felt that this was the beginning of a big adventure. King and Country beckoned.

On 9 January 1940, John Morgan did not go to work. Instead, he took off on his motorbike to the nearest recruiting office in Pontypridd, where he volunteered for the Armed Services. He desperately wanted to join the Royal Air Force, but the Regimental Sergeant Major had other ideas when he read John's qualifications. John held a driving licence, was an experienced driver, he had passed banking examinations, he was good with figures, and he spoke a bit of French. There was only one way to go—the Royal Army Service Corps.

John was no doubt disappointed. He could see the RAF uniform and the wings on his shoulder slowly vanish into thin air. However, at least he would not be stuck at home like his father had been, pen-pushing in a dingy office.

John's civilian life was over for the foreseeable future. He was now Private John Percival Morgan, Army No. P160250. He had swapped his bank clerk's suit and tie for a khaki uniform and cap.

3

The Passionist Way

Red, white and blue bunting fluttered between tents and stalls as people busied themselves setting up trestle tables, laying out their wares, arranging sideshows, and preparing refreshments. The 1st Whitstable Scout Group Band was playing a medley of patriotic tunes, adding to the festive atmosphere as the general public started to gather in the grounds of La Sainte Union Convent High School, Herne Bay, for the annual Catholic Church fête. Perhaps this was going to be the last peacetime fête to be held.

Father Clement O'Shea, the parish vicar, had been in charge of the annual event for a number of years, and locals still remember these occasions today. He was a local legend, famous for his organisational skills, originality, and effectiveness in getting people to part with their money. That day, Saturday 29 July 1939, his magic touch would ensure, once again, that crowds from miles around would come, especially to see the guest of honour invited to open the fête.

Everyone loved 'Father Clem', as they called him. Everyone who knew him, Catholic and non-Catholic alike, said the same—they felt better for just being in his company. As he strolled around the grounds, checking that everything was in order, he was frequently stopped by members of his congregation who wanted to show their appreciation of his work with invitations to come for a meal or a drink. Former altar boy Tony Pozzetti remembers Father Clem coming to his house regularly for supper or taking a tot of whisky, being offered the comfortable armchair in front of the fire:

> Catholics are very inward-looking, and it was a close community but I always felt that priests were lonely people. It was a bit of company for Father Clem away from the Retreat House, where he lived.

There was a good deal of excitement and anticipation at the choice of celebrity. Once again, O'Shea had managed to secure someone special, a real crowd-puller—'The Fastest Man on Earth', Captain George Eyston MC, *Légion d'honneur*, current holder of the World Land Speed Record.[1] Everyone had heard about the man in his wonder car, Thunderbolt, which had reached 357 mph on the Bonneville Salt Flats, Utah, finally beating Sir Malcolm Campbell's record in his own immortal Bluebird. The man whose face had appeared on the front page of every newspaper and magazine, on posters and advertisements for cars and motor oils, was now in their own little Kent town.

Everyone needs a hero. There were dark, threatening clouds gathering on the horizon. The great machinery of war was already oiled and fuelled, ready to follow its inevitable path. The country needed brave men to face the approaching Armageddon. What was better than a couple of hours of fun and laughter, basking in the glory of a moment, in the presence of a person of courage and tenacity—someone to inspire and look up to? He was a war hero and a living legend.

However, heroism comes in many forms and courage is displayed in many different ways. O'Shea, who stood quietly at the side as Capt. Eyston took centre stage, would also soon find himself called Captain, and his vocation would be tested in the harshest of circumstances.

The congregation had rushed straight off after Sunday mass, with barely a wave or a thank you to their parish priest—everyone had to get home in time to hear Prime Minister Neville Chamberlain address the nation on the BBC Home Service, What a choice! The Lord's Day, the Sabbath, the one day set aside in the week for rest and for families to pray, play, and share a meal together—but there was nothing but war talk everywhere, the state of the country, how we could be spared, how we could not. Newspapers and wireless broadcasts were full of it and preparations well in progress. Sandbags were piled up on street corners in Herne Bay, barbed wire strung along the sea front and gas masks ready in local depots. War was inevitable after the invasion of Poland. It was now a matter of waiting.

The last time anyone had taken such an interest in a news broadcast had been when Edward VIII had abdicated in December 1936, which had stunned the nation. No one was expecting good news this time either. Everyone knew there was no turning back, even though they hoped that war could be avoided at the last minute. The winds of change had blown up the Thames Estuary from the Channel, and a deep chill spread into every body and soul.

O'Shea had been preparing himself for months. As a reservist chaplain, he had received preliminary papers of his imminent call-up. He would soon swap the habit he wore for that of an Army officer. He would continue to wear his precious crucifix round his neck to indicate his position as chaplain.

The country was set on the inevitable path to war. How could anyone believe that a solution would present itself to the grave situation in Europe? The line had been crossed. The promise to protect the Poles against the German aggressor had to be honoured. Tyrants could not be allowed to flourish. There could be no peaceful resolution.

The words of Leviticus hung in the air from his morning sermon: 'You shall not take vengeance or bear a grudge against the sons of your own people, but you shall love your neighbour as yourself: I am the Lord.' Would anyone heed such words?

It had happened before, only there had not been radio broadcasts in 1914. News was broken by messages over the telephone or in telegrams. If you were not one of those to hear the reports, the newspapers left you in no doubt: 'Britain at War', the front pages declared, published only hours after the announcement. Some people actually celebrated, cheering that they would jolly well give the Kaiser a bloody nose! Surely no one would cheer at the prospect of war again.

Compassion and suffering were the tenets of O'Shea's faith, and no doubt he prayed all the more on the eve of the outbreak of war, reciting the words of his favourite prayer:

> My crucified Jesus, I devoutly adore the wound in Thy Sacred Side. Ah! By the blood, which Thou didst shed from it, enkindle in my heart the fire of Thy love, and give me grace to persevere in loving Thee to all eternity. Glory be to the Father.[2]

How long before seats in the pews of Our Lady of the Sacred Heart were empty where young men and boys would have sat? How soon would he be administering to other boys far from home, in need of comfort in a strange and hostile land? The world would suffer again. '*Bella, horrida bella, et Thybrim multo spumantem sanguine cerno*'—'Wars, horrible wars, and the Tiber foaming with much blood'. O'Shea knew about bloodshed, and not just from studying Virgil.

Father Clement was born Maurice Francis Dominic O'Shea in 1897 into a military family in Aldershot. His father, Timothy O'Shea, was Irish, while his mother, Edith Lovelace, was English. They had three sons and a daughter. Maurice's father was born in 1856, joined the Army at eighteen, and had a distinguished career in the King's Royal Rifles Corps (KRRC). He was Quartermaster to the 9th Battalion of the London Regiment and served in Burma in 1891, for which he was awarded the Campaign Medal with clasps. During the Boer War, he was awarded the Queen's Medal with four clasps; in the First World War, he was mentioned in dispatches twice and awarded the DSO, achieving the rank of Lieutenant-Colonel.

Maurice's two brothers, Dermot and Alec, also served in the Army; they lost their lives in the First World War. Lieutenant Dermot O'Shea, the eldest, was killed in August 1918, crossing the German lines as a tank officer, whilst the younger brother, Alec, died in March 1921 from wounds he had received in the same campaign; his was a long, lingering death. His father died soon afterwards, aged sixty-two—war-weary and full of grief. *The Tablet* reported a correspondent's tribute to him on 30 June 1921:

> Riflemen throughout the Empire will learn with deep regret of the death of Lieut-Colonel Timothy O'Shea, D.S.O. ('Tim'). For many years he served with the 60th Rifles, being with them in campaigns in India, Burma, and South Africa. Later he did invaluable work with Queen Victoria's Rifles. With this battalion he went to France on 4 November, 1914, and stayed with them till illness forced him to duty in England in September, 1918.

Military life was in Father O'Shea's blood and bones. Discipline, duty, and pride in one's country had been instilled in him from an early age. Suffering and sacrifice were the cornerstones of his upbringing. The memory of his brothers' deaths and their bravery lived on in his mind and always in his heart.[3]

He had no earthly family now; he was pledged to God. He felt that God was calling him to war, asking him to follow a path that had been chosen for him.

O'Shea had entered the Passionist Congregation in 1913, aged sixteen. Following his education at St Aloysius College, Highgate, and at seminaries in County Waterford and Dublin, Ireland, he received the Passionist habit four years later, along with a new name—'Clement'. The initials 'CP', standing for '*Congregatione passionisti*' ('Congregation of the Passion of Jesus Christ'), were placed after his name, and he wore the heart-and-cross symbol of the order embroidered on the left breast of his cassock. He vowed to serve his Lord in memory of the Passion and his suffering on the cross, following the example of St Paul of the Cross, founder of the order.[4]

He continued his philosophical and theological studies at Mount Argus in Dublin and was ordained as a priest in 1922. He then joined orders in Ilkey, Yorkshire, and Highgate Hill, London, finally moving to the Passionist Brothers community in Herne Bay in 1934, aged thirty-four.

There was no pleasure to be had from listening to the radio on 3 September—there was not the usual dance band music or laughter from a variety show to lighten the recreation period the Brothers were allowed. There was just the speech from the Prime Minister, making his fateful announcement.

In the Retreat House, the Superior, Rev. Father Malachy Gavin, led the prayers after the broadcast. 'May the Passion of Jesus Christ be ever in our hearts. Let us pray.' Each head bowed and each said a silent prayer. O'Shea's choice of prayer of comfort throughout his life was one that reminded him of the vows he had taken on his ordination.[5]

> To live in the midst of the world with no desire for its pleasures; to be a member of every family, yet belonging to none; to share all sufferings; to penetrate all secrets, to heal all wounds; to daily go from men to God to offer Him their homage and petitions; to return from God to men to bring them His pardon and hope; to have a heart of fire for charity and a heart of bronze for chastity; to bless and to be blest forever. O God, what a life, and it is yours, O Priest of Jesus Christ![6]

The words would carry him through each of death's dark vales. 'Yet will I fear no ill. For Thou art with me, and Thy rod and staff my comfort still'. His crucifix was always near his heart.

O'Shea was about to enter a different world, yet it was still familiar in many ways. Having served in the Army Cadet Force at school, he knew how to drill, march, and take orders; he had also watched many men on the parade ground near his home during his childhood. Even though he had travelled widely as a young man, moving to Ireland for his education, novitiate, and ordination, and he had visited Rome and Assisi, Lourdes and Lisieux, a different journey awaited him. War would take him away from the security and tranquillity of a retreat house and the familiar and comfortable work of the parish priest. He would be pastor to a different flock.

He had no close family to concern him. He would do his work in memory of his father and two brothers, and he treasured their medals—some of his few worldly possessions. He would serve his country like them, in the only way he knew. He had promised himself to God and would continue his work as a Passionist wherever he was sent, drawing strength from his faith and trust in God.

A month later, having been granted permission by the Congregation Superior to serve during the duration of hostilities, Father O'Shea returned to his hometown of Aldershot. Always a busy place, it was busier than ever, full of men, movement, and purpose. He went to visit the Rt Rev. Monsignor Dey DSO, Bishop to His Majesty's Forces, about his enlistment, meeting him at St Michael's House, which was the garrison church office on the camp.

With the Bishop's endorsement to the Royal Army Chaplains' Department, on 9 October 1939, O'Shea went off to the Military Station, where he registered as Chaplain to the Forces 4th Class (RC)—equivalent to the rank of Captain. He was allocated Army No. P100700. He was able to tell the desk sergeant that he had already written his will, a prerequisite for all new recruits to the armed services at times of conflict. Of course, it wasn't a long will—he had no material possessions to leave.[7]

Things moved quickly as he obtained paperwork and passes, getting ready for his duties abroad. He was issued with his British Red Cross ID card two days after enlisting, and he was attached to the 118 Field Regiment. He would soon be accompanying the British Expeditionary Force on its way to France. As far as training went, he was thrown in at the deep end—although his familiarity with the military life was undoubtedly an advantage. Besides, there was no choice; Territorial, Reserve, or Emergency chaplains were rushed through as they were desperately needed.

Chaplains soon learned how to adapt to new parishes and parishioners. They would not depend on buildings such as churches or chapels to hold services, instead finding space on unknown territory to hold mass and take prayers—shifting sands and muddy fields, craggy hillsides and barren wasteland. Their altar would be a table in the mess hall, an upturned box, the tailgate of a truck; their congregation would be the wounded and dying, military and civilian, as well as ordinary men simply in need of comfort. They would give succour to all who called out for help. They might not be able to heal damaged flesh or mend broken bones, but they could administer to the mind and soul. Their words and comfort would give balm to the lost sheep of the wartime flocks and strengthen the spirits of those far from home, parted from loved ones.

In any company, battalion, regiment, or corps—whatever the size of the attachment, however varied the denominations—a chaplain's duty was the same, to treat all men as equals, to give spiritual guidance and comfort, and to create and sustain a sense of unity, pride, and wellbeing amongst all men. This was jokingly referred to by some who thought the padre had a cushy job—'He was paid a pound a day for smiling'.[8]

Being in the Army was not very different for O'Shea, who had spent most of his life in institutions, following the customs and rituals of his particular order. He was used to the company and friendship of men and living in close quarters with them. However, it was unusual to meet a Passionist. There were only seven other Passionist chaplains out of over 600 Catholic chaplains who served during the war. Perhaps their sense of mission, of reaching out to people in need and keeping the suffering of Christ at the centre of their faith, brought other qualities. O'Shea had a wonderful way of connecting with people through wit and humour, and wherever he went he was a popular, well-loved, and much-respected figure.

O'Shea's good humour, generosity of spirit, and high moral standing would be the foundation of his wartime ministry. He did not need to be paid £1 for smiling; he was always smiling anyway.

With his portable altar, typewriter, camera, and watercolour painting box, dressed in his officer's uniform and with his beloved cross around his neck, Father Clement O'Shea CP went off to war.

Behind the Lines

2 February–4 June 1940
Northern France

Major Philip Newman, a twenty-eight-year-old surgeon with the Royal Army Medical Corps (RAMC), posted to the 12th Casualty Clearing Station (12 CCS) in northern France, sat down to write his diary after another long, busy day. The weather was dreadful and there was lot of sickness around, but he had not expected the Catholic padre to be one of his first patients.

16 February 1940

Rumours and orders for move. Wild expedition to Lancé to see 9th General (Hospital)—my first ward round for a very long time. Met Major Thompson from Liverpool and saw many of his fractures—also a case of frostbite. Tea very good in mess. Wiggens not well—O'Shea for tonsillectomy next day. Back to Le Mans ... Rapid fall of snow—some doubt about going.

Father O'Shea arrived at Le Havre in early February with the British Expeditionary Force (BEF) to join the 12 CCS. In spite of feeling under the weather and not being quite his usual jolly self, O'Shea managed to meet the officers and visit the men in the company within the first few days of arrival. He had taken a couple of church parades before his voice finally gave out; he could no longer ignore the painful throat, swollen neck glands, and high temperature, and so he reluctantly submitted to a medical examination. Newman immediately ordered the removal of his tonsils.

Even though the BEF had been in readiness since before the declaration of war and the first troops were sent to France as early as October 1939, it had seen no action. It was the period known as the 'Phoney War'—eight months of inactivity before the beginning of the German offensive on 10 May. French and British divisions were currently camped behind the Belgian border and the Maginot line, waiting for the Germans to attack. The 12 CCS was standing by in readiness.

Casualty clearing stations were one of a number of front-line medical units established to receive the sick and wounded. Their job was to classify casualties, provide emergency treatment, and move the serious cases to a general hospital behind the lines. The 12 CCS was made up of twelve officers, including the commanding officer, two specialists (one being Newman), four general duty doctors, three chaplains (O'Shea and two Church of England priests), a dental surgeon, a quartermaster, and 100 or so other ranks acting as medical orderlies and general support.[1] They were billeted in a variety of places in and around Coulombiers, a small village between Alençon and Le Mans.

An Army chaplain's primary job was to meet the spiritual and pastoral needs of the men in his company; for O'Shea, that was primarily of the Roman Catholics. He heard confessions, said prayers, and celebrated mass. On active service, on the front line, he tended to the sick and dying, performed the last rites, wrote to families of the deceased, and arranged funerals. However, every padre was expected to roll up his sleeves and get on with whatever was required, especially in an emergency. Nobody knew what lay ahead; everyone needed to be ready to deal with whatever came their way.

One of the first things O'Shea did on his return to the unit after his spell in hospital was to make contact with the local clergy—something he continued to do wherever he was stationed during the war. He was invited to join the Curé in celebrating mass at the village church and accompanied him on parish visits to the sick and dying. He was good at connecting with people immediately, clergy or layperson; his deep faith, humanity, and good humour shone through.

Newman developed a special relationship with O'Shea, who appears frequently in diary entries. He is referred to by his nickname, 'Cockie'—a sobriquet that O'Shea clearly embraced, even incorporating a cartoon cockerel's head into his signature. From Newman's first mention of O'Shea on 16 February 1940 to the last reference to him on 1 June 1940, when O'Shea left for Dunkirk, he was a constant companion, strengthening the bonds of friendship with the other officers.

Newman recorded many of their activities over the first few months, which were a mixture of work and leisure, including a lot of shopping ('Shopping with Cockie again—an almost daily routine now.'). They went to Amiens to buy twenty-five pairs of shorts and vests and bought Narcissi for one of the wards. They played 'some very good deck tennis' and enjoyed 'quartet opera singing in the garden'; on 5 May, they went 'to ceremony of confirmation at Annezin. Cycled round canals. Photos taken with confirmees'.

O'Shea was obviously good company, and his naughty schoolboy behaviour livened up many a mundane activity:

Saturday 23 March

Erbi, Bunny, O'Shea, Gordi, Lissy and I to Arras. For haircuts—very rowdy party in carriage much fighting and horseplay. All stops crowded—didn't manage to get haircuts. Returned back for dinner—full of discussion about new move.

Newman and O'Shea's friendship lasted after the war. They and the other members of the 12 CCS kept in touch, meeting every year for a veterans' reunion in London. They even held it at O'Shea's retirement home in Birmingham when he was too ill to attend in 1965; he died soon after. It is certain that they remembered the good times and the fun they had together before the bombing and bloodshed began.

What kept the officers going were the meals and parties, which helped them relax as well as keeping up company morale. When the station moved location, the officers usually found a suitable café or local bar for their mess and made friends with the patron. Mess dinners were particularly memorable occasions, thanks to O'Shea:

> St Patrick's Day, 17 March 1940
> Miramount, near Amiens

> After tea decorated [the mess] for dinner. Table looked first class. Caps and medals by O'Shea set out on view and looked most attractive. Guests arrived at 7 and straightaway made short work of Tim's two pints of 'Sidecar'. Then to dinner—a really good dinner, lots of fun—'OS was after proposin' the towest to ol' Oireland' (After the toast to Ireland a glass was thrown at the radiator—it was not known at first where it came from). CO, Erbi, Tim and Sam made speeches followed later by football and darts. Prizes presented by Sam. Had circumstances permitted it might have been a lot rougher. A very good evening.[2]

After another shopping trip, Newman and O'Shea brought back a very large bottle of champagne and 'squibs' (fireworks) for a dinner party. Another lively evening was promised.[3]

> 29 April

> An evening that started off by us all appearing as padres, with black paper fronts and some of Cockie's collars. Dinner extremely lively and very good. Live frog passed round in potato and carrots. Gave cause for a lot of fun, but some criticism next morning.
>
> Speeches by Erbi (Cardinal of the evening with red paper tabs) Tim (Sous Cardinal), myself—to explain the origins of the party and distribute Joyce and Michele [the patron's daughters] from the hatch. Lambley Ellis, Cockie and almost everybody else. An evening that got wilder and wilder with the squibs—Major Gilchrist sat on one of the squibs and burnt a hole in his trousers.

However, things soon began to change, and the laughter and hijinks ceased. The Germans invaded the Netherlands, Belgium, and Luxembourg on 10 May, and on the 13th, German troops crossed the River Meuse at Sedan, on the French Belgium border. By the 15th, the French Prime Minister, Paul Reynaud, had informed Churchill: 'We have been defeated; we are beaten; we have lost the battle.'[4] Everyone was propelled into action, and all the hanging around came to an end. The CCS was thrown straight into the middle of the German offensive, and chaplains O'Shea and Lisemore found themselves assisting the doctors, as Newman records:

14th May

Well here goes! We must change our CCS from peace to war basis. The CO takes his coat off and we all get down to work to make the new theatres. Major Tooey of 7 MAC [Motor Ambulance Company] comes to make acquaintance—he has no ambulances left. Lissy assisted me—he will make a first class ThS (Theatre Staff)—and Cockie did much 'scrubbing'. An appendix finished the evening ... There is going to be a hell of a scrap in front of Brussels.

The next day, O'Shea was busy making bandages and helping with the casualties, which began to arrive. He faced the reality of front-line action and what his real vocation was—to alleviate pain and suffering and bring comfort to those in need.

German troops reached the Channel at Abbeville on 20 May. On the 23rd, the decision to save the BEF was taken—against the wishes of the French commander, Gen. Weygand. As Calais and Boulogne had already fallen to the Germans, plans to evacuate troops from Dunkirk to England were set in motion.

23 May

Told to open again as MDS [Main Dressing Station]. Up at 4.00 a.m. Bombing attack this morning—my first experience of the sound of bombs nearby. Civilian casualties kept coming in to us. Cockie and I went to say last words to a dying chap. Camp machine gunners—two ambulance drivers wounded. We all felt very near to tears—with the sight of wounded and dead children—Tired bewildered and hungry refugees and dog tired ourselves with conflicting orders coming in 'very often'. One message told us that it was vital to stay where we were. Two hours late a staff officer appeared and gave us 20 minutes to clear out. By this time the camp was getting most unhealthy rushing into the trenches every 10 minutes. Before we left three kids with head wounds came in and the mother of one implored us to take her and the kids with us. We were all very close to weeping that day.

As the Germans moved towards them, the 12 CCS were ordered to move to Annezin, in the Béthune region, where they set up their facility on the sports ground. Suddenly the marquees were full of the wounded, and the sports ground was being strafed from the air and shelled from the ground. The unit found itself out beyond the rapidly retreating front line.

On 26 May, they were ordered to fall back to Dunkirk and to set up a hospital. The CO, Col. Plank, received orders to go to Le Chapeau Rouge, a large redbrick chateau situated on the outskirts of Dunkirk. Newman's diary provides a vivid account of events:

Tuesday, 27 May 1940

I was in charge of the second party with three lorries and about 40 men—we lost our way and found ourselves up near the Belgian border. We returned onto the proper road in failing light but the journey was very slow with all the refugees, abandoned vehicles, and stray cattle. Every quarter of an hour the road was strafed by low-flying aircraft. We arrived in Dunkirk at 1.00 a.m. at the start of an air raid. We found a house with the rest of the unit and I slept on the floor of the basement.

Wednesday, 28 May 1940

In the morning there was a hectic drive to Chapeau Rouge just after another air raid. Picked up two soldiers burnt to a cinder and arrived at the Chateau in Rosendael on the outskirts of Dunkirk. We now knew that we were left holding the baby and that the BEF were pouring as hard as they could out of Dunkirk. Straightaway I organised a theatre in the drawing room of the Chateau and within two hours had two operating teams going.

It was hard to find the energy to start all over again, in another place, when others were leaving to go home. The noise of the bombing was relentless and the feeling of being cut off from everyone else was hard to bear. However, when an officer arrived and told them to expect 700 wounded, they had no choice but to get on with their work. Casualties started pouring in at 5 a.m. the next day, Thursday 29 May.

There was no time to sleep or eat proper meals over the next few days. Bully beef and hardtack biscuits (eaten standing up) were the most anyone could expect.

Shelling and bombing became worse; a 500lb bomb fell within 50yds of the house and a smaller one within 20yds. Wounded increased until the house was packed full and the driveway was full of ambulances loaded up. I shifted my operating theatre to the cellar with one electric lamp.

The building shook and windows shattered as a shell just missed a direct hit, landing a few metres away in the garden. How many more men would O'Shea give the last rites to? How many more grieving parents would he have to write to? He was so tired, barely having time to wash and shave, never mind eating or drinking. He had managed to snatch brief periods of sleep—an hour here, half an hour there.

He would comfort the men with a sip of water, a drag on a cigarette, a smile and a squeeze of the hand, and spiritual consolation, prayers, and blessings. For those near the end of their lives, absolution before the last rites were given.

So many casualties were piling up that Newman decided to take things into his own hands.

I drove the CO down to the Mole and saw Dunkirk for the first time in 3 days. It was a sight of great devastation and one drove very fast to lessen the risk of getting hit by shells. The jetty itself was a sight for H. G. Wells alone—dead horses, overturned ambulances, columns of German prisoners, sunken boats and God knows what else. An ammunition dump went up just close by to add to the variety. I spent from 10–1.30 and 2.30–5.00pm on the Mole and on that day we got rid of some 700 wounded.

On the evening of 30 May, everyone was expecting to go home, with everything packed and ready to go on the ambulances, but a message came through early the next morning: '12 CCS to remain open, only patients to go'. It was another disappointment. It couldn't get any worse, with the thunder of bombing, the wounded crying out in pain, and the fear of being captured or killed.

New orders arrived the next day; everyone was to pull out except for one medical officer and ten men for every 100 patients. A ballot was held that afternoon. Lisemore went off to supervise the men's ballot and O'Shea was put in charge of the one for the officers. It was decided that the last four names out of the hat would be the officers to stay behind. There were seventeen officers, excluding the chaplains, and over 230 casualties, but the latter number was expected to increase—hence the need for four officers. Newman wrote: 'I shall not forget the secret agony as the names were read out'. The last four names were drawn: Herbert, Hewer, Williamson, and Newman.

Time dragged on as they waited for final orders and news of a hospital ship. Lisemore and O'Shea decided to hold a farewell service. 'Perhaps', Newman wrote, 'they wanted to attempt to bridge the gap between the good and bad fortune and to offer a prayer for the survival of all those destined to stay'.[5] It was a moving occasion; afterwards, everyone shook hands and said goodbye.

O'Shea was unusually quiet, standing in a corner at the back. He came forward to speak to his friend. 'Cockie and I had a talk and a weep', Newman wrote, 'and he gave me his cross, which I value more than anything in my possession'. O'Shea handed over his precious crucifix, saying, 'This will get you home safely, Pip.'

The only recorded account of what happened to O'Shea during the period leading up to the evacuation of Dunkirk appeared in *The Catholic Herald* on 8 November 1940.

The Curé's Best Wishes

At dinner the other night with Fr. Clement O'Shea, the Passionist of Herne Bay, who is now Chaplain to the Forces, I was kept amused by some of his reminiscences of the Dunkirk withdrawal. I particularly liked his story of the night spent sleeping in a graveyard, when he and his unit had to be on parade at 4 a.m. It was then that the CO told them that he had received word that in two hours they would all be taken prisoners. This was no comforting thought for Fr. O'Shea, who at once made himself busy hearing the confessions of his men. When he had finished he decided he must have his own confession heard. It might be his last.

While the bomb blitzkrieg raged unremittingly about him, he made his way to the house of an old curé he knew and to whom he made his confession. 'I asked him to make a real good job of the Absolution he gave me:' said Fr. O'Shea, 'as I felt I might never get another. But the old curé said to me, '*Ah, bon courage, mon pére, bon courage!*' and then in broken English he went on: 'I will give you what is your consolation.' With that he handed me a holy picture, which I at once slipped into my breviary and hurried back to the unit. It wasn't till a few hours later that I was able to glance at the picture, and on it said: 'This day thou shalt be with me in Paradise.'

14 May–17 June 1940: Northern France

Driver John Morgan disembarked at Le Havre in the morning of 14 May with the advance party of the RASC company of the 2nd Armoured Brigade. After having been moved from town to town by orders and counter-orders (an early symptom of the general confusion and indecision that was to affect the French campaign), the advance party finally joined the rest of the company at Caudebec-en-Caux on 17 May.

John was feeling elated. After a lot of asking, he had been reassigned as driver to the company in April. Like many young men who had enlisted, he did not want a cushy job in a depot at home; he was keen to see action, and now his prayers had been answered. He was in France, ready to give the Germans a bloody nose.

In England, the brigade RASC company had been stationed in Poole in preparation for going to France. As always, the men were not left idle. For those not away on embarkation leave, the day was filled with training and various activities. Squad drills were followed by guard and sentry drills, painting duties, maintenance demonstrations and tasks, lectures on personal decontamination, war duties, and motorcycle training. Even at the weekend, the men were kept active with vehicle inspections on Saturday mornings, organised games on Saturday afternoons, and church parade on Sunday mornings. One day, as a special treat, the commanding officer requested a mobile gas chamber, ordering all personnel to pass through it in their respirators. It is no surprise that by the time the movement orders came through, John and his friends were looking forward to a change.[6]

In spite of the efforts of the CO and the other officers, the company was not fully equipped for service overseas. There was a shortage of almost all types of equipment, from anti-gas clothing to vehicles, cookers to pistols, and machine-gun ammunition to mess tins. It was not until the company had arrived in Southampton, a day or so before embarkation, that some equipment was finally received.

In early May, the Germans finally ended the Phoney War by attacking Holland and advancing through Belgium. No sooner was this threat contained than another German Army unit broke through the poorly defended French line through the Ardennes, which had been thought impassable to tanks. The German Army captured Sedan and crossed the River Meuse, threatening to encircle the British and French armies in the north. British and French troops had been rushed in to try and contain the attack, but they had been mauled by continuous air bombardment by the Luftwaffe acting in coordination with ground troops. Reinforcements were badly needed, and so were the tanks of the 2nd Armoured Brigade.

That May was unusually hot, and British soldiers were not dressed for the weather. As a consequence, a number of the men went down with sunstroke and had to be taken off duties. During this time, John was busier that he had ever been. In addition to refuelling and maintaining his vehicle, he had to mount guard at night as part of an in-lying piquet (the group on duty to warn of enemy advances). During the day, John had to run supplies (everything from petrol, lubricating oil, tinned rations, and fresh bread) from the distribution depot at Le Havre and the large Army bakery at Bolbec to the fighting units of the brigade.[7] He occasionally had to collect food bought by the Army from French suppliers, and this is when his school certificate French came in handy.

It was clear to all that the Germans were getting closer as the sound of guns could be clearly heard. The day began with air raid warnings, and there were frequent but unfounded reports of enemy parachutists landing nearby that had to be followed up.

Over the following days, the company was constantly on the move, supporting units of the 2nd Armoured Brigade engaging the enemy. They moved forward to Aumale, but later they had to fall back to Bois Heroult, near Rouen, to avoid being outflanked by the advancing Germans. Driving became a slow and very dangerous task. The main roads were congested with columns of displaced refugees and there were numerous air attacks by dive bombers, although some were beaten off by the RAF. In the confusion, individual units often got separated. At the same time, there were acute shortages of fuel and ammunition. Nevertheless, the officers strove to maintain order where they could; vehicles were maintained, latrines were dug, and, when possible, the men were sent off in bathing parties, necessary to maintain the minimum of hygiene and provide relief from the oppressive heat.[8]

However, the retreat continued, and a move back towards Le Mans followed. The job of supplying the units had now become very dangerous. The main roads were clogged up with refugees, and drivers were using the smaller and narrower country lanes to escape the congestion and the Luftwaffe planes, which had taken to bombing and strafing the fleeing French population. By now, allied aircraft were very rarely seen. The fighting units were constantly on the move to the extent that, on occasion, even brigade HQ was in the dark as to their whereabouts. In spite of these problems, the RASC company did its job and managed to get through what supplies it had.

The fluidity of the front made encounters with infiltrating German forward units a real and frightening possibility. Drivers were not heavily armed. On paper, the driver had his Lee Enfield rifle and the co-driver a Tommy gun; in reality, however, this was not always the case.

Like many others, John was in the thick of it, but life was about to become far more difficult and dangerous for him. Little was known about this until years later, when John told the story to his children. The company was about to retreat further through Brittany, and John went on one of the last supply runs. He was on his way back in a country lane, miles from anywhere, when, in a cloud of steam, the engine stalled and refused to start in spite of many attempts to get it going again.[9] There was nothing else to do but abandon the vehicle and try to get back on foot. Before leaving, John and his co-driver had been told that the company was expecting to receive evacuation orders very soon and that the probable route would be through Laval and Rennes to Brest.

Armed with a map, a rifle, and a few rounds of ammunition, John and his co-driver left the empty lorry and marched east, hiding in the bushes or fields of corn. They soon heard the droning sounds of planes. That night, they slept under the trees, deep in a wood. When they woke up the next morning, they heard men's voices and laughter, recognising a few words of German. The German soldiers were between them and the road. John and his companion crept in the undergrowth, ready for a fight. They looked up and struggled not to laugh at what they saw—the backs of two soldiers who were crouching, trousers down, relieving themselves and cracking jokes.

A few yards away stood a grey motorcycle with a sidecar and a mounted machine gun. The two men were obviously a scouting party. John could not believe his eyes; as a motorcycle enthusiast, he was confident that he could start the vehicle and drive away to safety. He and his co-driver silently crept towards the vehicle and John began to fiddle with the carburettor and ignition while his companion kept watch. Eventually, the engine roared into life; John leapt on and his companion got into the sidecar, and they were off in a cloud of smoke. They did not look back to see what the Germans were doing—the two men had been caught totally by surprise.

After having driven for a couple of hours they came to the outskirts of a village and decided to take stock. In the rush of the escape, they had left their weapons and emergency rations behind, and they suddenly felt hungry and thirsty. The motorcycle tank was over half full and, fortunately, John still had his map with him. They decided to uncouple the heavy machine gun and ditch it with its ammunition—they did not want to scare the French population or risk being shot at by their own troops. The village was deserted, but they found a fountain and quenched their thirst. They could not find any food, so they decided to carry on. They drove on north west for the rest of the day, witnesses to the devastation that war had brought—burning farmhouses, corpses rotting by the side of the road, and countless civilian vehicles left destroyed. They heard the screaming sirens of the Stukas in the distance and the explosions that followed.

They passed countless civilians walking west and even some French soldiers. Nobody took any notice of them or tried to stop them. They spent another night in a derelict barn. It was the following morning, on the outskirts of a small village somewhere between Pontivy and Baud, that they ran out of petrol. They abandoned the motorcycle and continued on foot again. They were hungry and thirsty, with their only food being fruit picked from the hedgerows and orchards. They decided to risk going into a village.

As they approached a junction, an old man in blue dungarees appeared from nowhere. He had been watching them for a while and waved at them to stop. He hobbled down the road to speak to them. Having confirmed that they were British, he beckoned them to follow, taking them to his home. Inside the farmhouse, an elderly woman was ladling out soup and cutting slices of bread. They didn't hesitate to take up their invitation to join them for a meal.

John and his friend stayed the night. In the morning, the old man took them around 1 mile to a neighbour's house; the neighbour looked after John and his friend in the same way, feeding them and giving them a bed for the night. This went on for a couple more days until they were told that they were going to meet a special person to help them get home.

They were introduced to another French man, one who spoke good English and had obviously been helping other allies. He said that everyone was moving to Brest and he had seen many English soldiers going that way. He promised to take them there.

He arranged transport and took John and his friend to Brest. When they arrived at the outskirts of the town, they were stopped by the Military Police and taken in. After lengthy explanations—corroborated by the French man—they were told that their company was indeed in Brest and due to leave for England that very evening. They thanked their French friend, who wished them good luck, and they were reunited with their comrades. They set sail that evening, Sunday 16 June, on *Lady of Mann*,[10] arriving in Plymouth Sound early the following morning. John's War Diary records:

Monday 17 June

05.30 Boat arrives in the Sound
10.30 Embarkation
21.00 Train to Warminster
18 June 48 hours leave granted[11]

The evacuation of Cherbourg, Brest, St Malo, and St Nazaire was known as Operation Aerial, and it was deemed a success by the War Office; over 41,770 fit men and 732 wounded had managed to escape France.[12]

On 18 June 1940, John sent a message to his parents on a plain postcard inscribed with 'BEF Detail'. It read: 'Arrived safely in England yesterday and feel very well after my holidays in France!'. Perhaps John was not quite Steve McQueen in *The Great Escape*, but the tale of this small wartime adventure was always enjoyed by his children in years to come.

Two Paths, One Direction

Canvas Camp,
Lavington Down, Wilts.
1 July 1940

Dear Father & Mother

It has been extremely hot here during the last few days and it makes the perspiration pour off one. At the moment they don't seem to know what to do with us … As things are, with nothing much to do, and being miles from anywhere I would much rather be on active service in France. One did feel that one was doing something towards winning the war then, and one certainly was, and had a bit of excitement, which kept us amused.

John disliked hanging around doing nothing. 'Just let me get a grip at Jerry, that's all. Gosh, what wouldn't I do!' he wrote in another letter. Of course, he was not really doing nothing; he was unable to mention his current duties, which involved helping to solve the problem of a shortage of vehicles. So many had been damaged, destroyed, or left behind in France after the British left that it was the Army's priority getting itself back to full fighting force. A special branch of the War Office General Staff had been formed to control supply and prioritise needs; orders soon made their way to the RASC.[1]

The transport of men and equipment was an important part of the work of the corps. Troop-carrying vehicles had become a priority, and even more so with the fear of invasion at its highest since Germans forces had marched into Paris and France had surrendered. As northern and western France were occupied, defence of Britain's coastline was vital. Troops needed to be sent quickly and in large numbers to guard and protect English coastal stations mainly in the south and southeast.[2] Two and half thousand vehicles were needed immediately for adaptation and refurbishment. If local businesses (such as coach companies) did not offer them freely, the War Office simply requisitioned them.

In order to deal with this emergency, a number of RASC units were reformed into specialist Motor Coach Companies.[3] John was posted to No. 2 Motor Coach Company Depot.[4] His knowledge of engines and his maintenance skills were put to good use converting single-decker motor coaches, which arrived in the workshops, to military use. Regardless of the age of the vehicles or their previous owners, they were all converted in similar fashion, being made accessible for troops and all their gear. They were repaired, serviced, and sprayed in their standard service colour; the coaches were ready for use.

The War Office had met its target in less than a fortnight.[5] Work still continued day and night as other types of vehicles and specialised equipment were now required, such as ambulances, mobile workshops, and bakeries.

John worked hard, and his good conduct, level of performance, and above-average educational standard meant he was put forward for a commission in July. He wrote home with the good news:

> The Major (or OCV of 10Co) read out a list of about 20 names including we six [*sic.*] He told us we had definitely been accepted as Cadet Officers and we would very soon be sent to our OCT (at Bournemouth, I believe) (OCTU—Officer Training Unit) ... The training course lasts 6 weeks and is absolute hell. If you fail in the exam you get sent back to your unit but I have little fear of that. When I get there, I intend going at it like 'a bull at a gate'. At the end of 6 weeks, if successful you get made 2nd Lt and then, I believe, attend a MT (Motor transport) course for 2 weeks. After that you are a full-blown officer!

He was sent to the Cadet Officer Producing Centre at Boscombe Down, where he undertook his training:

> As the invasion is expected any time now, we have to do defence work as well as training. At the moment, the programme is as follows: Lunch 12.30pm. In the afternoon one is supposed to lie down and rest, preferably in one's bedroom. From 5.30pm to 7.15pm you are allowed out within 1½ miles of the hotel. At 8pm you turn up for parade in light battle order and have to sleep with your clothes on, and equipment by your side, ready to proceed at a moment's notice. You are awakened at 4.30am, put on your equipment and stand by until 7am. You then wash and shave and get breakfast. Training then lasts from 9am until 12.30pm consisting of drill and lectures etc.

Cadets complained amongst themselves about the course, and especially about not getting a decent night's sleep. They missed their families and home comforts, but cadets like John learned that hardship and stamina were necessary to survive. They were being toughened up for whatever lay ahead, helping them to become future leaders of men. In September 1940, John wrote: 'Believe me, the Army has altered my whole outlook on life and made me realise what a fortunate chap I am. This has done me the world of good'.

Now with the rank of 2nd Lieutenant, John was posted to the Deputy Director of Supply and Transport HQ. His previous employment at the bank, his eye for detail, and his head for figures were an asset as he learned how to negotiate the complex system of sourcing, storing, and moving supplies, whether toothpaste or fuel, buttons or bully beef. He was meticulous with paperwork, making sure that figures tallied and records were kept up to date. He was gaining a very good understanding of the full extent of the work of the RASC at home and abroad, and that cooperation and communication were key to keeping the Army supplied in order to perform its duties effectively.

John's own experience in France showed him how reliant a soldier was on the work of others. He knew what it was like to run out of fuel and break down in the middle of nowhere, and he knew what it felt like to go hungry and to have no roof over his head. He also knew how to accept help when it was offered. The corps' motto was fitting—'*In Arduis Fidelis*', meaning 'Faithful in Adversity'.

Meanwhile, John leapt at the opportunity to undertake an instructor's motorcycle course. He attended further ammunition training; this was unusual as it was normally the work of the Royal Army Ordnance Corps (RAOC), but it probably made good staff sense for a transport expert to learn more about types of ammunition, safety, and regulations. John was able to put his newly acquired knowledge to good use after being posted to 3 Corps Ammunition Park. This was a kind of moveable warehouse, normally under canvas, where all the ammunition for the corps' divisions, from pistol rounds to heavy artillery shells, was stored before being moved to individual fighting units as required.

In October 1941, John transferred to 89 General Transport Company. He was appointed Acting Captain in January 1942. He was eventually posted to 3 Corps Troops Transport Company as Temporary Captain and War Substantive Lieutenant in readiness for active service. In February 1943, he went with the Central Mediterranean Force (CMF) to join forces with the Eighth Army, which was fighting in Tunisia to overpower the remaining foothold of the Axis powers in North Africa.

John arrived as the Allied offensive against the Axis Forces was entering its final phase. Tripoli, the last bastion of the Italian North African Empire, had been captured by the Allies that January. The enemy had retreated westwards into Tunisia, where the terrain was suited to defence, and the supply routes from mainland Italy were shorter. Under Rommel's direction, the enemy still packed a considerable punch; before long, a strong counter-offensive was launched. The enemy could now be resupplied overnight from Italy, and its heavy tank strength actually increased.

After a very short period of acclimatisation, John was detailed to the RASC unit organising the movement of supplies from the port of Tripoli to the front. Before long, more than 3,500 tons of supplies per day were discharged at Tripoli and had to be sorted, put on lorries, and dispatched to the depots and, from there, to the fighting units. In July 1943, John was posted to a heavy anti-aircraft regiment in charge of supplies. Anti-aircraft units were essential at this stage of the war to protect military installations from attack by the German and Italian bombers and fighters based in the fortress island of Pantelleria and Sicily. Because of his ammunition training, John was later posted to the 498 Artillery Company.

He was not happy behind a desk, and he joined ammunition, fuel, and water-carrying convoys as frequently as he was allowed. For the most part, the convoys travelled on roads, but they sometimes had to drive through minefields, keeping to the paths cleared by the engineers. This was a dangerous job. Occasionally, lorries either strayed from their narrow paths or the paths had been obscured by sandstorms; despite taking great care and travelling very slowly, the lorries could sometimes hit a mine. The consequences of this were disastrous.

When travelling off-road, everyone scanned the route ahead as the lorries crawled at a snail's pace, watching the ground for changes in depth or height in the sand, looking for obstacles or anything suspicious. If something was spotted, John would jump out, halt the vehicles, and then walk slowly ahead, checking the area with a stick. He would carefully and slowly defuse each device and then move it away from their path. Occasionally, the odd Messerschmitt or Italian Macchi—escaping interception by the Desert Air Force—would attack, strafing the vehicles before turning quickly homeward.

Aside from the enemy threat, the things that John remembered most about North Africa would be the heat, sand, dust, wind, and flies. The flies had descended on him as soon as he had disembarked the troop-transport ship from England, and they stayed with him throughout his tour. The heat could melt corned beef in its tin; he would pour the contents into his mess can and eat them with a spoon, details that he recounted to his parents in letters home. The sand got into everything—food, clothes, and every possible crevice in the body. Washing oneself and one's clothes was sometimes difficult as water was rationed—even down to 0.75 gallons per man per day at one point.

Transporting water caused as much anxiety to the RASC as carrying fuel and ammunition; it required huge resources, and this had not been taken into account during the planning.[6] It is said that to deliver 1 gallon per man per day to a division of 18,000 men, around twenty-seven additional 3-ton vehicles were required. However, as 3-tonners were seldom loaded to that weight in the desert, many more additional men and trucks were needed.

John served in the region for nine months, travelling in Libya, Algeria, and Tunisia, through deserts, rocky landscapes, and woods. The nearest thing John had to a mention in dispatches was an unsigned, handwritten note that was found among his papers after he died. It seems to be a citation: 'For organising the expeditious delivery of ammunition over long and difficult routes by day and night to forward positions'. John showed courage and determination in fulfilling his duties to the artillery units in the front line and leading his men safely through hazardous conditions.

When John was not loading and delivering supplies with his men, he would be working in his 'office'—often a tent at the camp or the back of a truck, as shown in photos John took at Sid Mabrouk, Constantine. The Army could not run without its extraordinary system of communications; the RASC was a part of this, alongside the Royal Engineers, who were responsible for laying and maintaining field telephones, repairing roads and bridges, and construction work. Everyone relied on a fully operational telegraphic and postal system. Administrative work kept John busy, dealing with messages, orders, and letters, filling in forms, and keeping records. He always tried to do the best he could and expected others to do no less. He was regarded as strict but fair.

Everyone was a cog, however small, in the big machine of war. Everyone worked to support the vast network of people, vehicles, resources, supplies, and their movement, whether to forces on the front line, field medical services, or NAAFIs (The Navy, Army and Air Force Institutes).[7] Officers fulfilled a number of roles; John also looked after the welfare of his men (as chaplains did), making sure that they had access to sport, education, and entertainment where possible.

The common pattern of war for those on active service was periods of intense, often dangerous activity followed by long periods of inactivity and boredom. This gave officers the opportunity to sightsee in their spare time. John's photos show places such as the ruins at Drea in Souk Ahras Province, Algeria, and the Temple of Jupiter at Teboursouk in Dougga, Tunisia. There is also a photograph of him with a pet tortoise, which John adopted from nearby Le Krib.

After the defeat of the Axis forces and the conquest of North Africa, the Allies invaded Sicily and then mainland Italy. John's long journey with the Eighth Army continued to Italy, eventually leading to the small hilltop village of Civitella many months later.

Meanwhile, Father O'Shea was also busy with his camera, recording life with No. 3 (UK) Mobile Casualty Clearing Station (3 CCS). He had been in North Africa for two years by the time John Morgan arrived, appearing on the officers' list as early as September 1941. He had witnessed the British retreat into Egypt, Rommel's advance being finally stopped at El Alamein, the German retreat that followed, and the capture of Tripoli.

He was an experienced officer and chaplain after his time in France, although the theatre of war, the climate, and the conditions were very different now. He fitted easily into whatever situation presented itself, visiting other hospitals and field stations, supporting 3 CCS medical services, and attending to the sick, wounded, and dying. He was living with and supporting Catholics and non-Catholics alike on the front line; there was not always the luxury of chaplains of different denominations to meet the particular needs of other faiths. He was part of the medical team, but he also worked independently, using his initiative according to whatever circumstances presented themselves and taking orders for whichever jobs were deemed necessary.

On 24 October 1943, in San Severo, Italy, the 3 CCS War Diary stated: 'Padre O'Shea departed for Taranto for the purpose of ascertaining the whereabouts of the unit missing vehicles and personnel'. Sadly, there is no note of the outcome of his mission.

Medical units were never short of work, and not just in dealing with the casualties of war. Hospital wards were full of cases of malaria, sandfly fever, and jaundice, and this required many extra nursing staff. 'Practically everyone who has been in the desert has come down with one of those ailments at one time or another,' wrote Clifford Saber, war artist and volunteer American ambulance driver with the British Eighth Army, after a spell in hospital himself.[8]

As a priest, O'Shea may have considered the irony of his position, holding church parades, hearing confessions, giving communion, and preaching God's eternal love, in the cradle of Christianity. The beauty of the landscape, the ancient cultures, and the indigenous tribes were side-by-side with the death and destruction of modern warfare. However, O'Shea was able to combine a continuing spiritual development and quest for knowledge as he travelled along the Mediterranean coast through Tunisia, Egypt, and Transjordania (present-day Jordan), covering thousands of miles during his three years of service. He provided pastoral and spiritual care to the wider community, meeting other chaplains and local faith leaders and holding retreats (a time for relaxation and reflection for the faithful at war). He also took services at various RC churches, including the Garrison Church at Ataka, Suez, and the Garrison RC Church, Christ the King, at Sarafand al Amar, Palestine—places O'Shea photographed.

In addition to military life and the men he was working with, O'Shea particularly wanted to record the landscape, architecture, and local communities. There were also special occasions such as a visit by Field Marshal Montgomery, Middle East Commander-in-chief, who gave him a pack of cigarettes, as a scribbled note in his photo album affirms.[9] Sadly, his attempt at a photo resulted in a blur of figures. However, his mind and eye were always focused on the places of religious significance, such as the Tomb of St George at Lydda, the Mosque of Omar, the Dome of the Rock, and the Garden of Gethsemane in Jerusalem, as he travelled this ancient land in the course of his duties and during periods of leave.[10]

Fortunately, there were others who took photos of their padre. There are images of O'Shea perched on a jerry can at a small table in the middle of the desert, eating from a mess tin; it is entitled 'Camel caravan at back, hungry man in front (3 CCS, Kantara). O'Shea is also seen surrounded by Berba children at a palm-fringed watering hole. Another image, entitled 'Burials at Medinine', shows rows of graves marked by crude wooden crosses and, in the distance, O'Shea helping two men dig a grave. Another picture stands out in which O'Shea is striking an unusual pose for a chaplain—standing to attention, a rifle by his side. The title reads: 'El Alamein 1942'.

As chaplains were non-combatants, they did not bear arms. As with all officers, a chaplain was assigned a soldier who was a combination of bodyguard, personal servant, and driver. A February 1943 entry in the War Diary lists Gunner James, RA, as 'Padre's Driver and Batman'.[11] There were undoubtedly times when O'Shea did not have the luxury of his own armed protection, especially in the middle of a battlefield.

One of the most poignant photographs initially seems mundane, showing four men, including O'Shea, relaxing in the desert, playing some sort of game with counters on the bonnet of a truck. O'Shea's caption reads 'Playing cannibals and missionaries', with the added line: '2 fellows on right killed 10 minutes later'.[12]

In addition to taking photographs, O'Shea enjoyed painting, and he captured some desert scenes in watercolour sketches; three are preserved in his album. One depicts a close convoy of vehicles on the horizon, silhouetted against a dramatic sunrise sky, next to which O'Shea has placed a black-and-white war photograph postcard of a similar view without the vehicles, entitled 'El Alamein on the eve of the offensive, 23 October 1942, which forced the enemy to retreat'. O'Shea's picture has a vivid reality that is more powerful than that filtered through a camera lens.

The 3 CCS Medical Diaries cover nearly six years of service, from September 1939 to April 1946, presenting a daily snapshot of the complex and challenging circumstances of their work. Resources were dwindling, but there was a constant stream of casualties and the sick, moving from field ambulances to dressing stations, to general hospitals, to evacuation ships.

After the success in North Africa, it was planned that mainland Italy would be occupied to give the Allies a stronghold in Europe. As such, 3 CCS headed for Malta, where they waited for the order to launch the invasion of Sicily. This would be known as 'Operation Husky'. The Medical Diaries from this period give an indication of Father O'Shea's movements:

1 July 1943

Unit still in Malta awaiting further instructions for onward move. Present site situated on the shore has enabled swimming to become the main recreation of Officers and men.

13 July 1943

A few copies of the Order of the Day were distributed to the troops, also handbooks on Sicily ... Enemy aircraft in the vicinity of the convoy at 21.10 hours and through the night at varying periods. Some bombs were dropped but no casualties among the unit personnel.

16 July 1943
Catania

112 cases were evacuated ... Unit lorries were asked to convey sitting cases. Embarkation at the docks was supervised by the Unit Dental Officer. 3 unit lorries

detailed to help move Field Ambulance should hold slightly wounded and normal sick, leaving room in the C.C.S. for serious wounded ... There was a large number of P.O.W's [*sic*.] in the day's admissions. Owing to the large number of surgical cases being admitted to the C.C.S. it has been decided that the unit surgical team together with the 21 F.S.U. [Field Surgical Unit] team should work in Eight-hour shifts.[13]

Casualty clearing stations were constantly adapting to the circumstances of the war, which were changing daily—if not hourly. They would have to move premises, acquire new equipment, and delouse mattresses in premises vacated by the Germans, alongside setting up blood transfusion centres and maintaining the men's morale: 'A unit concert was held in the evening, unit artistes being augmented by Italian civil artistes'.[14]

O'Shea moved with the CCS, along with everyone else, following the path of the British Eighth Army and US Seventh Army. He went from Messina into southern Italy, onto Taranto on the east coast, Bari, Foggia, and eventually on towards Rome. The city had been taken by the Germans in September 1943 and was not liberated by the Allies until nearly a year later, on 4 June 1944.

John Morgan remained in North Africa until RASC reinforcements were needed after the main invasion of Italy at Salerno, on 9 September 1943. John left Bougie (present-day Béjaia), Algeria, at the end of October 1943 for Naples. One of John's photos shows him with members of his company—Captain Shirley and his batman, Driver Milne, sitting in front of their tent in the transit camp at Bougie before embarkation. He was delighted to be leaving Africa, as he told his parents:

> 1 Dec 1943
> HQ 498 Arty Coy RASC, CMF
>
> Gosh! Am I glad to leave N Africa. Once the campaign finished I'm afraid I lost nearly all my interest in that country. Now, at least, I hope we'll be doing a useful job of work again. I'm afraid that there is a lot I could say but censorship regulation won't permit, so once more, having run my stock of rather uneventful news completely dry, I must say cheerio and again.
>
> Love from John

> 21 Dec 1943
> HQ 498 Arty Coy RASC, CMF
>
> My dear Father & Mother,
>
> Sorry you've been kept waiting rather a long time for a letter. As you can guess, I expect, I'm in Italy at last and what with all the moving about there has been no time for letter.

Fortunately we've had grand weather for the last few weeks and that has been a great help. Well, I'm certainly seeing quite a spot of country at the Government's expense. Believe me the scenery we've passed through has been grand. The sight of greenery, trees, fields, hedges etc, is a great relief from the rather barren, vast expanses of N Africa.

His delight, however, was short-lived, as he soon faced the horrors of the Battle of Monte Cassino, the protracted five months of bitter fighting to break through the Gustav Line from January to May 1944. Years later, he was only able to tell his son a little about the horror of seeing men blown up in front of his eyes. The hilltop Benedictine monastery that dominated the town and surrounding countryside was destroyed, and John's photographs of the devastation left behind speak volumes.

Jack Cassidy, a driver with the RASC, wrote the following in his diary on 1 June 1944:

Past through Cassino. Nothing left of it. It's gutted with shell holes. Not a wall standing and dead Germans under rubble but too risky to move them for mines and Booby traps. They'll be finding them next year at this time.[15]

Morgan and O'Shea continued to follow their own paths in Italy, eventually meeting in June 1944 in Tuscany, when O'Shea was attached as padre to John's company. Captain and chaplain embarked on what historian Peter Doherty termed 'the long hard slog'. Captain Alan Whicker of the Army Film and Photo Unit, who served in Italy, went on to describe the period as '666 days of fear and exhilaration'.

John and Father O'Shea were two men from different backgrounds and faiths, but they had a common purpose to serve king and country and the men in their company. They also both felt an overwhelming desire to relieve the suffering of innocent civilians.

In July 1943, Benito Mussolini, *Il Duce*, lost the confidence of the Grand Council of Fascism. He was dismissed as Prime Minister and arrested by the King of Italy, Victor Emanuel III, who replaced him with General Badoglio. Although the new Italian government was ostensibly continuing the war on the side of the Germans, it was secretly negotiating an armistice with the Allies. Hitler, always suspicious of his Italian allies, ordered several divisions into Italy with the excuse of protecting Italy from Allied landings.

After protracted secret negotiations, the Italian government signed an armistice to come into effect on 8 September 1943. However, Italian troops and the population were not informed of this, and the first they knew of the armistice was an announcement made by Allied radio. The King escaped from Rome and took refuge in the south of Italy, which was in the hands of the Allies by then. On 13 September, Italy changed sides and declared war on Germany. The Germans encountered only token resistance by the Italian troops in the rest of the country and quickly occupied these areas. Mussolini had earlier been rescued from his prison in the Apennines and taken to Germany. He was to form a puppet Fascist state under German control, the *Repubblica Sociale Italiana*, covering the part of Italy not occupied by the Allies.

The Germans began to wreak revenge on the country that had been their ally but was now their enemy; there was plenty of suffering to come for the Italian population and Italian soldiers at home and abroad. Under the command of Field Marshal Albert Kesselring, the Germans fought a brilliant and tenacious defensive campaign in Italy, aided by the mountainous terrain and the weather, which was hot in summer and cold and very wet in autumn and winter. The German troops were thus able to retreat slowly up the peninsula, from one fortified line to another.

Tuscany was one of the most damaged regions of Italy as a result of what was called the *sosta*—the pausing of the war on its territory. The hilltop village of Civitella, along with the whole region, suffered dreadful reprisals for the action by civilians and partisans (the equivalent of resistance fighters) against the Germans.

'My Village, My Home'
Lara's Story, Part I

Lara Lammioni was born in 1924 and lived in Civitella with her parents, Dante Lammioni and Armida Caccialupi, and sister, Maria Grazia. She was encouraged to write her memoir in 1994 by fellow survivor Ida Balò Valli. She begins with an account of her life before the war:

Civitella della Chiana, the medieval fortified village, situated with its tower on top of a hill at the edge of the Val di Chiana, was the place of my wonderful childhood. I lived there for twenty years.

My paternal family owned a great old house near the church, right at the centre of village life; I have very sweet memories of my first years. I was surrounded by the great love of my parents, my grandmother, my uncles and aunts, and also of the other villagers. I felt like a queen in my own little kingdom.

Perhaps all childhoods are happy, but I thought that mine had something special. I remember clearly all the games, from the simplest, when I was very young, to the more elaborate ones of my early adolescence—from ring-a-ring-a-roses and hide and seek to attempts to recite and dramatise stories and novels.

The girls who lived near me enthusiastically helped me in all these activities. We enjoyed maximum freedom in each other's house and we used to play in our lofts and gardens. The lofts were very large, airy, and full of many different objects, from old furniture, paintings, old books, and newspapers, to clothes of all types and fashions. They were the ideal places for our games.

When the weather was good, there was the garden. It abutted the village walls and was a very good place to enjoy ourselves. The vegetation offered hiding places for our battles, which, perhaps unconsciously, recreated the old war sieges that had taken place in Civitella over the centuries.

There was also the *colorino*, a type of grape with a very bright red juice, which, mixed with flour, was the basis for our homemade stage makeup.

When I started middle school, I had to stay in Arezzo during the school year. On my return for the holidays, cherries welcomed me—so many cherries that I can still remember them, red, plump, and shiny, filling the large wicker baskets. And the garden full of fruit. And the sunsets on the side of the *Trove* and the hills of Valdarno. And the screeching of the swallows who had their nests under the eaves.

And the walks with my best friends towards the sports field with the obligatory stop at the *girata fresca*—an airy glade where, even in the height of summer, one could enjoy the cool shade and view of the Val di Chiana, screened by the tall cypresses, or towards the spring of the *Selva Grossa* that generously gave its pure water, an ideal place for us to eat our snacks (two slices of homemade bread with oil and salt, or homemade jam).

We used to stop in a quiet wood, sit on a rock, and read a book—very often a thriller (my great passion) that had been carefully hidden to avoid the disapproval of our families, who did not want us to ruin our eyes on holiday by reading useless books.

Meanwhile, the circle of my loving family had grown larger: my two little twin cousins Vittoria and Giuliana were born to my dearest Uncle Gigi and Aunt Marietta. My aunt had a lot to do and I used to go and help her as soon as I could.

I remember the complex feeding arrangements and the ritual of dressing and undressing the babies. When the twins were a little older, my aunt used to let me look after them and take them out. I used to show them off in the village and women stopped and paid polite compliments to the twins. Afterwards, we used to sit under the trees together with a girlfriend of mine and eat tasty snacks that my aunt had prepared for us.

These memories crowd my mind with such intensity and clarity and painful regret that I could carry on about them for much longer.

That state of peace, innocence, and absence of any disturbance or worry, made up of thousands of little happy moments, that feeling of security and extraordinary love, was not to repeat itself in later life. This is normal and represented without doubt my little private paradise from where I got the strength to face the sad times that were to follow. The fact that my world was broken and trodden upon in such a cruel way does not detract from the sweetness and the yearning of its recollection.

Village life that took place around me was simple and peaceful.

Civitella has always been a poor village, owing to the lack of any form of industry or commerce and because of its isolated location and difficult roads. However, its inhabitants, although almost always poor, always behaved with dignity, intelligence, and respect—never with servility.

The women were always very busy, spending every minute of the day looking after the home, the garden, and the many domestic animals. They used to go far to get fodder for these animals and carry it back to the village on their shoulders in enormous bundles, which weighed them down so much that they almost disappeared. The same thing happened with firewood to keep warm in winter and to light the bread ovens for the weekly bread-baking session. Then there were the clothes to be washed—far from the village because in Civitella, water was as scarce as everything else.

I have always thought that the women were the real leaders of village life, where a kind of matriarchy was in place.

The church bells gave rhythm to our day, beginning early in the morning, announcing the first mass, at midday, signalling lunchtime, and towards sunset, signalling evening activities and the Ave Maria that ended the day.

On Sundays and on the great religious festivals, the sound of church bells was more solemn, more joyous, and accompanied the three morning masses, the evening services. and, once a month, a procession around the village.

Holy Week was such an attraction that I used to spend whole days in church. We used to prepare little jars to decorate the Holy Sepulchre, with grains of cereal kept in the dark as they were sprouting to make them become white and diaphanous. On Holy Thursday, all the bells were tied together and the altar boys used to go around the village to announce the forthcoming religious events by the shrill sound of a special instrument. On Good Friday, all holy images were covered with purple cloth and the priest wore black vestments.

At night there was the procession of *Gesú Morto*—the death of Jesus—to the cemetery, in which the whole village took part. The long line snaked through the roads, the darkness punctuated by the light of flickering torches. Finally, at midday on Holy Saturday, the resurrection of Christ, radiant, solemn, full of promise and joy. I took part in all of this with a mystic spirit and profound emotion, and a certain and unspoilt faith.

Sometimes the bells tolled for a mournful event or to stop the dark, hail-bringing clouds, as it was a popular belief that the sound of bells would scatter clouds.

At home, we used to be worried by the sight of these whitish clouds. My maternal grandmother, a woman of great faith and devotion, fretted if the tolling of the bell was late, and the other villagers used to go to ring the bells themselves if the Archpriest or the altar boys were late. The economy of the area relied entirely on the meagre profits from the crops, which the hail threatened to destroy.

I remember the long line of women who, at set times during the day, used to get water from the *cisterna* with a hand pump. The well was situated in front of my house in the main square and I would watch the women with their copper jugs, always kept highly polished, waiting for their turn. This break was an occasion for socialising, a time when all that happened in the village was analysed and commented upon. The women of Civitella, like all the other villagers, liked to exchange news and opinions on what was happening. This was the only distraction available.

However, the women did not waste their time while chatting; they were sitting down in groups, but always with something to do in their laps—darning, sewing, or embroidering. The only time for idle chatter was on a summer's evening in the main square, from 8 p.m., when everybody had finished eating, to 9.30 p.m., when everybody retired to bed. We all sat on the many small stone walls and on the *cisternino*, a large, round stone in the centre of the square. The men used to take part in these gatherings, and they gave a sense of jollity to the occasion with exchanges of quips and phrases with double meanings.

Then war was declared.

At first, village life did not undergo many changes. Serious matters were discussed in addition to the usual gossip—who had been called up, what news of them there was, and animated comments about the daily war bulletins—but on the whole, the situation was rather calm. We showed sympathy to those who had lost loved ones and were sad at the news of Italian defeats, but this was all as onlookers. We were living in a safe place; the aerial bombardments did not threaten us and not even the food situation was worrying us. We all had more than enough wheat, oil, and wine. The gardens were supplying all the vegetables we needed and we had many animals.

My father, who was an Army officer based in Grosseto, kept telling us that cities were dangerous and that we had to remain in the village, so I stopped attending university. On 8 September [1943], the day the armistice was announced [shortly after Mussolini was deposed and Italy surrendered to the Allies], Civitella had a day of pure joy; it was all over, and all the threats had gone.

In the evening, large bonfires were lit around the village. In that euphoric moment, all the firewood that had been gathered for the winter with such difficulty was consumed. Everybody was very optimistic and nobody seemed to be aware that our position had become a lot more difficult, with the German Army fully operational among us; the Germans now considered us to be traitors.

Some people, however, did understand this great danger. I remember that I was excitedly running from one bonfire to another, among so many people who were noisily expressing their joy and relief, when I noticed a villager, an artisan of great intelligence and ability, who sensed the approaching danger. He was speaking loudly and cursed the other villagers, calling them blind and stupid and telling them that they did not understand their position. He was gesticulating and looked like a prophet of doom against the light of the fires. Sadly, his foresight did not save his life on 29 June.

Soon afterwards, Allied bombardments began in areas close to Arezzo, Castiglion Fiorentino, the Palazzina Bridge, and the railways. We learnt to distinguish the deep rumble of the four-engine bombers and, sometimes, we could actually see the bombs falling on their objectives and the columns of smoke that rose afterwards.

Those were anxious days; the village was filling with evacuees from Arezzo and Florence. My aunt, uncle, and maternal grandfather came to stay with us in search of safety and peace. In spite of this, we never felt that we were not in a safe place, nor did we ever feel unlucky.

The Shooting at the Club

17 June 1944
Orders from General Field Marshall Albert Kesselring:

New rules in the war against the partisans.

The partisan situation in the Italian theatre, particularly central Italy, has recently deteriorated to such an extent that it constitutes a serious danger to the fighting troops and their supply lines, as well as to the war industry and economic potential. The fight against the partisans must be carried on with all means at our disposal and with the utmost severity. I will protect any commander who exceeds our usual restraint in the choice of severity of the methods he adopts against partisans. In this connection the old principle holds good, that a mistake in the choice of methods in executing one's orders is better than failure or neglect to act.

Civitella, Sunday 18 June 1944

'Look what the Germans gave me,' said Lara Lammioni's grandfather, Federico Caccialupi, as he showed her the multi-coloured sweets he had been given by a German soldier in the square. There had been cigarettes too, but he didn't smoke. Lara couldn't resist taking a sweet.

Four German soldiers had been hanging around Civitella on and off all day. They were dressed in light-coloured tunics and wore service caps with the emblem of the Luftwaffe, an eagle in flight. They were part of a group of seven or so who had been separated—or had decided to go off on their own—from a parachute division that was in the area. They had billeted themselves in the hayloft of a farmhouse near the entrance to the village at Madonna di Mercatale.

Young Alberto Rossi (known as 'Palombo') had been playing football with his friends Angiolino, Valdo, and Enea in the Piazza. When it started to rain, they took shelter under the ancient Portico, the arched walkway running the length of Via di Sopra from Piazza Becattini down to Piazza Vittorio Emanuele III.

They stayed there until the rain started to clear. They then saw the four German soldiers walking along the Via di Sopra towards them, looking around and greeting anyone they met with a loud and heavily accented '*Buon giorno*.' They seemed to be of a similar age, in their early twenties, though the tallest and most upstanding one appeared to be the senior officer.

Palombo decided to play a trick on the senior officer, creeping up behind him and sticking the toy gun in his side. '*Camerata, mani in alto!*' he said ('Comrade, hands up!'). The officer instinctively reached for his pistol as he turned around, but he burst out laughing when he saw Palombo. He offered to take the young Italian for some sweets, and Palombo pointed the way and led the men to Emilio Marsili's shop in Il Pozzone, the only sweetshop open on a Sunday.[1]

The shopkeeper would have been disconcerted by the arrival of the boy and an armed German soldier. Sweets were very scarce and strictly rationed, but he served them nonetheless.

On the way back up to the main square, Palombo took the Germans along Via San Francesco and showed them where he lived. As they came round the back of the nursery school to return to the main square, one of the men suddenly took out a flare gun from a holster on his belt and let off three coloured flares up into the air in quick succession. Palombo's friends and some other children nearby ran towards them, delighted by the sight of this impromptu firework display.

After distributing sweets to the children, the German asked Palombo about the social club, and Palombo told them where it was, pointing to the Portico. The senior officer thanked him and asked him to come to the club later that evening. When Palombo said that he was too young, the officer told him that it would be all right as he was in charge.

Sunday Evening

A light rain was falling, cooling the air. The main square was empty and people were gathered under the shelter of the Portico by the Podestà Palace. The population of Civitella had recently grown with the arrival of a number of families evacuated from Arezzo and Florence, many of whom were out that evening, enjoying the cool breeze after the hot and humid day.

A young partisan from the Banda Renzino, currently thought to be camped in the hills near Cornia, had recently been seen in the village, trying to get money and looking for food and weapons.[2]

German soldiers had been seen in the area recently, but they rarely came up to Civitella, so the presence of the four Luftwaffe non-commissioned officers caused some concern. Even though they had appeared friendly, blacksmith Gino Bartolucci had felt nervous about them and had hurried home. Lara Lammioni saw the flares in the sky from her house on the corner of the square and Via Francesco.

At approximately 7 p.m., Lara's uncle, Luigi Lammioni (the town clerk of Civitella), was walking home with his wife and three daughters when he saw three German soldiers go into the *Dopolavoro* (after-work social club). It was on the ground floor of a building in the middle of the Portico, and the elementary school was housed on the floor above it. There was only one entrance and exit to the premises. The club occupied two rooms—the large recreation room contained tables and chairs and a radio set on a small table in the corner by the window, and a smaller and narrower room, where wine and snacks were sold, was on the left. The two rooms were connected by a door and some steps.

The club was managed by Torquato Menchetti and his wife, Alduina. The three German soldiers joined the locals in the club, but they were not an immediate concern—despite the fact they were armed with automatic pistols and submachine guns. They settled down in the recreation room and played cards, with their weapons propped up against the wall.

After dinner, young Palombo left his home with his mother, who was going to visit Luigi Lammioni a few doors along from the club. They parted company when they arrived at the square, and Palombo stood under the Portico and waited for his tall German friend. When he arrived, the two went into the building. Eliseo Bonichi tried to prevent the young boy from coming in, but the German soldier told him that Palombo was with him. Palombo joined the Germans at their table. One of the officers fiddled with the knobs of the radio.[3]

Just before 8 p.m., Edoardo Succhielli (also known as 'Renzino'), the founder and leader of the 'Banda Renzino', arrived at the outskirts of the village with a squad of partisans. Succhielli had heard that malicious rumours were circulating about partisans running away from the Germans, and he wanted to put a stop to them. He had been told that a group of Germans had been molesting the inhabitants of a farmhouse close to Civitella, where they were billeted, and he wanted to go there and confront them. However, Dr Gambassini, the village physician and partisan medical officer, had warned him off. The Germans had strong positions and many automatic weapons, he was told. They would certainly be able to defend themselves and inflict heavy casualties on the attackers. Also, it would be a mistake to fight German soldiers so close to the village—it could make matters much worse for the villagers. Instead, Succhielli decided to go Civitella, disarm the Germans that had been seen there, and return to the hills. He left half of his men by the edge of town and took the rest up towards the main square.

As he was walking up towards Via della Mura, some locals stopped him and told him that four Germans were drinking in the social club. It was an opportunity to catch the men off-guard; Succhielli and his men would act so quickly that no bullets would be fired and not a drop of blood spilled.

As they were approaching the Portico, Succhielli directed Dario Polletti, Angiolino Nappini, and Quintilio 'Bibi' Bacconi to stay outside and guard the door while he and Vasco Caroti went inside.

The young seminarist, Daniele Tiezzi, was sitting on the balcony of his family home, above the carpenter's workshop in Piazza Becattini, when he saw three men dodging from doorway to doorway, going in the direction of club, trying to avoid attracting attention. His older brother, Bruno, was in the club.

At around 8.15 p.m., Vasco Caroti entered the recreation room and saw the three Germans seated at their table. Some of the club members would have recognised Succhielli, and others would have known that he and his men were partisans from the red stars on their hats and red neckerchiefs. Succhielli strolled across the room, hands in pockets, and stood with his back to the window, facing the table where the Germans were sitting. He then drew out his pistol and shouted in Italian, '*Mani in alto!*' ('Hands up!'). One of the Germans immediately pushed Palombo down under the table and into the corner, behind the radio. The other two looked surprised and did not immediately react to the order. Succhielli shouted again, this time in German—'*Hände hoch!*'

Events then moved very quickly. The Germans went for their weapons and Succhielli and Caroti opened fire. Everyone else tried to avoid getting caught in the crossfire, some rushing for the bar next door.

Dario Polletti ran in to see one of the Germans moving towards the partisan leader with his bayonet, so he shot him in the head, killing him. Succhielli himself managed to kill another German, but then the lights went out. A third German was on the floor, seriously wounded and groaning with pain. Bruno Tiezzi and Guido Bidini were injured in the crossfire and were looking for a means of escape. Someone shouted, '*Italiani, fuori!*' ('Italians, outside!') and the lights came back on.

Francesco Fiorani got up from where he had hidden, behind a small table in the bar, and made his way out through the recreation room. He saw three German soldiers lying on the floor as he passed through the recreation room, and he assumed that they were dead. As he approached the exit, he told the partisans his name and was allowed to leave the club.

Francesco Marzoli also left the club safely, walking out of the bar through the recreation room with his hands above his head. He saw four or five men dressed in khaki and carrying rifles, but he did not recognise them. They ordered him to pass behind them so he could not see who else was in there. Bruno and Guido managed to escape soon after with the help of some other men.

Alba Bonichi had gone to look for her father, Eliseo, who was in the club. She was approaching the club when she heard a burst of gunfire. Soon afterwards, there was a scramble from the club doorway and her father came running up to her and told her to go home.

As Polombo made his way out of the club, he was swept aside by one of the armed partisans. The others had all gone, taking the German soldiers' weapons and leaving the dead bodies and injured soldier behind. Palombo sneaked along the Portico, keeping close to the wall, and then hid behind a column. He watched one of the partisans go towards the war memorial, where Dr Gambassini was standing, having been alerted to events by the noise. Palombo went to meet his mother at the Lammioni's house and, when he met Luigi at the door, he told him what he had seen. Mrs Rossi grabbed her son and marched him home immediately.

Daniele Tiezzi heard the sound of gunshots. On looking out of the window, he saw eight men running out of the club and heard them cursing. It was too dark for him to see them properly. His brother Bruno came home bleeding from a head wound. Fortunately, the wound was not severe, and Dr Gambassini was close at hand to tend to it at the infirmary opposite the war memorial. Guido Bidini was lucky too; he received only a superficial wound in his buttocks, which the doctor also treated.

The noise of the gunfire had been heard across the village. Lara Lammioni, who had earlier watched the coloured flares from her house, a few doors down from club, had heard a noise like the sudden and violent lowering of a metal shutter.

Laura Guasti Sabatini was at home with her children when her husband, Paolo, rushed in. He was accompanied by Gen. Del Buono, who was their evacuee guest and lived on the top floor of the house. Paolo had seen the partisans running in the direction of the club, and he had just finished telling his wife about it when they heard the gunshots.

After everyone had escaped the club, the uninjured German officer, who had been hiding in the bar, picked up his wounded companion and made his escape. Later that night, the injured soldier was taken by truck to the hospital at Montevarchi, where he died the next day.

There was concern as the news of the shooting spread through the village, along with questions as to what would happen next and fear of a reprisal. Many citizens fled the village that night to shelter with friends or acquaintances in the countryside nearby. Some waited until the next day to decide what to do.

Lara Lammioni was one of those who came out to see what had happened. She was worried because news of the massacres of Partina and Valluccione in Casentino, north of Arezzo, had reached her. When she returned home, her family were arguing about what to do, eventually deciding to leave after a few hours' rest to stay with friends at their farmhouse near Casa al Pazzo, around 3 km from Civitella.

The weather had worsened and it was now raining heavily again. Laura Sabatini put her children to bed while Paolo kept watch all night from an armchair facing the window, which looked out on the square.

The next morning, with the rain over, Francesco Fiorani left Civitella with his father and mother to go to a farm at Casa al Pazzo. He did not return until 17 July. Other villagers left their homes, some taking to the woods. Luigi Lammioni, his wife, Maria Sandrelli, and their three daughters left, seeking refuge at the farm of Fortunato Ciardi, around 2 km from Civitella.

Gina Magini was undecided about what to do. Everything went quiet after the shooting and everyone went to bed soon after. She had a house full of relatives to look after and a café to run with her husband, Rinaldo, who was also the village butcher. However, she was assured by a friend that nothing would happen, and so she decided to stay.

Giuseppina Caldelli, whose brother Adolfo had been in the club at the time of the shooting, came downstairs the next morning to find that he had left the village with his wife and children, leaving just her mother, Rosa Chinazzi Caldelli, in the house. Curious about what had happened at the club, Giuseppina went to have a look at the bodies. She reached the club at approximately 10 a.m. and saw the two dead Germans lying on the floor. She found that she was not needed as there were already people tending to the bodies and cleaning up the place.

Monday 19 June 1944

Two nuns from the Passionist community, which ran the infirmary, were already busy in the recreation room of the social club when Nurse Domenica Dondolini arrived just before 10 a.m.[4] One was on her hands and knees, cleaning the floor; the other was using a pitcher to fetch water from the sink in the bar next door. Abandoned playing cards and glasses of red wine were still on the tables, but the broken glass that had littered the stone floor had been swept to the side. There was a pile of clean white sheets in a basket by the window, and a small altar cross and two candles had been placed on the radio table.

Nurse Domenica had received a message from Don Alcide Lazzeri, the village priest, asking her to go to the *Dopolavoro* to clean the bodies and wash the blood from the floor. The German soldiers lay where they had fallen. Flowers had been placed by the side of one of the bodies so that as she bent down to look more closely at the corpses, the sweet smell of jasmine and roses filled her nostrils. She observed that one man had a bullet wound on his temple and one on his chest; the other had a wound on his temple and one on his face.

Domenica directed the Sisters to rearrange the tables in order to lay the bodies on them. Together, they washed the soldiers' hair, faces, and hands and sponged the blood on the uniforms to smarten them up. As they were finishing, Don Alcide arrived with Mrs Cau, a Swedish woman living with her Italian writer husband and children in nearby Gebbia. She occasionally acted as interpreter for the Germans at their headquarters at Villa Carletti, Monte San Savino, around 15 km away.[5] They stood in front of the makeshift altar for a moment and, when everything appeared ready, the priest blessed the dead men and placed a single lily on each man's chest while the Sisters recited prayers. There was nothing else to do but to wait for further instructions.

Later, Mrs Cau and her husband went to the Maginis' café for a meal and told their friends Rinaldo and Gina not to be afraid as nothing was going to happen. She told them that she had tried to get a lorry to take away the bodies that day but failed. It was getting late and they lived quite far away, in Cornia, so they spent the night at the Magini's house.

During the rest of the day, locals came to pay their respects and leave more flowers.

20 June 1944
Orders from General Field Marshal Albert Kesselring:

It is the duty of all troops and police in my command to adopt the severest measures. Every act of violence committed by partisans must be punished immediately. Reports submitted must also give details of countermeasures taken. Wherever there is evidence of considerable numbers of partisan groups, a proportion of the male population of the area will be arrested; and in the event of an act of violence being committed, these men will be shot.

Tuesday 20 June 1944

At approximately 7 a.m., Luigi Lammioni, who was the secretary of the Civitella hospital as well as town clerk of the commune, returned with his family. He needed to reassure the inhabitants—especially the elderly and infirm—that everything was all right. He also wanted to find out exactly what had happened on Sunday night at the after-work club.

He met Mrs Cau as she was leaving the village, and she told him that she had sent a letter by Rinaldo Magini to a German officer billeted at the farm of Dorna, near Badia al Pino, informing him of the death of the two Germans soldiers in the club. She also stated that the people guilty of the killings were not from the village. Luigi decided to go and see the bodies, try to identify the men, and enter their names in the register of deaths.

At approximately 10 a.m., some Germans arrived in a dusty Fiat Balilla and went into the *Dopolavoro*, accompanied by Mrs Cau. Don Alcide was sent for and he watched while the *Soldbuchs* (pay books) of the dead soldiers were examined. The men were identified as *Obergefreiter* Gustav Bruettger, aged twenty-one, from Rheinhausen, and *Obergefreiter* Ernst Menschig, aged twenty-three, from Braunsdorf.[6] Luigi was ordered to go and prepare coffins for the funeral, and one of the officers told Don Alcide that they would return to bury the bodies at 5 p.m. The priest and Mrs Cau tried to persuade the Germans that the people of the village were innocent and that nobody knew the perpetrators of the killings.

Luigi set to work on the coffins with some wood that the Sabatinis had donated. At approximately 2 p.m., a German truck drove up to the main piazza by the church. Inside were fifteen soldiers armed with submachine guns. Aldo Tavarnesi was watching from the window of his house. He was a civil engineer and had served in the Italian Army, and he took an interest in the Germans, noting the vehicles and uniforms.

Luigi went to speak to the soldiers, who told him that they had come to bury their comrades. One of the men spoke Italian very well, and Luigi explained to him that if they were to be buried in the local cemetery, he needed the names of the deceased and their next of kin to write down in the register. The soldiers agreed, and two of them accompanied Luigi to the house to fill in the register; the others went to collect the bodies and put them in the coffins, which were now ready.

Don Alcide arrived to bless the bodies; they were then loaded onto a lorry by the German soldiers and driven down to the cemetery at the bottom of the hill. People from the village followed the cortege, bringing flowers as a mark of respect. After a '*Requiescat in pacem*' from the priest, the coffins were lowered into the graves, accompanied by a ceremonial volley (the population had been warned in advance so as not to take fright).

After the burial, the soldiers returned to the village, looking for something to drink. They went from house to house, knocking on doors and politely asking for wine, which was given to them. Laura Sabatini felt reassured by these little courtesies on both sides; it made her think that everything would be resolved for the better.

As the wine began to take effect, the soldiers began driving around and shooting from various places. Nurse Dondolini looked out of her window and saw them firing into the valley beneath. She thought that this was done to entice the partisans to show themselves. She later found that the village was surrounded as Gen. Del Buono, a guest in her house, attempted to leave and was ordered back inside. Aldo Tavernesi, who was sitting in the square, heard someone shout in German and fled. The Germans spotted him and set off in pursuit, eventually tracking him down. He gave myself up and was escorted to the bottom of the village, where two other men were being detained.

Meanwhile, Luigi Lammioni had heard gunfire and, soon afterwards, heavy knocks at his front door:

When I opened the door, there were German soldiers pointing their weapons at me. They took me to the old tower, where they told me that they had seen a man with binoculars looking from the top as they were leaving Civitella. They had returned and searched the tower but did not find anybody. The soldiers then marched me to Porta Senese, where they were holding three men as civilian prisoners [one being Aldo Tavarnesi]. I explained that they all belonged to the village and had nothing to do with the shooting and so they were released.

Aldo was still within earshot when the German sergeant took Luigi to one side and interrogated him about the partisans. He demanded that Luigi give him the names of those responsible for the ambush and threatened terrible reprisals if nothing was forthcoming. He gave Luigi twenty-four hours to come up with the names.

I was allowed to go home but I was desperate and I rushed off to Guido Mammoli, the Mayor, and told him: 'I am a dead man because if I say something the partisans will kill me and if I don't say anything the Germans will take their revenge on me and my family.'

Mammoli advised Luigi to tell the Germans that he had been unable to get hold of any names. The Germans would think that fugitive prisoners of war were responsible.

The village remained quiet until approximately 6 p.m., when the Germans returned once more. Aldo Tavarnesi saw a 626 Fiat lorry carrying around thirty soldiers. He rushed home, hid in his attic, and watched out of the little roof window as soldiers dressed in camouflage jackets and helmets and armed with pistols and stick grenades in their belts jumped from the lorries and scattered through the village. They began to shoot again. Laura Sabatini was not sure what was happening now:

> They made us come out of our houses and rounded us up to check our identity cards. In the small square by the post office, we noticed a row of cars. We were all put in a group and the German officers examined my husband's papers and the ones of the other men and then they let us go.
>
>   They are finally satisfied, we thought, and hoped that the whole thing would be forgotten, especially as the Allies were not far away. There had been frequent strafings [*sic*.] from Allied planes and the German Army was retreating with vehicles of all types, including carts pulled by oxen. Later, the police chief who deputised for the Mayor came and told us that he had understood from the German Command that the population could come back to the village because it was recognised that they were innocent.

The Germans left, but more arrived in the area soon afterwards. They pitched tents in the woods and billeted themselves in farmhouses in the countryside surrounding the village.

Wednesday 21 June 1944

Very early in the morning, Don Alcide decided to go and look for the partisans in the woods of Cornia to tell them not to organise any more attacks on the Germans and stir things up again. The Germans had been impressed by the way the local population had behaved during the funeral and by their hospitality afterwards; they seemed to have abandoned the idea of reprisals. However, Banda Rezino activities continued in the area. They shot and wounded two Germans travelling by car near San Pancrazio, and they also attacked a small German unit in retreat and took fourteen prisoners. The Banda Rezino leader, Succhielli, said that four of the prisoners then joined the partisans.

After a few days, an official statement was issued by the Germans:

> The German Command has realised that the population of Civitella is not responsible for the killing. This is attributed to the rebels [the term used to indicate the partisans] and so the Archpriest Don Lazzeri is ordered to announce from the pulpit that the inhabitants of Civitella can safely return to their homes.

Lara Lammioni was pleased:

As soon as the news got out, we all started to return to our homes. We felt, reassured and confident since we did not have any part in what happened and became blind and unquestioning despite the reality of the frightful reprisals that had already taken place elsewhere.

A few days passed in relative calm. The front was getting nearer. Towards the south, flares lit the sky and we could already hear the rumble of guns and see their flashes [the Allies bombed Arezzo from 21–23 June].

During the night, long lines of retreating German lorries were heading north through the Trove Valley. We observed all this with some detachment. The nearing of the fighting was like a very dangerous unknown, but we thought that we, inhabitants of Civitella, a village so far away from the main roads and devoid of any military installation, would escape unscathed.

Then we started to hear announcements like: 'It is advisable that, during the passing of the front, all inhabitants remain in their homes as a security and safety measure,' and, 'All inhabitants are ordered to stay in their homes even if shots are heard.' Nobody thought of putting a more sinister interpretation to these announcements.

Nothing more happened until another party of German soldiers came six days later.

Tuesday 27 June 1944

Alba Bonichi saw members of the German *Feldgendarmerie* arrive in Civitella, accompanied by some local Fascists. 'They were taking lots of photographs,' Alba later remembered, 'especially of the ramparts and of Porta Senese. I stayed indoors.'

Nurse Domenica was in the hospital that afternoon. 'They came to take away our radio and to talk to me about their dead comrades. I told them that we did not know anything and that we heard that it was a partisan action.'

Maria Assunta Lammioni reported that two soldiers came to her house asking for radios and typewriters. One searched the house while the other showed her a list of names of those they suspected of having radios or typewriters and questioned her about them. She denied any knowledge, and the soldiers left.

At approximately 4 p.m., Oscare Giovannetti was in Piazza Vittorio Emanuele, where he saw two German soldiers arrive in a cream-coloured motorcar. They made him carry a radio set from the priest's house to their car. Lina Rossi was at home with her uncle, Don Alcide, when the soldiers came banging at the door:

Two Germans were in front of me asking to be let in. They wanted to requisition the radio that we had in the house. They held in their hand a sheet of paper on which I could read the names of all those who possessed a radio set. My uncle went to fetch the set, which we had stored in the cellar, wrapped in newspapers. We had done this to protect it from damage during the passing of the front, and, jokingly, he said to the soldiers, 'I am a poor country priest, the radio set is my only wealth,' which was true in a way as it was worth 3,000 lire. They laughed and told us that the radio would be returned soon, said goodbye very politely, and left.[7]

The soldiers eventually left the village, having confiscated all the radios they could from the local population. Lina recalled that no one suspected the truth:

That visit was the start of the extermination plan. With that innocent excuse they had come to the village to study its geography and to find out how many inhabitants had come back. I felt very anxious and implored my uncle to leave the village but my words fell on deaf ears. On the contrary, to scold me for my anxiety, he told me that the German military command had made known that the population of Civitella was considered innocent and that everybody was free to come back and would be left in peace. The trap worked.

On the evening of the 28th, the village came back to life; salvation seemed certain.

The church bells were ringing on the evening of 28 June, a comforting reminder that tomorrow was the great feast day of St Peter and St Paul. Everyone would be celebrating with their families; everything was returning to normal in their small, happy community.

PART II

PART II

Death in the Morning: 29 June 1944

The Germans came early in the morning, in large numbers and ready to kill, armed with machine guns, submachine guns, pistols, flamethrowers, and stick grenades. They wore long, camouflaged smocks and protective rubber aprons. Local Italian Fascists also joined them, dressed in German uniforms and with their faces masked—fearful of reprisals. They flooded Civitella and the surrounding countryside. Troops were positioned at crossroads, where they positioned machine guns mounted on the back of trucks. They waited there for locals to be rounded up as they went up to early mass in Civitella. Machine-gun nests were also set up on the highest points of the medieval ramparts and tower.

By 11 a.m., members of the 1st *Fallschirm* (Parachute) *Panzer Division Hermann Goering*, commanded by Hauptmann Heinz Barz, had killed 115 people and burned down three quarters of the buildings in Civitella.[1] At the same time, in the nearby hamlet of Cornia, fifty-eight people had been killed and nearly all the houses had been destroyed. By the early evening, in neighbouring San Pancrazio, seventy-one people had died; sixty had been lined up and shot in the wine cellar at Pierangeli Farm, where they had been held as prisoners for refusing to betray the partisans.

In Civitella, after the executions were over, the bodies were collected and thrown inside the burning houses in an effort to make them unrecognisable. The soldiers then sat on walls and steps, basking in the sunshine, eating their breakfast and drinking their stolen wine. Some former members of the disbanded *Hermann Goering Musik Korps*, who had been reassigned to the *Feldgendarmerie Abteilung 581* (the military police) took up the instruments belonging to the *Filarmonica Santa Cecilia* orchestra, which they had found in the school hall. The sound of popular German songs and marches echoed across the blood-soaked square.[2]

Feast of St Peter and St Paul, Thursday 29 June 1944

It was cool and dry in the early morning of 29 June. There would be another fine, hot day ahead, and there was just a light early morning mist settling over the valley below. The day marked the feast of St Peter and St Paul, the patron saints of Italy.

The women in Civitella were already up, preparing breakfast and getting ready for the busy day ahead. Many went to early morning mass and then returned home to begin cooking for their families. The men rose soon afterwards—some with work to do on their farms, in their workshops, or in their businesses. Others remained at home, travelling to a second mass before coming back to join their family for the special midday meal, which was held to celebrate the feast day and give thanks to God for their food and their continuing good fortune.

At 2 a.m., Emilio Bonichi had been woken by a great deal of noise and activity on his farm at Spoiano di Sopra. For the past year, German soldiers had been living in and around his farm, seven of them occupying rooms inside the house and the remainder camping in the woods around half a kilometre away. He heard vehicles and men moving out, and it wasn't until approximately 4 a.m. that things quietened down and he could get back to sleep. Emilio probably thought that the soldiers were going north, towards Florence, joining the troops retreating from the Trasimeno Line. At approximately 8 a.m., Emilio woke up again and looked out of a rear-bedroom window towards Civitella, which was clearly visible on the hilltop. Thick black smoke was rising from the village.

At 4.30 a.m., Giuseppe Bernini and his brother Vittorio started work on their farm at Palazzina, in the valley just below Civitella. They noticed that the surrounding countryside was full of German soldiers. Although they were worried by the sight, they assumed that the soldiers were just passing through the area as they had done many times before. One brother went off to cut corn while the other went to work near the farmhouse. Two hours later, they were both facing truck-mounted machine guns at the nearby bridge. They were held alongside seventy other men who had been rounded up at gunpoint by the Germans.

At the same time, Metello Ricciarini left his home, *Casa Alla Costa Di Tuori*, around 5 km from Civitella. He was taking bags of grain to be milled at the flour mill at Ciggiano. He said goodbye to his wife, Augusta, as he left. It would be the last time she saw him alive.

At 5 a.m., at Pierangeli, near San Pancrazio, farm manager Ugo Casciotto looked out of the window and saw two trucks coming towards the village. A short time later, he saw the men of the village being assembled by German soldiers in Piazza della Chiesa.

At 5.30 a.m., Maria Assunta Lammioni was busy around her house in Civitella. She had heard that the British were not far away and she had a few precious things that she wanted to hide from the retreating Germans. She helped her daughters, Luigina and Maria Rosaria, get dressed in their best frocks and sent them off to church. Shortly afterwards, her husband, Giovanni Battista, heard the noise of loud German voices just outside the village and went to investigate. When he returned, he told her to leave what she was doing, fetch the children from church, and leave the village at once. That was the last time she saw her husband alive.

Farmer Aldolfo Caldelli went out early that morning to gather mushrooms; that was the last time his sister, Giuseppina Giorgina, saw him alive.

Over in San Pancrazio, Laura Ciofi was at home with her husband, Alfredo, and brother-in-law, Altimo, when they heard vehicles arriving in the village. Two German soldiers burst into their house and, speaking Italian, ordered the men to go to the main square. Later, she took breakfast to them in Piazza della Chiesa, where they were lined up with other men in front of a machine-gun post. It was the last time she saw them alive.

At 6 a.m., Giuseppe Balò said goodbye to his wife, Maria, and went to look for his hat before leaving home to go to the local quarry, where he worked as supervisor. He wanted to dismantle some machinery to prevent it from being taken by the Germans. He woke his thirteen-year-old daughter, Ida, whom he knew loved removing anything that looked out of place. He was looking for his hat. That was the last time Ida saw her father alive.

At 7 a.m., Gina Magini was preparing breakfast for her husband, Rinaldo, when she heard gunfire. Soon afterwards, three Germans came in and took her husband away at gunpoint. She was ordered to leave at once and fled the village with her children.

Lina Rossi was eating breakfast and drinking coffee with her uncle, Don Alcide Lazzeri. He was going to be busy that day with special celebration masses at his church, Santa Maria Assunta. Lina and her uncle walked to church together at 6.30 a.m. An hour later, she watched him give the final benediction to the congregation before they were all pushed out of the church and into Piazza Vittorio Emanuele III. The women were sent away and the men were lined up in the square by the old cistern. That was the last time Lina saw her uncle alive.

Young Daniele Tiezzi was getting the church ready for mass—one of his jobs as a seminarist. He had to light the candles, set out the vestments, and check the communion wine. A few people had arrived early, including Sisters from the old people's home, and they were already seated, mouthing their Hail Marys as their fingers worked their rosary beads. Daniele had left his parents and his two brothers, Bruno and Dino, at home. Two hours later, he would be lying in the undergrowth, beneath the walls of the castle, having escaped his execution; he was injured by a bullet that passed through his body.

Just after 7 a.m., Francesco Marzoli was on his way back to his farm at nearby Capo Contra di Sopra after visiting the butcher in Civitella. Everything was quiet until he reached Porta Senese, the west gate, where he saw a large group of German soldiers coming towards him, shooting anyone that they saw trying to leave. With one hand in the air and the other holding the meat he had just bought, he walked on. When the moment was right, he ducked and ran into a vineyard just off the main road, avoiding a hail of bullets.

At approximately 7.30 a.m., Augusto Felicione, a farmer in Solaia, Cornia, heard gunfire and women screaming in the distance and went to the woods for safety. The machine-gun fire continued and he saw houses and barns burning nearby. At around 4.30 p.m., he finally felt safe enough to come out; he found all the houses on fire and a large pool of blood outside his barn.

Don Natale Romanelli left his mother, Emilia Tavanti, and disabled sister, Emma Romanelli, at home in Cornia at 7.30 a.m. He was on his way to say mass in nearby Verniana, but he heard rifle shots and machine-gun fire. He looked in the direction of the sound and saw that a smokescreen had been laid in the valley. He then met Brazio Mugnai, who warned him to return home as the Germans were burning houses in the area and he had heard shooting and screaming from the direction of Burrone. Don Natale rushed back to his village to warn his parishioners to leave the place immediately. His mother refused, believing that the Germans would not harm her as she was too old; she also stopped Emma, who was wheelchair-bound, from leaving. Don Natale would not see either of them alive again. He went in search of higher ground to find out what was happening, and he could see Civitella burning in the distance. Gunfire sent him into the woods to hide.

Lara Lammioni described what happened to her family on the day of the massacre:

We were getting closer to 29 June, the day of St Peter and Paul. There was nothing that could lead us to predict what was going to happen.

To afford a little more comfort to my relatives who had been evacuated from Arezzo—my maternal grandfather, my brother, and one of my mother's sisters, and to help my aunt Marietta to look after her three little daughters, I was sleeping in my uncle Luigi Lammioni's house, in a small room facing the square Piazza Vittorio Emanuele III.

On the morning of the 29th at around 7.30 a.m., the sound of agitated women's voices outside awoke me. I did not know the reason for that agitation and ran to my uncle to find out why. He told me that armed Germans had gone into the church but he was not sure what was happening.

Then the shooting began. I ran to my aunt Marietta to help her dress my three little cousins. I was determined to stay with them, but I heard my father calling me, 'Lara, come down at once, your place now is here with us.' His voice had a sombre and authoritarian tone that I had never heard before and that made me feel uneasy. I could not object and I decided to go down the stairs to my home, which was situated on the ground floor of the same building, separating myself from the tragic destiny that was later to befall my aunt Maria Sandrelli and my two little cousins, Giuliana and Maria Luigia Lammioni.

Things were coming to a head. My uncle Luigi, appearing at the window of the room facing the back of the house, was shouting, 'Uncle Bista [Giovanni Battista Lammioni] is here below the cellar door. He wants us to let him in.'

I flew down the stairs to the cellar and tried to unlock the stiff locks of the large wooden door. At that moment I heard a shot very near me. I was not yet aware of what was happening. Finally, I managed to open the door and found myself in front of Uncle Bista, who was lying on the ground, terribly pale, but with a serene expression on his face. Believing that he was only wounded, I tried to go to him, but the strong hand of my other uncle, who had come down after me, held me back. 'Don't go out.

The Germans will kill you too!' he said. I replied, 'But Uncle Bista cannot be dead, he is only wounded, perhaps by mistake. Why should the Germans kill him?'

The impact of the death of that very dear person was too strong. I could not accept it. For years I was obsessed by the thought that if I had gone downstairs faster, if I had been able to open the door faster, perhaps my uncle would have been saved. My mind kept going over the seconds that elapsed between the shot and the opening of the door.

Uncle Bista had left his house very early in the morning, alarmed by what he had seen from the windows facing the *piano di Civitella* [the valley to the south of the village] towards the Val di Chiana, perhaps an unusual movement of German troops.

He had saved himself by going over the village walls in a spot in my garden where it was easy to go across. Then, the thought of his family and his brothers made him come back to the village and to his death.

I ran back upstairs to persuade my father to come down with me and bring Uncle Bista in. By then, my family had congregated in the large room that was facing the back, just over the cellar door. There was my father, Dante Lammioni, a retired Major in the Italian Army, my mother, Armida Caccialupi, my little sister, Maria Grazia, and Uncle and Aunt Caccialupi (my mother's brother and sister), who had been evacuated from Arezzo.

My grandfather Federico Caccialupi was missing. He had gone to the first mass and I would never see him alive again.

I said to my father, 'Father, they have wounded Uncle Bista, we need to go and get him right away!'

He answered, 'Uncle is not wounded; he is dead. There is nothing we can do for him now. Believe me, I have seen many die in the Great War.'

My relatives began discussing the possibility of my father and Uncle Giuseppe escaping through a trap door that led from the room where we were to our old cellar. Eventually, this solution was rejected—I don't remember why. Perhaps it was not thought to be sufficiently safe, or perhaps my father did not like the idea of leaving us alone in that moment.

The sound of shots was intensifying and Aunt Assunta, the wife of my Uncle Bista, ran in, carrying her youngest son. She was followed by the other three children. She knew about her husband's death and was crying in desperation. My father embraced her and said, 'Assunta, remember that as long as I live, my brother's children will be my children.' These were his penultimate words.

We heard loud banging at the front door. My father saw the terror and dismay in my eyes and told me, 'Lara, you always told me that you had courage. This is the time to show it.' These were his very last words.

I went to open the door and was faced by four Germans. They pushed me to one side and pointed their weapons at my father, who had followed me. My father lifted his hands, and that gesture hit me painfully; it was as if the support against which I leant with so much confidence had suddenly collapsed, leaving me defenceless.

They made us leave the house, I was holding my father's arm; my mother, my little sister, Maria Grazia, and the others were following. They led us towards the square and the church. The square was full of German soldiers and echoed with commands shouted in German.

I thought that the shooting had stopped. I noticed that many soldiers were wearing a sort of long apron of camouflaged rubber over their uniform. I did not realise the macabre significance of that accessory at the time.

We had been walking towards the church and we had just passed the *cisterna* [well], when a German separated me from my father. When I resisted, he pushed me away and showed me where we were supposed to go, towards the war memorial in Piazza Becattini. Out of the corner of my eye, I saw my father trying to speak to a soldier. He took off his watch and gave it to him.

As we were walking through the porticos on the right-hand side, I noticed that something was out of place. There was a short, dark-haired soldier in German uniform, leaning against an arch while an officer with a gun in his hand was yelling at him. The little soldier was desperately shaking his head and there was terror on his face.

Naturally, I did not stop; I only registered this strange scene. After a few paces more, I heard a shot being fired very close to me, and I was immediately sure that the little soldier had been shot; however, I did not see him fall, nor did I see his corpse, because the well was in the way. Nobody else in the group seemed to have noticed what had happened—they were ahead and on the left of me. I started to think that I had been mistaken; anyway, other things were happening.

We passed the war memorial and went towards Porta Senese. There were fewer soldiers in this part of the village and the sound of shots was muffled. I noticed a few old men walking away from the village.

Coming out of Porta Senese, we continued to walk for a while and then we stopped under the cypresses of Maesta' Tonda, around 1 km from Civitella, to wait for news. There was profound distress and we could not clearly understand what had happened and why. At the bottom of our hearts there was still the hope that our dear men had been spared.

Very soon the news arrived—everyone killed, all the houses on fire.

Dino Tiezzi was ten years old and lived in Civitella, above the carpenter's shop in Piazza Becattini, with his father, Pilade, mother, Giuseppa and brothers, Bruno and Daniele. Daniele was away, training to be a priest. Dino still remembers the events of the massacre in detail:

Our house was adjacent to the house of our local doctor, Luciano Gambassini, who was so active in the Resistance that the Fascists often came over to look for him. To help him and also to earn a little money, we let him have a room in our house and we crowded into the remaining rooms. We built a partition wall between our quarters and this room while he made a hole in the wall that separated his house from ours, so that he could get quick access to his hiding place. He concealed the hole with a wardrobe. When the Fascists came to look for him, he would go through the hole into the room and escape from there through a bolthole, which led to the ground floor and to a door on the side of our house.

On the morning of 29 June, my mother had gone to mass at about 7 a.m. Not long after, we began to hear shots fired in the village and my mother suddenly returned having been warned that the Germans were coming. She had gone to the early mass so that she could prepare dinner for the whole family afterwards. She rushed into the house shouting, 'The Germans, the Germans, the Germans!'

My father took the ladder, intending to climb onto the roof to get a better view of the situation from there, hiding behind the chimney. However, he became worried that the Germans would discover Doctor Gambassini's hiding place, so he decided to come down again to the bedroom where we all slept. I had another brother, Daniele, who was studying to become a priest and did not live with us then.

My father tried to calm my mother, telling her that it was better if we all kept our heads because we had not done anything wrong. At that moment a hand grenade exploded outside, destroying the supports of our large balcony, which collapsed in a heap below. We were suddenly overcome by the acrid smell of the explosives and choked by the masonry dust. Two armed German soldiers forced their way into the house. My mother went below to meet them and we could hear her shouting. I don't know whether they could understand her, but I hoped they could since there were many German-speaking Italians from the Alto Adige region among the German soldiers in the area.

My mother was shouting, 'My little child is sick, please do not go upstairs, he is sick!' I wasn't sick, but she was trying to protect me with an excuse to keep the Germans away. The next sound I heard was of footsteps as the soldiers started to climb the stairs, which they were doing very carefully because they were climbing a very steep staircase and did not know what they would find at the top. I was in the double bed in front of the door and my father and my brother were sitting on the other bed. The soldiers looked up when their heads were just in line with the bottom of the door and I could see their helmets. They saw me in the bed and then saw my father and brother.

They were very young—teenagers. They lifted their rifles and fired. I immediately climbed out of the bed and one of the bullets passed so close to my head that I can feel the sensation even now. As my father moved, an explosive bullet hit him in the face and he dropped on the bed, crying in pain. The other bullet hit my brother in the head and he fell without a sound. I found myself alone, facing this terrible tragedy. I felt the bad smell of the gun smoke in my lungs and throat, and I threw myself face-down on the bed because I did not want to see my father choking and with his face destroyed by the explosive bullet. I don't know how long I remained there.

On the ground floor of our house there was a carpenter's shop that was full of timber. The Germans set fire to it with a flamethrower and the house started to fill with smoke. I did not move. My mother came up as soon as the soldiers had gone and saw her husband in that appalling condition. She went to get a towel to cover his face, which had been cracked wide open. She desperately tried to keep it together, trying to stem the blood flow. She was so busy trying to help him that she forgot about me. Before coming upstairs, my mother had called for help. My aunt, the local schoolteacher, arrived. She dressed me as best as she could and took me away as the house was filling with smoke and starting to burn.

We came out in Piazza Becattini, which is the square with the War Memorial. They had thrown a hand grenade at the Old People's Home and some of the residents had been killed, and their corpses were on the stairs and inside the entrance. The place was covered in blood. My family owned a hut, where we used to keep firewood, that abutted the castle walls. Months earlier, we had managed to knock a hole in the walls to provide an escape route in case of danger. We decided to go there and leave the village, unseen, through the hole. We found the body of my uncle lying outside the hut. We saw that the Germans had already been inside and had taken away the firewood. We went through the hole and came out on the other side.

As soon as we came out, the machine gun that was on the tower started to shoot at us. At first we held back, but then we decided to run and kept low under the precarious cover of the walls supporting the terraces. The Germans kept on shooting, but finally we ended up in a place where the vegetation was very dense and gave us shelter. In the end, we reached a track that led to some fields and got to the main road, the Via Senese. There we met all the other people who were fleeing from the village.

Women and children were running screaming and crying. The Germans positioned in the castle started to shoot at us. They probably did not recognise us as women and children because if they had, they would not have tried to kill us. There we met my aunt's good friend Elda Paggi with her sons. Still in her nightdress and covered in blood, she was screaming, 'They have killed my husband. They have killed my husband.' She had tried to come to the rescue of her husband and was going crazy, trying to get her children away. Then we lost sight of her. We arrived at a villa that was used as a holiday home for a female college in Arezzo, and we stopped there.

The next day we tried to go back to Civitella, full of fear of what we would find. While we were walking, we heard the noise of engines and ran to hide in the woods. As soon as we came out of hiding, we saw a huge column of smoke rising from Civitella. The village was just a burning brazier in this clear morning. The Germans had set fire to the village to try and eradicate all traces of the massacre. They killed people where they found them, took the bodies to the houses, and then set fire to the houses. Many bodies were half-burned. After that, all we had left of my father, Pilade, and brother Bruno were two carbonised corpses.

9

Escape From the Massacre

Some might say that it was thanks to the grace of St Peter and St Paul that little Luigi Bigiarini was spared death that fateful day, and that he had been singled out for salvation. Others would say that it was pure luck that he lived. Luigi certainly had the good fortune of looking young for his age. Having been lined up with all the other men in the square to be executed, one sharp-eyed soldier thought he did not look fifteen. Not wanting to breach the order to kill every male over the age of fifteen that they found, the soldier pulled Luigi out of line and told him to get out of Civitella as fast as his little legs would take him. Luigi would later report what he had witnessed outside the church in Piazza Vittorio Emanuele III.

Gino Bartolucci, the village blacksmith, and Daniele Tiezzi, the young seminarist, were two other males who escaped just as they were standing in line in the central square, about to be executed.

Gino was on his way to church to join his family at about 6.45 a.m. when his wife came running towards him. She told him that the Germans were coming, so they needed to go home immediately with the rest of the family:

A short while after we got home, I heard the sound of shots and looked through the back window of my house to see Giovanni Battista Lammioni lying on his back in the road. I did not go out and look at the body but realised from the way he was lying—his eyes closed, arms outstretched and not moving—that he was dead.

I went to the front window and saw about twenty Germans fixing up machine guns on tripods in the piazza facing the church. After a few minutes, villagers started to stream out of the church with their hands above their heads.

There was a loud banging on my door and I went downstairs with my wife and family. My wife opened the door and was confronted by a German soldier pointing a rifle at her. He was wearing a camouflaged smock reaching down to his knees, gathered at the waist by a belt, and dark coloured trousers and a steel helmet. He also carried an automatic pistol.

Seeing me, he grabbed me by my jacket lapels and dragged me out of the house. At the same time he shouted in Italian, 'Go away, women!' I am certain that he was

Italian. My wife and daughter went off down the street and I was dragged by the soldier into the piazza and lined up with another twenty to thirty local men who were standing near the old cisterna.

Men and women were still coming out of church with their hands up above their heads. After they had walked a little way into the square, the men were forced into line by the German soldiers and the women and children were hustled away.

There were about twenty-five Germans in the square, all dressed in camouflaged smocks. There were three machine guns with German gunners positioned behind them. They all carried rifles or pistols.

One German appeared to be in charge. Tall and well-built, he was dressed the same as the others but armed with submachine gun and pistol and giving orders to the others.

While we were standing in the square, the German soldiers frisked us and took our wallets and wristwatches and put them in their pockets. My wallet, which contained 500 lire, was taken and pocketed by one soldier.

The German in command shouted in Italian, 'Five!' So five Italians were led towards the back of the school in Via San Francesco, where I could see more machine gun posts. When the Italians reached the back of the school, I could see some German soldiers forming them into a line facing the wall.

A German soldier then stepped forward with a gun, aiming it at the back of the head of our priest, on the right of the line, and he pulled the trigger. Don Alcide Lazzeri fell to the ground. The soldier passed along the line, behind the men of the village, from right to left. He shot and killed each of the Italian citizens.

In the square, we were arranged in groups of five and led towards the back of the school. I was in the second lot of five and we were marched right behind the five in front of us. We were stopped at the back of the school, about five paces away from the first five. I kept my head down and stared at the ground because I was afraid to look, but I could not help seeing the bodies of the first five. They were Don Alcide Lazzeri, Torquato Menchetti, Paolo Sabatini, Giuseppe Pasqui, and Agostino Tavarnesi. There was blood pouring from their heads and they were obviously dead.

The Germans lined up the five men in front of us, facing the village wall. I saw the soldier stand behind the civilian on the right and raise his revolver to the back of the man's head. As he did so, I saw Daniele Tiezzi, one of the five men about to be executed, hurl himself to the left and run for his life. One of the Germans fired a burst of bullets at him with his machine gun but did not hit him. He fired again, but Daniele kept running until he was out of sight.

The German with the revolver continued to walk behind the other four left in line and fired one shot directly into the back of each man's head. Each dropped dead to the ground about 3 metres away from me.

Our line of five was pushed forward up against the dead bodies. I was second from the left, on my right Dante Lammioni, on my left Dario Scaletti. I watched again as the same German with the revolver stood behind the man on the right and raised his weapon. I heard an explosion and the man fell. He raised his weapon once again and there was another explosion, and the other man dropped to the ground.

Dante Lammioni, overcome with terror, then fell back onto the ground and started groaning and crying out, covering his eyes with his hands. The German with the pistol stood over him and fired three shots into his chest, and then there was no more movement or sound from Dante.

It was my turn. The German stood behind me, and I saw him raise the pistol to the back of my head out of the corner of my eye. I put my hands on the sides of my face, anticipating the shot. As he fired, I turned my head to the left. I felt the muzzle of the gun against my hand and heard the recoil. Immediately I felt a burning pain in both my hands, my face, mouth, and throat, and—realising that I was still alive—I slid down to the ground and lay there, pretending to be dead.

The shot had passed through my left hand, which was covering my face, through my throat and cheek, coming out through my right hand.

I stayed there without moving until the Germans had gone. As I lay there I heard many shots fired—all single, distinct shots—and heard many bodies fall near me. When the Germans had gone, I opened my eyes and saw the bodies of my fellow villagers all around me.

I managed to crawl across the street and over the village wall, making my way into the woods, where I was helped by a friend who treated my wounds. I gradually made my way to the house of Amerigo Volpi and stayed there for nearly a month, treated by Doctor Gambassini.

About ten days after I got there, I was picked up by the Germans and forced to carry logs for them for a day, despite my wounds.

I returned to Civitella some days after its liberation by the British. My house was completely destroyed. As a result of my injuries, I was left with a paralysed left thumb and unable to eat any solid foods.

Daniele Tiezzi was assisting Don Alcide Lazzeri at the first service of the Feast Day at the Church of Santa Maria Assunta. It was around 7.30 a.m., and the service was nearing its end:

I was aware that the large congregation had become restless. People were murmuring and whispering and I heard what I took to be rifle shots in the distance. Some women left the church, but the service continued and the sound of firing got nearer and louder. The priest interrupted the service and told us all not to worry as the Germans were retreating and, if they attempted to take any of our property, we were not to resist but to let them take whatever they wanted and avoid any confrontation.

The service was practically over when there was an explosion that sounded like a grenade bursting outside the church door. A local man rushed in and I heard him tell Don Alcide that the Germans had fixed up three machine guns in the Piazza, covering the church door. 'The Germans are shooting and killing everyone.'

Everybody was alarmed and tried to move back towards the presbytery. There was much noise and confusion.

Most of the congregation remained inside the church. Four German soldiers entered the church, three carrying pistols and one a sub machine gun. They all wore the same dress—steel helmets, camouflaged smocks, and each had a red band with black lettering on this sleeve between their shoulder and elbow.

They were shouting at the congregation in Italian, ordering them to get out of the church and menacing the people with the weapons they carried. They even searched the confessional boxes. People started to file out of church with their hands above their heads, and I was one of the last to leave, still dressed in my cassock, which I was wearing for the service.

When I got to the church door, I saw seven or eight machine guns ready to fire, with German gunners in position behind them. I heard a voice shouting, 'Keep your heads up!', and I moved forward with the women as I thought my cassock might conceal my identity.

There were also about twenty-five more Germans in the Piazza, mostly armed with pistols, and I saw that the women were being sent away down the street while the men were being lined up near the water cistern.

I was still amongst a small group of women when I saw the same sergeant who had dragged me out of my house two days before (following the incident in the social club) stopping people to check their identity papers. He saw me, grabbed me by the arm, and hustled me over to where the men were lined up. As I stood there, I saw that several houses in the village were burning.

He called out to some soldiers in German and they came over to where we were standing and searched us. They took wallets and wristwatches from the villagers and placed them in their pockets, but I did not lose my wallet, which was in my hip pocket. I was searched, but luckily they didn't find it. The soldier who searched me said in an obvious Tuscan dialect, 'Have you got anything?'

After we had been checked, I heard another voice coming from the direction of the school, shouting in Italian, 'Fire!'

It was then that I saw a German shove our priest, who had been lined up with us, in the direction of the school. Don Alcide told the German, 'We are innocent. We have done nobody any harm and have done no wrong.' The German shrugged his shoulders and carried on pushing the priest towards the school.

The Sergeant with the pistol in his hand said something in German and dragged four more men out of the group. They were menaced on each side by German soldiers armed with sub machine guns, and they were forced to march down the road and behind the school, out of sight. A minute or two later, I heard several shots.

A German soldier came up the road from the direction of the back of the school, and in broken Italian he shouted, 'Another five!' The sergeant caught hold of me and pushed me forward. I walked towards the back of the school, followed by another four men.

When I reached the back of the school, I saw a manned machine gun facing the Piazza. There were three other manned machine guns, two on one side and one opposite the first one, all occupying three sides of the square.

I then saw the bodies of the first five Italians to leave the Piazza—Don Alcide Lazzeri, Torquato Menchetti, Paolo Sabatini, and Agostino Pasqui. All of their faces were covered in blood and they appeared to be dead.

The five of us were formed up in a rough line by soldiers, and another soldier armed with a pistol followed behind us. We were standing with the bodies by our side and with our backs to two machine guns. I was so afraid. I was young, and my survival instinct was strong. I had to try to get away. I remember that escape plans were flashing through my mind and I can still see the German who was aiming his machine gun at me. At that moment I made up my mind, realising that I had only a few seconds left.

The German soldier with the pistol stood clear of us and raised his weapon as a signal to the machine gunners. I saw the machine gunner on my left smile and nod to the machine gunner on my right, and I heard the click of the machine gun being cocked. For a moment, my feet were paralysed; I felt like a statue. Then, a second later, I sprang forward, turned to my left, and ran.

I passed the German with the pistol, who was caught off-guard and made no attempt to stop me. The squad commander saw me and tried to stop me but I hit him in the stomach with my elbow and ran as fast as I could among a burst of gunfire, along the back road of the village, zigzagging as I went. I kept going and didn't stop to look back. There were bodies on the road and I stepped over them.

I heard a burst of machine-gun fire behind me and bullets whistled past me. Later, I discovered two bullet holes in my cassock and one in my trouser leg, but I was not hit by that burst of fire. I carried on running and then felt a blow on my right side. I fell down, but feeling no pain and hearing somebody running after me, I got up quickly and continued running. I dodged behind a building about 100 metres from the school and jumped over the village wall. This wall was not high from the roadside, but on the other side there was a very steep drop into the vegetation beneath.

As Civitella is built on top of a hill and the hillside at this point was terraced for growing grapes, it was a dangerous area to land on. It was full of stakes sunk in the ground, holding the wires that held up the vines, but I managed to kick them away. As I left the shelter of the wall, I was fired upon and hit in the side. Eventually I threw myself into some dense vegetation and the Germans could not see me despite looking down from the ramparts.

I hid for a while as I was bleeding quite a lot and felt faint. When I was sure that the coast was clear, I made my way into the woods, where I managed to hide before losing consciousness. I came around to the sound of the voices of two German soldiers evidently searching for locals. They were having fun firing shots into clumps of bushes, including the one where I was hiding, but fortunately I was not hit again.

I was not far from Civitella and could still hear explosions and the anguished cries of the women echoing across the valley. After things quietened down, I attempted to move but found that I could not do so. I was discovered later that the day by some relatives who treated my injuries. I had wounds in my back and in my chest on the right side of my body, caused by a bullet that had passed through my body from the back to the front.

My uncle hid me in a small farmhouse and put my cassock in a chest so that when a group of Germans came to search the house and found the garment, they mistook it for a woman's dress. I pretended to be an evacuated student. They belonged to the Hermann Goering Regiment and they were very young. We even chatted a little bit in Latin and made jokes. Two days later, Doctor Rosai from Badia al Pino visited me and treated me.

Soon afterwards, after hearing that the Germans were preparing to defend Civitella against the British, I left the house and took to the woods again. A few days later, I was picked up at night by members of the Hermann Goering Regiment and forced to dig trenches near Arezzo.

Even those who managed to escape being shot or got away from their burning homes suffered further terrible losses.

Town Clerk Luigi Lammioni had dealt with the German officials soon after the killings in the social club and after supervising the burials. In spite of not revealing any names of partisans to the Germans, there were no repercussions other than soldiers coming to search houses, check identity papers, and confiscate radio sets. Like many in the village who had returned after the initial fear of reprisal, Luigi had been lulled into a false sense of security.

The days after the shooting passed without incident, and most people just got on with their lives. They had no reason to fear a reprisal; after all, they were not partisans and had nothing to do with them or the shooting.

The next time Luigi saw German soldiers in Civitella was on 29 June 1944:

My wife Maria [Marietta] Sandrelli went to Mass at about 6.45 a.m. At about 7, I heard my brother, Giovanni Battista, calling me from the back of the house. He told me to get out immediately because the Germans were coming. I rushed downstairs, but as I was descending, I heard rifle shots very close by. These rifle shots frightened me, so I opened the door very carefully and saw my brother lying in a pool of blood in the street. I did not dare go to him in case the Germans were still there. I closed the door quietly and went back into the house. My wife had returned from church in the meantime, and she suggested that we all hide in the loft.

I got my children, Giuliana, Maria Luigia, and little Vittoria, and we went up to where we stored the fuel for our stove. The loft was half-full of charcoal and there was only a small window in the roof. We heard a lot of shooting around the village, but no one was shooting where we were. I started to feel ill and short of breath after a while, and I opened the roof window to get some fresh air. It was then that I realised the house was on fire. I turned to look at my wife, and I saw that she was foaming at the mouth and that the girls were lying perfectly still. I grabbed my wife, but I could not help her because she was already dead. Giuliana and Maria Luigia had been killed too by the fumes. I picked up my only living child, five-year-old Vittoria, and pushed her through the roof window. I followed my daughter, and, walking across the tiled roof, we got into the house next door.

The shooting continued in the village, so I waited a little time before going outside. When I did, there were just two Germans left in the square. I went to them and asked them if they would take pity on my little girl and spare us. They turned their backs and left without saying a word. Then I went to sit outside the school, where I saw four bodies. I recognised one as Virgilio Caldelli. I stopped there for a little and afterwards I went to the hospital, where I stayed the rest of the day.[1]

Giuseppa Bozzi lived with her husband, Conforto, and four sons—Bernardo, twenty-eight, Alighiero, twenty-six, Fernando, twenty, and Pietro, nineteen—at the farm Podere alla Fonte, approximately 1 kilometre south of Civitella. The family were not particularly worried about repercussions from the shootings on 18 June as they did not live in the village. Some German soldiers had come to the house two days later and ordered them outside while they searched the house, but the family was not harmed. They later found out that the Germans had taken five ducks and 15 kilos of chestnuts.

However, on the day of the massacre, the Bozzi family suffered terrible losses. Giuseppa described how she and one of her four sons managed to escape death:

The next time I saw any Germans was at about 6 a.m. on 29 June, when I saw German lorries on the Civitella road and soldiers in the fields. About an hour later, I saw some of these soldiers coming towards our farm and thought that they were going to take some more of our livestock, so I sent my son Alighiero off with the oxen while I saw to the sheep. When I looked back at the farm to check what was happening, I saw my husband and my other three sons walking away with the Germans.

I was about 500 m away when I heard shots, and I turned to see my husband and sons fall to the ground, one after the other. I ran to find Alighiero to tell him what I had seen. He was hiding behind a rock as he too had been fired upon, but he was not hurt. As he had no boots or a coat, I told him to wait there while I went back home to get them for him.

When I got back to the farm, I went straight to the bodies of my husband and sons. All of them had bullet wounds in the head. My two youngest sons were still alive, but I couldn't help them as they were too big and heavy for me to lift. I went inside the house to get the boots and coat, but as I was looking for them, six German soldiers came in and asked if there were any men hiding in there. I told them that all my men were already dead. They ordered me to get out of the house. I refused to obey them and sat down on the doorstep. The Germans proceeded to set fire to the bedroom and leave, but I managed to put the fire out.

I went back to my son, gave him his boots and coat, and told him what had happened and that he must run away and hide in the woods. I returned to the house and saw that my two youngest children had died. At about 5 p.m., two men called at the farm. I didn't know them, but they helped to carry the bodies into the barn, where we washed them as best we could. A few hours later, my son Alighiero appeared and he helped the men make three rough coffins—a job that took most of Friday.

At about 3 p.m. on Saturday 1 July, we managed to put the bodies of my husband and sons into their coffins and then into a handcart, which we pushed to the cemetery. There was no priest present when we buried them.

Gemma Falsetti was lucky to escape from the church with her three children while the massacre in the square and at the rear of the school was in progress. She had left her husband, Settimo, at home. She never saw him alive again:

The service had just finished when a German soldier walked into the church. He started waving his rifle around and shouting, so we understood that he wanted us all to go outside....

I went out of the side door of the church with the nuns and my children and then into the latrines at the rear of the Asilo Sacro Cuore—the Nursery School of the Sacred Heart. There were eleven of us hiding in there and we stayed there until about 11 a.m. We could hear a lot of gunfire, but we did not know what was going on.

When I left our hiding place and came into the village, I saw a lot of houses burning and some lying in ruins in the street. I went with the sisters up to the hospital in Piazza Becattini for company as the village was deserted. At the hospital door, I saw my first bodies—those of four old men. I wondered what had happened to my husband at home while I was at church.

I didn't find my husband at home and I couldn't find him anywhere in the village, so I thought that he must have gone back to the farm to work. I then took to the woods with my children and left them there so that they would be safe while I went to look for my husband.

Angiolino Alberelli, a farm labourer from Dornia, was walking along the road to Civitella at approximately 7 a.m. on the 29th when he met a group of what appeared to be terrified women coming out of the village. They told him that the Germans were in Civitella, so he decided to turn back and go home. As he set off on the road near the cemetery, a party of around fifteen German soldiers stopped him and his uncle Settimo Falsetti, whom he had just met making his way out of the village. He and his family had been staying with his uncle at the farm the past week since the shooting on 18 June, and he had only just returned to Civitella, thinking it was now safe.

They were both searched and then taken to the Floriano crossroads, where they saw fifty more Germans.

We were taken to a field around 50 metres from our farm, and one of the Germans told us that we could go, so my uncle and I began walking towards our farm. We

John Percival Morgan,
Temporary Major, on leave in
Merthyr Tydfil, October 1945.
(*Morgan Family*)

Reverend Clement O'Shea,
RC Chaplain to the
Forces, France, April 1940.
(*Newman Family*)

A view of the hilltop village of Civitella in Val di Chiana, 2013. (*Dee La Vardera*)

Keith Morgan at the unveiling of Costa Capitano John Percival Morgan, Civitella, 2001. (*Morgan Family*)

The Church of Santa Maria Assunta, Civitella, 2013. (*Dee La Vardera*)

John Morgan's photograph of soldiers among the ruins of the Church of Santa Maria Assunta, Civitella, July 1944. (*Morgan Family*)

Cyfarthfa Iron and Steelworks *c.* 1900–1910.
(*Cyfarthfa Castle Museum & Art Gallery, Merthyr Tydfil.*)

Arthur and Louisa Morgan with John, Barry Island, 1922. (*Morgan Family*)

John Morgan with his father,
Arthur, at the rear of No. 9 The
Parade, Merthyr Tydfil, *c.* 1920.
(*Morgan Family*)

John with his mother, Louisa,
on his motorbike, Merthyr
Tydfil, 1936.
(Morgan Family)

Cyfarthfa Castle School photograph, *c*. 1930. Physics teacher and form master Evan Davies is in the middle row, while John Morgan is at the far right. (*Morgan Family*)

BLACKWOOD (Mon.) (8).
Telephone No.—46.
Office Hours—10 till 3 ; Saturday, 9 till 12.
Staff.—B. MOUNTJOY (*p.*), *Manager.*
    T. Thomas
    J. E. Griffiths (*F.*)
    J. P. Morgan

Above: Lloyds Bank Blackwood staff, 1935.

Left: A Lloyds Bank advert from 1947. (*Lloyds Banking Group Archives & Museums*)

Then you won't require my husband's signature?

The day has gone when husbands regarded their wives as chattels. Among the customers of Lloyds Bank are many married women who have their private accounts and manage their own monetary affairs in complete independence. They enjoy all the facilities the bank offers ; and, of course, their transactions with the bank are treated with inviolable confidence.

Let LLOYDS BANK
look after *your* interests

The wedding of John Morgan and Barbara Jenkins at St Woolos Church, Newport, on 30 March 1946. (*Morgan Family*)

A day out in the Morris Oxford for the Morgan family, with their neighbour, Mrs Morris, 1962. (*Morgan Family*)

Mount Argus Superiors with 1922 Ordination Class
Front Row - Frs. Austin Tierney, Kieran Farrelly, Oswald Donnelly, Richard Curran, Ambrose Hayes, Lambert Hayden, Sylvester Palmer.
Middle Row - Alexis Boyd, Conleth Boothman, Thomas Mackenzie, Paul Cyril Doherty, Columba Daly, Michael O'Donnell, Clement O'Shea, Rupert Lennon.
Back Row - Stephen Lafferty, Victor Louchran, Gerard O'Neill, Stanislaus Cross, Cronan Doyle, Bonaventure Thom.

Mount Argus Superiors with their 1922 Ordination Class, Dublin. Father Clement O'Shea is in the middle row, second right. (*Mount Argus Archive*)

A Passionist banner at the Church of Our Lady of the Sacred Heart, Herne Bay, 2014. (*Dee La Vardera*)

Father O'Shea's legacy—the Lourdes Grotto at the Church of Our Lady of the Sacred Heart, Herne Bay, 2014. (*Dee La Vardera*)

Father O'Shea visits the grave of his brother, 2nd Lt Dermot O'Shea, Tank Corps, at Newfoundland Park, near Beaumont Hamel, France, on 3 April 1940. His brother had died on 10 August 1918. (*Newman Family*)

Left: The 12 CCS St George's Day menu, France, 23 April 1940. The menu was drawn by Father O'Shea and signed by the company. (*Newman Family*)

Below: A section of Father 'Cockie' O'Shea's wanted poster, 12 CSS, France, May 1940. (*Newman Family*)

WANTED.

A REWARD of 10 cents will be given for information as to the whereabouts and known abodes of C. O'Shea. 12ᵗʰ. C.C.S.

FOUND GUILTY BY GHQ. COURT MARTIAL for stealing car – KIDNAPPING HETTY PLUS ONE EGG – ABSCONDING WITH FUNDS of the PURITY LEAGUE – AND INTERFERING WITH THE RELIGIOUS beliefs of the gold fish.

Friends at 12 CCS. O'Shea is at the right, standing, while Philip Newman is squatting on the front right. France, April 1940. (*Newman Family*)

Father O'Shea (left) outside the RC Garrison Church, Ataka, Suez, 1943. (*Douai Abbey Library and Archive*)

O'Shea (centre) relaxing at Ben Gardene, Tunisia, 1942. (*Douai Abbey Library and Archive*)

O'Shea (right) with a soldier from the Arab Legion, Transjordania, 1943. (*Douai Abbey Library and Archive*)

Left to right: Capt. Shirley, John Morgan, Maj. Birkmyre. Sidi Mabrouk, September 1943. (*Morgan Family*)

A poster illustrating the difference between Italian life under occupation by the Allies and under German National Socialism. (*Bundesarchiv*)

A view of Monte Cassino. Photograph taken by John Morgan in May 1944. (*Morgan Family*)

Capt. John Morgan at HQ Casa Reale, Italy, 1944. (*Morgan Family*)

A picnic with jerry cans. John Morgan and Driver Hammond near Naples, 1944. (*Morgan Family*)

John's photograph of Mussolini's former headquarters, Pallazzo, Venezia, Rome, after the city's liberation on 5 June 1944. (*Morgan Family*)

The view from John's office window, Area 55 HQ, Poste Centrali, Arezzo, 1944. (*Morgan Family*)

Poste Centrali, Via Guido Monaco, Arezzo, 2013. (*Dee La Vardera*)

Above left: A membership card for the *Opera Nazionale Dopolavoro* (National Association of After-Work Clubs), 1944. (*Dee La Vardera*)

Above right: 5 lire—Allied Military currency.

Edoardo Succhielli, the leader of the partisan *Banda Renzino*. He led the attack on the Germans in the *Dopolavoro* on 18 June 1944. (*IWM, NA 16855*).

The children of Civitella in Piazza Vittorio Emanuele III, *c.* 1920. (*Civitella Archive)*

Boys and girls of Civitella, 1942. Dino Tiezzi is in the middle row, second right. (*Dino Tiezzi*)

A 1934 family photo recovered by Lara Lammioni from the rubble of her house after the massacre and fire. *Left to right*: Father Dante, Lara, Maria Grazia, and Armida Caccialupi. (*Lucarelli Family*)

Lara Lammioni aged twenty. (*Lucarelli Family*)

Don Alcide Lazzeri, the parish priest of Civitella and the first man to be executed in Piazza Vittorio Emanuele III, in front of the Church of Santa Maria Assunta, 29 June 1944. (*Civitella Archive*)

John Morgan's photograph of the interior of the Church of Santa Maria Assunta, Civitella, July 1944. (*Morgan Family*)

Above: Members of
the 4th Reconnaissance
Regiment viewing a map,
July 1944; Civitella is in
the background.
(*IWM, NA 16968*)

Right: The village of
Civitella, badly damaged
after the violence. A
British soldier walks up
Via di Mezzo with his
revolver drawn. (*IWM,
NA 16970*)

A British soldier walks through Piazza Vittorio Emanuele III, which is now named Piazza Don Alcide Lazzeri. (*IWM, NA 16972*)

Survivors of the massacre view the wreckage that was once their home. (*IWM, NA 17300*)

498 Artillery Company RASC. John Morgan is on the middle row, third from left; Maj. D. M. Birkmyre is on his right. (*Morgan Family*)

A photograph John Morgan took when he arrived in the main square in Civitella, July 1944. (*Morgan Family*)

Airgraph sent by John Morgan to his parents in Merthyr Tydfil, Christmas 1944. (*Morgan Family*)

Father O'Shea's design of the cover for the Area 55 HQ Christmas 1944 magazine. It depicts a Tuscan landscape with the hilltop village of Civitella in the background. (*Douai Abbey Library and Archive*)

Christmas party 1944, outside the church in Civitella. *Left to right*: Peter Ashton (REME), Maj. Angus Gray (RAMC), Lt Ronnie E. Weeks (G3) RA, Maj. Donald M. Birkmyre (RASC), and another officer. (*Morgan Family*)

The photograph that Keith Morgan first saw displayed in the church in Civitella in 1965. *Left to right*: Driver Mortimer, John Morgan, Driver Hammond, Father O'Shea. It was taken in January 1945. (*Morgan Family*)

A memorial plaque commemorating those who died in the massacre, Church of Santa Maria Assunta, Civitella, 2014. (*Dee La Vardera*)

The war memorial in the wine cellar at Pierangeli Farm, San Pancrazio, where sixty men were lined up and shot on 29 June 1944. (*Dee La Vardera*)

Alba Bonichi (right), who performed at the 1944 Christmas party, with Barbara Morgan in Civitella in 2001. (*Morgan Family*)

A reception to present a commemorative medallion, Civitella, 2003. *Left to right*: Dino Tiezzi, Keith Morgan, Gilberto Dindalini (Mayor of Civitella), Barbara Morgan, Jennifer Newcombe, Alison Newcombe. (*Morgan Family*)

Lara Lammioni with her son, Giuseppe Lucarelli, at home in Malfiano, 2010. (*Lucarelli family*)

Enza Marsili, a survivor of the massacre, with her son, Roberto Consales, and granddaughter, Nicoletta Consales, at the seventieth-anniversary commemoration, 29 June 2014, Civitella. (*Dee La Vardera*)

A memorial mural in the Church of Santa Maria Assunta. (*Dee La Vardera*)

The seventieth-anniversary mass in Civitella, 2014. *Left to right*: Don Tommaso Tononi, parish priest; Bishop of the Diocese of Arezzo, Cortona and Sansepolcro, Riccardo Fontana; and Monsignor Luciano Giovannetti, retired Bishop of Fiesole. (*Dee La Vardera*)

Keith Morgan delivers his speech at the seventieth-anniversary service, Civitella, 29 June 2014. (*Dee La Vardera*)

A bronze memorial to the massacre of Civitella by Mario Moschi. It is located outside the Church of Santa Maria Assunta. (*Alfred La Vardera*)

Ministers, ambassadors, and guests arriving at the seventieth-anniversary commemorations, 29 June 2014, Civitella. (*Dee La Vardera*)

Military Procurator Dr Marco De Paolis receiving honorary citizenship from the Mayor of Civitella, Ginetta Menchetti, at the Town Hall, Badia al Pino, 2014. (*Alfred La Vardera*)

'To the Fallen of Civitella'.
A medallion presented to
the Morgan family in 2003.
(*Morgan Family*)

Above left: Cockie's signature. (*Douai Abbey Library and Archive*)

Above right: Father O'Shea's crucifix, which he gave to Maj. Philip Newman at Dunkirk, June 1940. (*Newman Family*)

had only gone ten or eleven paces when I heard the sound of automatic small fire behind me and felt a burning pain in my neck and face. I fell to the ground, dazed but not unconscious. I saw my uncle fall to the ground. He didn't move again. The Germans didn't come up to us but walked back the way they had come.

About a quarter of an hour later, my mother and my sisters came across the fields to me and carried me into our house. They dressed my wounds, and later I was treated by an escaped British prisoner of war who said he was a doctor.

Apparently, a bullet had struck me in the back of the neck and passed right through and out of my right cheek. My speech has been affected and I am unable to eat solid foods.

Settimo Falsetti was found the next day by his sister-in-law in a field on their farm. She told her sister Gemma where her husband was, and Gemma helped her carry him back to her sister's house to prepare the body for burial.

One of those told to go to the Palazzina Bridge was Luigi Gabrielli, a farmer from Bella Vista, Civitella, with his youngest son—fourteen-year-old Gino—and two others, Olinto Milani and Giovanni Bonicolini, who were working in a field at nearby Caggioli farm. At approximately 7 a.m., Gabrielli was instructed to move from his farm as it was now being used as a munitions dump by the Germans. They were marched over to the bridge and joined a large group of other men, women, and children. After around an hour or so, the Germans sent the women and children away:

> They made us walk up a cart track that led off the road beside the bridge while German soldiers followed behind with submachine guns. When they were about 30 metres up the track, some of the Germans opened fire.
>
> I felt a burning pain in my left foot, so I jumped off the track into a ditch at the side and lay still.

Olinto was also struck by a bullet; it went through his right ankle, but he managed to crawl behind a rock and into some bushes. Like Luigi, he heard the men behind him screaming and moaning. He heard the German soldiers walking among them, shooting the wounded, making sure that everyone was dead. Then the soldiers dragged the bodies off the track and threw them into a ditch near the one where Luigi was lying. They machine-gunned the bodies again, just to make sure.

Luigi stayed there for around half an hour, until he was sure that the Germans had left, and then he made his way to the farm at Malfiano, where he stayed for two days, later joining his wife at the farm at Ciggiolo. He never saw his son Gino again. His wife, Cecilia, eventually found Gino's badly decomposed body twenty days later in a ditch near the bridge, and she buried him in the local cemetery.

Unable to walk due to the pain in his ankle, Olinto remained hidden until approximately 10 p.m. the same day, when Gina found him and helped him home.

Counting the Dead

Thursday 29 June, Afternoon

It was the smell of burning that finally drove Giuseppina Caldelli out of the safety of her home. She was terrified. She had waited hours for the Germans to leave. Even after the gunfire, screaming, and shouting had died down, she continued to wait. Silence was worse than noise.

Giuseppina and her niece, Ada, had locked themselves inside their home along with their lodgers. Her mother had refused to return from church when the shooting had begun and Giuseppina did not know where she was. Her brother, Adolfo, had gone out early to pick mushrooms for the special feast day meal, and she did not know where he was either. Soon after the shooting began, Ada peeped out of the window and saw the bodies of two men lying in the road. When Giuseppina dared to look out later, she was so shocked that she fainted. When she came around, she could smell burning, and she decided to leave the house and go to look for her mother.

She plucked up the courage to open the front door and was presented with a terrifying spectacle; the gutters in the street were flowing with blood, and there were torn clothes everywhere. She forced herself to go out.

She crossed herself as she passed bodies covered in blood, some still burning where they lay. Piles of rubble, which had been houses only hours before, filled the streets, and Giuseppina could hear the moans of the dying trapped underneath the stones. She did not want to look at the corpses, but she felt compelled to, recognising Emilio Marsili, Leonello Tiezzi, Giuseppe Franci, and her dear cousin, Virgilio Caldelli. She walked on to further horrors.

It was a place of utter carnage and destruction. The men—husbands, fathers, brothers, sons, grandfathers, uncles, nephews, and cousins—were all gone. Families had been destroyed and the workers and elders of the community wiped out.

Giuseppina had no idea of the time or how long she stayed there. She did not remember how she managed to do it, but she mustered the courage and strength to move the bodies that she found heaped in Via San Francesco across the square to her house opposite the church. Of those she moved, she recognised Federico Caccialupi,

Giuseppe Caccialupi, Dr Lorenzo Giuliani, Cesare Gualdani, Dante Lammioni, Paolo Sabatini. Domenico Falsetti, Dario Scaletti, Giovanni Battista Lammioni, Torquato Menchetti, Ibo Caldelli, Don Alcide Lazzeri, Giuseppe Pasqui, and Luigi Menchetti. This was no time to think or mourn their loss.

A few women and older children came out of their hiding places as Giuseppina worked. They saw the young woman struggling to move the bodies and came to help her. Perhaps all they could do at that time was to provide dignity in death, laying the bodies out as best they could, away from their place of execution. However, a short time later, these same bodies were dragged away by a squad of soldiers commanded by an Italian Fascist, Sergeant-Major Contini, who had been sent to clean up the place.[1] They threw the dead men into burning houses nearby, as if they were animal carcasses. The first line of German troops was due in Civitella in two days' time, and the place had to be sanitised and made ready for them if needed.

Sister Maria Pierina Acitelli emerged from her hiding place in the nursery school toilets. She and two other Sisters, members of the Passionist community that helped to run the hospital and home for the elderly in Piazza Becattini, had attended early mass. The nuns had escaped through the back of the church along with Gemma Falsetto and her family. They all saw the devastation.

They stood there, in shock, when a dreadful sound filled the air; it was the heartbroken voice of Luigi Lammioni, crying and calling out his wife's name. His five-year-old daughter, Vittoria, was in his arms as he made his way towards Piazza Becattini. Sister Maria followed him towards the home for the elderly.

The others followed Sister Maria towards the cistern and up the street, passing burning homes, picking a path through the rubble and debris underfoot. The children were scared and crying, and the women did their best to comfort them. The front door of the home for the elderly was open and Sister Maria saw the bodies of four of their elderly residents covered in blood on the floor of the entrance.[2] The ceiling of the stairwell was stained with blood. Sister Maria and the others made their way upstairs to the hospital ward. Fortunately, the rest of the elderly and sick were still in their beds, and the rooms were seemingly undamaged. Sister Maria found Luigi, his face black with soot and arms and hands bloody with cuts and scratches, still clutching his daughter.

Sister Maria called for one of the Sisters, who took Luigi's daughter by the hand and led her into a side room. Luigi was a broken man, sitting with his head bowed, wringing his hands, and rocking back and forth. Sister Maria helped to clean him up, tended to his cuts, and then told him to do an inventory of the medicines and bandages, thinking that it would be best if he was kept busy. They needed to be prepared to help anyone else in need.

Soon after 1 p.m., Maria Assunta Lammioni left her four children in the care of the orphanage at Poggiali to return to Civitella and search for the body of her husband, Giovanni Battista.[3] She knew he had been one of the first men to be shot, having glimpsed his body in the street outside their house before being made to leave by German soldiers. Someone told her that her brother-in-law, Luigi, had escaped from the smoke-filled house and was recovering in the hospital. When she arrived there, she found him and little Vittoria were safe but both in a bad way. Luigi became even more upset when he told her what happened to 'Bista' and that all that was left to see were 'his hat and a pool of blood.' When she went to look at the spot outside their house, she found the burned bodies of Don Alcide, Ibo Caldelli, and Torquato Menchetti, who ran the *Dopolavoro* with his wife, Alduina.

Having come back from the orphanage to search for her husband, Alduina Menchetti found the three charred bodies. She thought they must have been doused with petrol or burned by a flamethrower. She recognised Torquato's face, which had not been badly burned, and the shreds of his clothing and part of one boot, which were all that was left.

There was a fear that the Germans might come back and kill the women and children, so Alduina sought refuge in her house, which did not appear to have suffered any fire damage. When she went in, she discovered her father-in-law, Luigi, dead on the floor in a pool of blood.

Augusto Felicone finally felt safe to come out from the woods near his farm at Solaia at approximately 4.30 p.m. When he did, he was confronted by a sight from hell. All the houses in Cornia were on fire, and outside his barn he saw a small river of blood. He could not approach the barn because of the heat, being forced to wait until the fire had died down for him to enter the building. He picked his way through the debris and found the body of a woman and then the bodies of six more people. Although they were badly burned, he recognised them as friends and neighbours—Benedetto Valli, fifty-two, his wife, Narcisa Merusi, forty-eight, and their children, Assuntina, seven, and Giuseppe 'Peppino', three, alongside Modesta Rossi, thirty, and her one-year-old child, Gloriano Polletti. The building was still burning, and when the roof started to fall in, Augusto left and returned to the safety of the woods. When the bodies were eventually buried, only one coffin was needed for what remained of the six people.

Don Natale Romanelli returned to Cornia late in the afternoon from the woods to find all the houses on fire, including his own. On his way, he passed the naked dead body of Rosa Pontenani in the road. Further on, in a hut adjoining his house, he found the body of his disabled sister, Emma, on the ground. There were five or six bullet wounds on her right side of her body and bullet marks on her overturned wheelchair, which lay beside her. The next day, in a nearby house, he found the partially burned body of his mother, Emilia Tavanti and, in another room, the badly burned bodies of Rina Orsolani and Olga Mugnai. The furniture of the house had been piled around them and set on fire.

Later that evening, Laura Sabatini, safe with her children at the orphanage, learned the extent of the German atrocities from other newly arrived refugees. She had not seen her husband, Paolo, since being separated at gunpoint from him and the other men outside the church. Someone produced a train season ticket and a postal pass in his name, retrieved from his body. She now knew his fate, that he had been taken away and executed in front of the nursery school. She was told that her house was still on fire and that her husband's body was lying in a house on the square.

The next morning, Laura Sabatini left the children in the care of the nuns and returned to the village with her maid, Irma Mori, to look for Paolo. Some women told her where her husband's body was and she found him lying in the passageway just inside the front door of a house. He had three bullet wounds in the side of his head. She found other bodies in the house. Later on, with the help of Irma and Iole Barneschi, they managed to carry Paolo's body to the church. She was able to cover him with a sheet that she managed to retrieve from a still smouldering house. She later remarked, 'Soon others copied what I did until our beautiful church was full of corpses laid out in rows covered in white sheets.'

Friday 30 June

The noise of planes overhead, artillery fire, and explosions had kept people awake all night. To the citizens of Civitella, it is unlikely that it mattered whether the noise meant advancing Allied troops or retreating Axis soldiers. What else was there left to destroy? Roads had been reduced to rubble, bridges had been blown up, farms had been ransacked, and fields and crops had been damaged.

The survivors called wherever they sought refuge home—orphanages, woodlands, or basements. The focus was on protecting children and finding out what had happened to the members of their family who they suspected were dead. The journey back to the village was frightening, travelling along damaged paths and roads in the open air, passing bodies on verges. The houses were in ruins, many still burning or too damaged to enter. Some women were brave enough to try to enter their still-smouldering houses to look for a lost relative. As they came across bodies—relatives, friends, and strangers—they began to move them away from the bloodstained and burning buildings to safer places. Doors, planks, bed nets, and anything else that could be used as stretchers were taken by the women and older children.

They washed the bodies as best they could with what little water they could find. They called for sheets to cover them, and the nuns from the hospital and orphanage brought or sent for supplies. Those who were fortunate enough to still have their homes raided their linen cupboards.

Nurse Domenica, who had been working in the hospital on the day of the massacre and had refused to leave, had seen four elderly residents dragged downstairs and shot by the Germans. The next day, with the help of some others, she moved the bodies of Crespino Crespignani, aged eighty, Luigi Guerrini, aged seventy, Andrea Rossi, aged seventy-two, and Angiola Poltri, aged eighty-two, from the ground floor to the church.

Gina Magini, who had fled the village with her children after her husband had been taken away, returned from the orphanage at Poggiali. Outside her front door, she saw a pool of blood leading towards an adjoining stable, which, like her house, had been set on fire and completely destroyed. She searched for and found the body of Giustino Marsili and then that of her husband:

> He had been badly burned and was a terrible sight. He had been laid upon a pile of straw, covered with straw and wood, then the whole lot set on fire. I recognised him by the clothes on his back, which had not been burned, and also by the line of his features, although the rest of his body was jet black.

Lina Rossi also faced a dreadful sight when she eventually found the remains of her uncle, Don Alcide:

> I saw a man's trunk in a doorway among many burned human remains. Only the shoulders and the head were recognisable; it was my uncle, whom I loved so much. One of his black shoes was on a low wall near the garden of the presbytery. The house was a mass of ruins. White bundles containing the mangled bodies of the victims covered the floor of the church. In that way, Uncle found his church again.
>
> Part of his mortal remains rest in that small cemetery, among so many of his unfortunate brothers; part is mixed with the earth of the square that bears his name. My uncle Don Alcide will always remain with his body and spirit in Civitella, the village where, when he first arrived, he exclaimed, 'I will never leave this place!' And so it was that he is always here in our hearts in Civitella.

Uliana Caldelli came back the next day to look for her husband, Ibo. After a long search of the entire village, through the destroyed streets and among the ruined buildings, she gave up looking for him. The last time she had seen him was when he had been seized from their house at gunpoint by two German soldiers. Even though he had been ill in bed, he was made to get up; with her help, he had got dressed and been taken away. She was exhausted and returned to the orphanage and her children. She later heard that Ibo's body had been found and laid out in the church.

What the widows and orphans went through during the identification of their relatives was remembered years later. Many were unable to talk about it at the time. They were traumatised by the sight of scores of bodies covered in sheets, laid out in rows on the floor of the church where they had been celebrating the feast day only a day before. They were forced to walk slowly along each row, lifting the corner of a sheet to see who lay beneath it. They could not avoid noting the nature of the wounds, the bullet holes, and the effect of fire on flesh.

When Uliana Caldelli lifted the sheet and saw her dead husband, she recognised him only from his trousers and boots. His face was black, like coal. His right arm was burned off and there was only a short, gruesome stump left. There were two bullet holes in his chest. It was small comfort that he had the dignity of resting in a holy place, having been retrieved from the doorway of a burned-out building.

Ten-year-old Dino Tiezzi, who had watched his father and brother shot in his home, had managed to escape, but he had become separated from his mother. He ventured back to look for her and came to the church:

> It was a very difficult time for me as a young child with all that was happening, but I remember this particular episode. The Germans had spared the women and children, so I was shocked when I lifted the corner of a large sheet in the church and saw the bodies of a woman and two little girls. I knew it was the Town Clerk's wife, Marietta Sandrelli, a great friend of my mother, and I knew Giuliana and little Maria. They had not been executed but asphyxiated at the top of the house, by smoke coming up from below in their burning house. I was afraid to look at the girls. I was very friendly with them, and like all the young people in Civitella, we were all very close, much more so than in a big city. I was so afraid that I would be hunted down and killed that I ran away and hid in the school. I stayed there for such a long time that people were looking for me. I came out eventually and found my mother again.

At 11 a.m., near Palazzina Bridge, Augusta Ricciarini found the body of her husband, Natallo, among a pile of corpses. He had been shot in the head, arm, and side, machined gunned with another sixteen men. Assunta Gualdani of Casanuova, Civitella, found the body of her father, Cesare Aurealia; half of his face had been shot away. At the same time, Bruna Biliotti was making her way through the ruins of Civitella to her home when she met a girl who told her that her husband, Mayor of Civitella Guido Mammoli, had been shot at the bridge. She went back down to the valley and found the body of her loved one.

Later, Don Modesta, priest at Badia al Pino, arrived and advised that all the bodies should be taken to the cemetery to await the coffins, which were being made. As soon as Dr Luigi Rosai arrived, he began to examine the bodies and record the nature of the wounds on each corpse. He was responsible for reporting the cause of death of each of those who had died on 29 June, evidence that was later submitted to the Special Investigation Branch (SIB).[4] This body had been set up the British Army to deal with serious crimes—both military and civilian—and testimonies of the survivors were later collected during the period from November 1944 to March 1945 with the help of the Italian police.

The same people who helped to move the bodies set about making coffins from what material they could find—planks, doors, and parts of cupboards and drawers. They were assisted by men from surrounding villages who had escaped the massacres. Some of the women even salvaged the wooden voting booths used in the local elections from the communal hall, which had been destroyed.

Bruno Cocchini was one man who came back to help. He was employed by the Provincial Council and Office of Economy in Arezzo, and after the shooting in the social club, he took his wife and children to Capo Contro, approximately 3 km to the south of Civitella. He had heard the massacre while hiding in woodland on one of his daily visits to get supplies for his family. There was so much to be done, and everyone was exhausted, starving, and still in shock. Bruno tried to help put out fires in the buildings or damp down smouldering embers, but without water—which was now a precious commodity—it was nigh impossible. He cleared debris and helped remove bodies, recognising many of his friends and neighbours.

Laura Sabatini helped Maria Assunta Lammioni to get some boards to make coffins for the seven dead members of her family. Everyone who was able to help did so, and even young Dino Tiezzi was given a job:

> All the corpses were put in the church and they had to be transferred to the cemetery. A carpenter—who was the one who had the shop below our apartment—managed to find some wooden boards and build some makeshift coffins. The people were afraid that the Germans might come back, so they put me as a lookout in the square and I had in front of me the image of my house, collapsing little by little through the heat haze, with the bodies of my father and brother.
>
> I was no good as a lookout and they soon realised this and sent me away to help the other boys transport the coffins to the cemetery with a horse and cart. And here there was another episode, which seems strange but it isn't so. In those days, the roads were not tarmacked and were full of stones. The cart was wobbling over the stones and the corpses were sliding out of it. We began to laugh hysterically, like mad people. After this, I said that I would not go back to help out with moving the coffins.

Saturday 1 July

At 4 a.m., Bruno Cocchini came back again to Civitella, bringing three farmers with him. They worked in the cemetery, digging graves until 10.30 a.m. He spent the rest of that day helping women to put out the fires in their homes.

Laura Sabatini returned late morning for the funeral of her husband. She had placed his body in a rough box made from planks of wood, which Paolo had stocked a few weeks before for repairs to the house and outbuildings. With the help of four locals who carried the box on their shoulders, she accompanied him to the cemetery:

> After the burial I went back to my house in the Palazzo del Podestà to try to extinguish the fire that was still burning in the basement. The roof had collapsed and most of the ground floor rooms were completely burned. Flames were coming out of the olive press, where the oil acted as fuel. The large salon with the fresco of the Madonna and child by Spinello Aretino was completely destroyed, and only the wall of the fresco was still standing. The furniture, the carpets, the piano, the knick knacks were all destroyed. On the ground floor, my husband's desk had been forced open and I could not even find 10 lire. All the money and cheques had been stolen. I

took everything that had not been touched by the fire to the hospital's basement as advised by the good Sisters.

That night I returned to Poggiali, but because the fighting was getting closer, I felt it unsafe to stay. So we crossed the Allies' lines and took refuge in Monte San Savino. Twenty-five of us lived in a house there until 17 July.

At approximately 4 p.m., Luigi Lammioni was able to recover the body of his wife, Maria Sandrelli, and Guiliana, one of his daughters, from his house. The floor of the loft, where the charcoal had been stored, had burned right through—the place where Maria Luisa had been lying.

In the evening, Don Ermanno Grifoni, the priest of Montegonzi, Cavriglia, was summoned to the Castello, Montegonzi, where Maj. Seiler and another German officer had just arrived and billeted themselves, along with eighty soldiers and all their equipment and transport. Another group of soldiers was already billeted in the local school, along with two military lorries and five motorcycles.

The Major spoke fairly good Italian, and introduced himself as the commandant of the German soldiers who had just arrived. He asked if there were any partisans in the area, warning that if there were, he would be forced to carry out the same reprisals as those seen in Civitella della Chiana.

The priest assured the Major that there were no partisans in the village and that the population was peaceful. Obviously satisfied, the officer allowed him to leave.

Sunday 2 July

The body of Ferdinando Salvadori of Monte San Savino had been hanging from a lamppost in Piazza del Legname for two days before it was removed by the civil authorities and taken to Misericordia Cemetery. There was a notice attached to the wall beneath the body, having been left by one of the three German soldiers responsible for the public execution. It bore the message: 'This way the partisans of Cornia are dying'.[5]

Tuesday 6 July

Maj. Graf arrived in Montegonzi with about eighty men two days after Maj. Seiler had left with his. As the sole representative of any authority in the village, Don Ermanno Grifoni thought it diplomatic to present himself at the Castello to the new Major. Dr Barnaba, an evacuee staying at the castle who spoke fluent German, helped with interpreting. The Major informed Don Ermanno Grifoni that he was going to requisition some local foodstuff for his soldiers because his supplies were very low. On 15 July, Maj. Graf and his men left as the advancing Allies breached the German defences.

25 July–5 August

Ugo Casciotti returned to San Pancrazio to help clear debris from the ruins of Pierangeli Farm. On 29 June, he had managed to escape from captivity in the cellar of the farmhouse, where sixty men had been held by the Germans for failing to denounce the partisans. All the men had been shot against the wall and their bodies entombed when an explosion destroyed the rest of the building. Over 200 soldiers had taken part in the attack on San Pancrazio. The massacre occurred at the same time as Civitella. Ugo remembered:

> The building was an empty shell, and as we cleared the cellar we discovered the human remains. They were in such an advanced state of decomposition I could not give an approximate number. I was able to recognise parts of the priest's robes amongst the ruins.

Consiglia De Debole watched the removal of debris from the cellar, where she eventually found the remains of her husband, Corrado—a corn merchant—in a standing position due to the weight of the numerous other bodies behind him. Also found were his two brothers, Ferdinando and Umberto, who were only identifiable from parts of their clothing and some personal effects.

Caterina Moretti was another woman who had last seen her husband (Renato, an electrician) on 29 June in Piazza della Chiesa, San Pancrazio, with the other men who had been rounded up by the Germans. She and the other women had been told that their menfolk had been taken to labour camps. She returned to the village from her mother's house nearby, where she had been staying for the last month. She watched the discovery of what appeared to be piles of burned bodies, and she was only able to find two keys and a cross that had belonged to her husband.

Bianca Panzieri recognised the cap of her husband, Francesco, a farm worker, and his cigarette lighter among the clothing and personal belongings that had been collected from the burned-out cellar and put aside.

It took twelve days for the excavation work to be completed. The remains of the victims were buried in a communal grave in the village cemetery.[6]

The Passing of the Front
Lara's Story: Part II

4–16 July 1944: Malfiano, Civitella

I do not remember much of the day when we walked to Malfiano, our farm, a few kilometres from Civitella. It was the only possible decision considering the circumstances after the massacre. It was reasonable to think that we would find at least a little food and a bed and shelter for the night there.

It had been a few days since my mother, Armida, my little sister, Maria Grazia, and I had eaten anything, and we spent the night sitting on benches at the orphanage in Poggiali. Aunt Assunta joined our group with her four children and three or four villagers who were willing to share our fate. However, as soon as we got to Malfiano, we realised that we had made a mistake going there. The farmhouses were occupied by a group of around twelve Germans who had also taken all the food.

The surprise was terrible. To see those uniforms again (even if they were not SS) increased our terror and shock.

We wanted to run away, but where could we go? There was no other place. The front was very close; the battle was raging not more than a kilometre away. Our starvation, lack of sleep and the shock that we had suffered was wearing us down and already weakened our resistance.

My mother and my uncle were numb with pain, my little sister was distraught, and my little cousin Vittoria (five years old, a survivor of the fire in her house) could not overcome the terrible shock of losing her mother and two sisters, and she kept reliving the moments of that tragedy in her sleep.

My family, which was my support, my reference point, had been destroyed. I felt alone now, facing an ominous future.

We avoided the Germans as much as possible. We kept ourselves to ourselves, hoping not to be noticed. We had told them that we were evacuees from Arezzo, where the allied bombing had destroyed our house, but they did not understand a word of Italian. We did this to try to make our cohabitation less dangerous, but even the few contacts we had with them were discouraging. They told us to go away when we asked them for a few blankets for the children and when we asked them for a little sugar, we were nearly shot at.

For the sake of truth, I need to describe another episode.

I was sitting alone in a corner one day when the NCO commanding the squad walked towards me. I could not tell his age, but he looked older than the others and appeared more human. There were no other soldiers around, and, using gestures, he commanded me to give him my watch. I reluctantly obeyed. The watch was the only thing that I had left, and it had been given to me by my father when I passed my exams and got my diploma.

He took it, hid it in the palm of his hand, and, to my surprise, gave it back to me, making me understand to keep it hidden to avoid the other soldiers being tempted. This little gesture of humanity was a great relief for me. This NCO was later to be of further help to us in far more dramatic circumstances.

In the meantime, the Allied offensive had grown more violent. The bombardments increased in intensity; the old farmhouses were hit continuously and the shrapnel was falling everywhere. Indeed, over the next fifty years, we kept finding a large amount of shrapnel. We continue to find pieces of it even today.

The situation was becoming dangerous. Rumour had it that the safest place was under the arches of a house that today is called Casa Edi. An arch is still standing today, while the other one collapsed some time ago.

There were thirty-five of us, including the tenant farmers sheltering under those arches. I was not afraid of the bombs and was the only one willing to go to the farmyard to pick up a hen or a goose that had been killed by the bombs and turned green or black under the burning sun. Then, after cooking it quickly, everybody had a little piece of it. It was really horrible, but we had been without food for so long and we had to eat something.

The Germans were keeping busy preparing to repel the Allied offensive. The men told us that they had only one machine gun and that they kept moving it from one window to the other of the farmhouse to give the impression that there were more of them than there were. In fact, in our refuge, we heard sounds of continuous movement above, heavy footsteps and the noise of things being moved. The situation had become unsustainable.

Our farmers were worried about the cows that were their only capital and that they had set free to deny them to the Germans. In spite of the danger, they used to go out at night to ensure that they had not gone. This cost the life of one of the farmers and increased the danger for all of us as the Germans suspected that we were spying for the Allies since we were so close to the front.

One night, we heard some very load bangs above the usual rumble of the guns, while the sky became as white as if we had been in the middle of the day. All this lasted for hours and was very hard on our ears. The Germans had set fire to the ammunition dump of Fogliarina, a couple of kilometres away, so the men told us. This was a sure sign that the Germans were abandoning their defensive lines.

What would our fate be? We were too isolated and completely at the mercy of the twelve Germans, who were becoming more and more hostile. What other acts of violence might they commit before leaving?

The following night, it was relatively calm. The guns had become steadily quiet and we could no longer hear the Germans. There was complete silence. We congregated in a cellar where large casks lined the wall. The cellar was the same room that is now the kitchen of Casa Edi and the wall was near the front door. The silence and the calm continued and we felt an increasing sense of relief. 'The Germans have gone.'

'Are you sure that they are not in the house asleep?'

'No, nobody is in the house.'

Our hopes of survival became more and more real. Somebody said that the Allies would come soon. Then, suddenly, I heard the sound of approaching heavy steps.

'Here are the liberators. Let them know that we are civilians.'

'Make the children cry so that we are not mistaken for Germans!' The children, on command, started to cry when the others shouted, 'Long live the liberators!'

I remember that it was pitch dark, we had no means of illumination, and the oil lamp that before had given us some light had extinguished itself. The soldiers had come. But, by the light of a torch carried by the soldiers, I recognised the familiar shape of German helmets.

'Shut up, for God's sake!' I screamed to make me heard over the shouting of the others. 'These are Germans!' Everybody stopped shouting and suddenly there was deep silence. However, the Germans had heard us, and although they could not speak Italian, they were well-aware of the meaning of the word 'liberators'. You can imagine their feelings towards us. They came in to the cellar and one of them accidentally hit Alessandro Lammioni, a big, tall man, with his rifle. Alessandro, annoyed, pushed the rifle away. The reaction of the German was swift and violent. The soldier shot him at point blank. Alessandro fell instantly, almost bringing us down with him.

We were terrified. I tried to hide behind a cask. This instinctive act, useless and absurd, gives an idea of what I felt as the survival instinct took hold of me.

The soldiers, with menacing shouts of '*Raus, raus!*' ordered us out of the cellar. They arranged us in a line, three or four abreast, and told us to walk towards the hay barn, a building that was a few hundred metres away (more or less where the boules pitch is now).

My mother leaned on the house wall and implored, 'Shoot me, but leave the others!' However, the Germans did not understand her and pushed her towards our group.

Every so often, they told us in their poor Italian, 'All gone, tomorrow morning, all black!' meaning that they would burn us all to death using the large amount of hay and straw that was stored in the hay barn.

I will never know if they really intended to carry out their threats, but Germans did not usually make idle threats. They made us go into the barn and two soldiers started to ask in poor Italian, 'Where is the young girl?' It was clear that they meant me. Facing a new threat that was unmistakably directed only at me, and despite the fear and anxiety that gripped my insides, my brain started to work again, and I looked for a means of escape.

It was completely dark, and I tried to make myself less conspicuous by sitting by some old women dressed in black. I was still wearing my dress with red poppies, which I had put on on the morning of the 29th—it was very bright and instantly recognisable material. While feeling the floor around me, I found a dark overall (which was used by the farmers to spray the vines) and I put it on to cover my dress. I borrowed a black scarf from one of the women sitting near me and put it on to hide my hair, and, to complete the transformation, I plastered my face with mud from the floor. Then I went to sit next to an old farmer and I hugged him tightly.

The two soldiers, who had since gone away, returned with a torch. They were looking around and kept saying, 'Where is young woman? No young woman, all *kaput*!'

Not seeing my red dress anywhere, they started a systematic search. Some uncharitable voice among the group was heard saying, 'It isn't right that we all die for you. Show yourself!' I don't bear a grudge against the person who said this because I understand what he must have felt.

I had no intention of coming forward and I was torn between wanting to defend myself and wanting to flee, which were both impossible. The two Germans kept searching, shining the torch light in the faces of the people. It was evident that my disguise would not have fooled them. I understood that there was no way out for me.

Then a miracle happened. The silence was broken by the sharp voice of the NCO, ordering the soldiers back. They obeyed instantly and turned towards the exit while making menacing gestures and repeating the word '*Kaput*!' indicating that they would return soon. They locked the door from the outside. We were not out of danger; we had only been given a short reprieve.

In spite of that, we were relieved. When one feels death so near, even a few more minutes of life are very precious, and these minutes feel as long as days.

The Allied offensive began suddenly and unexpectedly. It was an offensive that was so violent and terrible that I thought that all the military might of the Allies had been concentrated against a sole objective—Malfiano.

The noise was deafening, the sky was brightly lit, and shells were falling everywhere.

However, this lifted my heart and gave me courage because I thought that the Germans would not come back as long as the attack lasted. The possibility of a shell hitting the hay barn and setting fire to the straw did not worry me; it was better than seeing the Germans peering through the door. I don't know how long the attack lasted or for how long we had been prisoners in the hay barn, but that was certainly the longest night, our private 'D Day'.

Thanks to God, the light of dawn began to filter through the brick peepholes of the hay barn and the attack stopped as suddenly as it started. Complete silence followed. We could not hear the Germans. The men finally got up and started to look through the gap in the brickwork. They could not see or hear anybody. We decided that this was the moment to risk trying to break free.

The hay barn door was heavy and strong, but we had ten men, and after a few unsuccessful attempts, they managed to lift the door from its hinges.

The first thing I saw in the white light of the dawn were the bodies of three Germans, lying face down and with open arms, on the ground next to the manure heap (where the swimming pool is now). I did not stop to look at them, nor did I try to find out where the other Germans had gone; I only wanted to flee from this cursed place of terror.

So, after telling my relatives, 'Let's go at once towards the British line,' I started walking through the field and towards the plain. I did not stop to consider what the shortest way was or to look for a footpath to make the walk easier. There was somebody with me, but I have forgotten who it was; I only remember that I was running like a woman possessed.

Suddenly, we heard the whistle of machine gun bullets very near us. Evidently there was a machine gun post high up on the '*Guardiola*' hill (another farm belonging to the family, so-called because of the good view below) from where they were shooting at us. We knew we were the targets because the bullets followed us as we moved away. I remember that I jumped into a blackberry bush to hide and I got scratched and tore my dress. We eventually found shelter by a terrace wall and the shooting stopped.

Finally, after a few minutes, we met the Allied forces. We saw only one soldier. He was very calm and he took more interest in the wheat in the fields than in finding out the whereabouts of the enemy.

Seen up close, he certainly did not look like the 'liberating hero' whom I unconsciously hoped to find. He was wearing the helmet that I had learned to recognise from the posters that were all over Italy—the caricature of a British soldier wearing that helmet and with an enormous ear with the caption 'Shut up. The enemy is listening'. This helmet was covered in netting that was used to keep small oak twigs in place. Strangely, I thought that this wasn't an adequate camouflage. He was very young and had a bright red face, which made him look like a turkey's wattle.

After we saw him, we began to wave a dirty rag—which had been once white—as we got nearer. The soldier did not seem to share our enthusiasm, barely glancing at us, and carried on walking. Naturally, this meeting was not as important for him as it was for us.

We kept on walking, and some time later I found I was alone. Perhaps the others had taken a shortcut, but there was nobody around me. There was no point in going back, so I carried on, sure that I would reach the British line sooner or later.

The first sign that I had arrived were large bundles of wires lying on the ground, similar to multi-coloured electric wires (telephone wires, I was later told). There were so many of them that I kept stumbling on them.

Then I saw large urns (for the tea, I learned afterwards) and, finally, a few soldiers. I ended up in the camp kitchens. I later found out from a dear friend of mine that I had stumbled upon the 4th British Division. This, starting from Foiano della Chiana, had divided its forces to pursue two objectives—Civitella della Chiana and Tuori.

The soldiers were busy cooking. There were towels drying everywhere and large heaps of wheat flour dough similar to those that we made at home. Then I felt tremendously hungry as my last meal had been some rotten hen meat days before. Nobody had noticed my presence, so, plucking up my courage, I started talking to one of the soldiers, asking him for food using gestures and broken Italian.

I was immediately given what looked like feast to me—a large dish full of slices of roast beef and a huge chunk of white bread, a bowl containing what looked like *pappina* [white baby food], which I later found out was porridge, and a mug of tea. I threw myself on it with voracity, but my stomach, perhaps weakened by the long fast or for other reasons, played a nasty trick on me—it refused to accept any food. I felt like a hungry Pinocchio who was looking forward to the delicacies, but then found that everything from the roast chicken to the fruit was fake. I returned the dish to the soldier, who looked at me disapprovingly.

After a while, I was taken to the officer commanding the zone. He had his office inside a command lorry. He was sitting at a table covered in maps and with a swagger stick in the corner. He looked at me in an unfriendly way and started to ask me questions in a language that I did not understand, without even bothering to take the pipe out of his mouth. Naturally, I was not able to answer his questions. I cannot remember if I said something in Italian or if I remained there dazed. He sharply told me to go.

I climbed down from the lorry and, feeling thirsty, asked where the nearest spring was. They showed me a place half a kilometre away, at the bottom of a field. I got there easily, but when I turned around I saw a soldier with a rifle pointed at me through the tall grass. Why had he followed me, and why was he pointing his rifle at me? Was I judged to be a dangerous character, or perhaps a spy?

Then I became aware of my appearance; my dress was in pieces, blood from the scratches was trickling on my arms and legs, and my face and hair were dirty with the mud that I put on it to escape the Germans the night before.

I washed and tidied myself up as much as possible and followed the soldier towards the farmhouse where they were billeted. I found an empty stable with a lot of straw and immediately fell asleep, not even caring about the many horse flies and other insects that were buzzing around me.

I woke up some time later covered in a thick and rough military blanket that had been put over me to shelter me from the stings of insects. I don't know who was responsible for that kind gesture. Soon afterwards, they came to look for me as the interpreter had arrived.

He had arrived on motorcycle to question me, I don't know where from. He was speaking perfect Italian, without any foreign accent or hesitation. He looked to me to be an American of Italian origin. He began by asking me where I came from. He did not seem very affected by my impassioned account of the Civitella massacre and insisted on looking for military information.

'Exactly how many Germans were in the Malfiano farmhouse?

'What type of machine gun did they have?'

'Did they have any other weapons?'

'Were they in contact with other outposts?'

'Was the small building higher up a weapons dump?' (This was the little church of St Francis, protector of the farm, the ruins of which were 100 metres over Malfiano).

I could only answer these questions superficially as I knew almost nothing and I wasn't interested. I had enough in the end and gave way to the bitterness that was within me, saying in a rather aggressive way, 'What kind of an army is this? The whole Army have been here for days and days right in front of twelve Germans who were moving one machine gun from window to window to make you think there were many more of them. We have been waiting for you for days and days. Don't you know that they were going to kill us all?'

I continued saying critical things about the Allied armies.

The interpreter let me speak and then, with great calm, replied, 'The life of a single soldier costs us twenty years of sacrifices and expenditure. We cannot risk it and we need to move on with maximum safety.' It was evident that he meant, 'Put the soldier's life at risk to go and save you, who, until yesterday, were our enemy?'

His reply made me think. At that moment I understood that two worlds with totally different ideologies were clashing. My childish ideas of *soldato eroe* [the hero soldier] were destroyed. I could not help thinking about those three Germans over there in Malfiano, lying by the manure heap, left there to rot under the sun without even a decent burial or a prayer. They had determinedly fought a hopeless battle because of discipline, duty, or because of an innate love of war. They had been left with inadequate weapons, without food, and their lives had been sacrificed— and for what? For them, there was no tea ready or a kitchen at their disposal.

Despite myself, a vague sense of pity for my torturers was taking hold of me.

I said nothing more to the interpreter, only that I had lost contact with my family and asked if he could help me to find them. He knew that a few refugees from the hills had taken shelter in Dorna Farm, a few kilometres away. He made me get onto a jeep where there were other soldiers and asked the driver to take me there.

Bomb fragments were falling as we travelled, and one of the soldiers put his helmet on my head to protect me. It was then that some men on the side of the road started to curse me and shout unrepeatable insults. They probably thought that I was a whore following the Allied army.

This was too much for me. I tried to jump out of the jeep, run towards those men, and scream at them how wrong they were and who I really was and what I had gone through. The soldier nearest to me grabbed me by the arm while looking at me with a surprised expression on his young face. He thought that I was mad. He obviously had not understood anything, and I wasn't able to explain. On the other hand, how could that young man understand that yes, he was fighting, but with tea and porridge ready in the morning, just like at home, with somebody who was concerned not to risk his life unnecessarily. I sat back on the seat while he kept hold of me.

We arrived at Dorna Farm, where I found my relatives in distress because we had separated and, not knowing what had happened to me, thinking the worst.

We stayed at the farm for a few days and I remember that nearby there was an artillery battery with the guns pointed at Civitella, where the Germans were probably resisting. The gunners were all Canadians, all blond giants with berets rather than the typical British cap.

When they realised that we were afraid and deafened by the noise of the guns, they started to shoot like madmen because they found it funny to see us run away with hands over our ears. They were all laughing, happy to shoot, fighting their private war with great jollity, I don't know with what advantage for the conquest of their objectives. We were obliged to stay indoors so as not to provoke more shooting.

After a couple of days, a lorry of the CLN (the Italian Committee of National Liberation) transported us to the village of Foiano della Chiana, which had been left almost untouched by the passing of the front.

We lodged with some local wealthy people who offered us comfort and solidarity. Having achieved a degree of security and relative comfort, without danger from the Germans, the war, or of imminent death, my continuous state of tension subsided, only to be replaced by sorrow for the death of my dear ones and the desperation of having lost everything.

In the evening, I could hear the sound of unknown rhythms and music (the boogie-woogie, I later found out), and with them the happy voices of the girls from the village, who—having survived untouched by the horrors of war and having found their pretty dresses—were dancing in the square to the tunes of the 'liberators'. Instead, I was in a corner of my little room, crying—crying for my dear ones and for all the dead villagers whose words, gestures, and smiles I could remember but would never see again.

To this desperate sorrow was added a feeling of rebellion in the face of this insufferable injustice. Why could others be happy and laughing? Why was I denied this? After all, I was only twenty years old and I had the right to life.

I did not know then how time cures all wounds, lessens human pain, and dims even the most terrible memories. I believed that I would be crushed forever by what happened and that there would not be any future for me.

Our tragedy eventually became known in Foiano and we were given many gifts—clothes, shoes, and a great deal of food, such as bread, cheese, salami and hams, and fruit. We could finally satisfy the hunger that had gripped us for so long, but I could not enjoy this abundance for very long.

It began with a strange and unexplainable aversion to food—a strong nausea at the sight of it. Then I started to experience extreme pain in my abdomen, while my temperature was rising very fast.

I was lying on the floor of my little room (our hosts had been unable to find a bed in spite of trying), my teeth were chattering with cold in spite of the hot July day, and I was covered with rough army blankets, which felt as though they were made of thorns. Then my skin turned yellow like a lemon.

My uncle was very worried and went to Badia to look for a doctor. I don't know how he managed to find one, but he did, and the doctor came and examined me. He told my family that he wasn't familiar with these symptoms and that it could be gallstones or jaundice. In any case, there were no medicines available and the Foiano hospital was full because of a typhus outbreak. So he prescribed a large spoonful of olive oil each morning—very good medicine for the liver. He then left, shaking his head and leaving me to my fate.

Many years later, while reading a magazine, I saw an article that had interesting news. During the period in which the Allied troops were in Italy, there had been an epidemic of *morbo giallo*— yellow disease [most likely jaundice caused by severe malnutrition]—and a precise description of my symptoms followed. It had caused many deaths among the civilian population. Fortunately, I recovered completely. I don't know whether it was because of the olive oil or because I was young and had a strong constitution.

After my recovery, little by little, the surviving members of my family, united in the great love that bound us together, began to walk the long, hard, painful path towards a normal life again.

Liberation

4–17 July 1944: Civitella

There was a severe lack of water in Civitella. The citizens had none except that which they could collect from local springs, some of which were as far as 4 or 5 km away—a dangerous enterprise under the present circumstances. The hot and dry weather did not help. The countryside was full of hazards—barbed-wire barricades, mines underfoot, and shelling overhead—and one could find oneself between a band of retreating Germans and a group of advancing Allied soldiers. The village had no electricity so the pumps were not working. The cisterna—their central water-storage system—was polluted.

Sister Maria Pierina Acitelli was still at the hospital, and she witnessed the arrival of more Germans to the village. They were looking for food and shelter in the buildings that had not been destroyed. What they found, they took. The women had no power to resist, already defeated and struggling to survive. It was a further insult, playing host to the same people who had committed such acts of barbarism.

Sister Maria took charge of their evacuation:

> We went down to the laundry in the basement, which had two large wash areas, and we brought everyone we could down there. We laid mattresses on the floor and used leaves as bedding. We also carried down the wonderful picture of our Lord, Jesus with the Eucharist, from the chapel. Although there wasn't a suitable place for it —no altar or lit candles—with great love we placed it near one of the bathtubs. We prayed day and night for our salvation. The serene face of Jesus looking down on us gave us strength and security, and comforted everyone.

> *Jesu, Saviour, hear our cry;*
> *Thou wert suffering once as we:*

> *Hear the loving litany*
> *We Thy children sing to Thee.*

Over the next few days, the Sisters, residents, and those in hiding heard the sound of German soldiers around the village. There was the noise of drunken men shouting in the street, doors banging, and gunshots. Soldiers patrolled the walls by day and kept watch on the tower at night. There were men coming and going at all hours in Sister Maria's building. She and her colleagues could hear boots upstairs and downstairs, and they were never quite sure who it was and what they were doing:

> When the men changed guard, they would fling open our door to give us a fright. But we remained calm because sweet Jesus was with us, watching over us. This sad yet also wonderful experience always lived in my heart.
>
> The Allied bombardment continued all around us. Germans or British, it made no difference who was bombing us. Part of the hospital and chapel were destroyed, but we were safe with Jesus. All our food, what meagre rations were left, was on the top floor, and at night we brought it down when the coast was clear so that we could cook at least one hot meal.

Early on Saturday 15 July, Sister Maria was airing a mattress in the back garden when a German soldier appeared holding a dead rabbit. He called to her through the wire fence, telling her to prepare a great feast for tomorrow. He held up his trophy for the Sister to inspect. Everyone in her care would have been pleased to have meat on their plates, but Sister Maria was cautious about receiving this unexpected gift.

The sounds at night and movement of troops during the day had made the survivors nervous. The Germans were retreating northwards, mining and burning swathes of land, making sure they left nothing of value for the Allied army advancing on their heels. Life was cheap to the Germans as they slaughtered their way towards the river Arno and Florence.[1] Word had got back to the village of further massacres not 40 km away. The villagers were trapped in Civitella. What else could they do but wait for liberation?

Soon, however, things became very quiet:

> We thought we would all be killed, but at dawn the next day we ventured out to see if the Germans were still around or had fled. The streets were empty. We looked in the basement of the hospital where the Germans had set up their dining room. There was no one. But what a bounty of food they had left, by the grace of God— ham, sausages, cheese and white bread, which we rushed and gathered up in our arms to take back to our refuge.
>
> Then, a small group of us decided to explore further and we went along the street towards the main square, to the *asilo* [the nursery school]. Uncertain as to what we would find, when we went inside we found two rooms crammed with food where the Germans had set up a dining room. There were two tables set with embroidered tablecloths and piles of food on best china plates—everything stolen from people's homes. Now it was all abandoned. What joy to find the Germans had gone!

We returned to Becattini and then walked down towards the lower part of the village. As I walked along the street, there was a strong smell of wine. The houses that survived the fire had been looted. What the departing Germans had not been able to take, such as barrels of wine and olive oil, had been smashed open. I found myself walking in a stream of pungent liquid.

Suddenly, I heard the sound of army boots and saw armed men in uniforms, soldiers coming from Porta Senese, along the bombed walls. I was afraid for my fellow residents, and the people in my care, that they were no longer protected inside our makeshift sanctuary with Jesus by our side.

The soldiers who arrived in Civitella on 16 July were members of the 4th Reconnaissance Regiment of the British Army.[2] They had been observing the hilltop town for a while and had not seen any movement from German soldiers or local people. As they entered the place, they saw the damaged buildings and empty streets. They walked along the town walls, parts of which were now just heaps of stones and boulders by the roadside. When they saw some figures in the distance, their leader called out.

Though nervous, Sister Maria soon realised that the men were not going to harm them—they simply wanted to know where everyone was, to which Sister Maria indicated that they were all that were left. The leader then told her that he and his men were British, and that they had come to liberate them. The soldiers handed out cigarettes to the men and chocolate bars to everyone, reassuring them that their ordeal was all over.

As soon as she returned to the hospital, Sister Maria rushed upstairs to the top floor and grabbed a sheet off a bed, hanging it out of the window to signal to others that it was safe. 'Come back! We are all free!' she shouted. 'The Germans have gone.' She kept repeating the same words until she saw a few people gradually emerge from their hiding places in the nearby woods as well as from houses within the village walls.

Captain John Morgan, attached to the 498 Artillery Company, was sitting in his office in the back of a Bedford truck, having just finished a letter to his parents:

Well, as you've read in the papers and heard on the wireless, events out here are moving with speed and we are all seeing a little more of Italy on our continental tour financed by the government!

You'd enjoy this sort of climate if it could be transferred to England, beautifully sunny and warm and I really can't remember when we last had rain. Beautiful and sunny by day with clear nights, not too cold. In the darkness the fireflies flicker all around us. They are really amazing. During the day lizards run all over the place and there are quite a few snakes around too.

Well folks, censorship really doesn't permit me the writing of much news so I'm afraid that the majority of my letters must sound rather empty and uninteresting. I shall have to make up for it by rather more graphic accounts when I get home.

He thought about his fiancée Barbara who had written to him with news of her success in her pharmaceutical exams. Clever girl. He was a lucky fellow to have her waiting at home for him, after all the heartache he had experienced with Marjorie. John had not seen Marjorie for over two years and she had dumped him for an RAF chap. Her sister Barbara had asked his parents if she could continue the contact with their son. John's parents had been upset when they heard that Marjorie had been seen out with another man, and were glad that it was all in the past now. Barbara had always had a soft spot for John, even accompanying her sister on dates before the war. Barbara was eight years younger than John, but she knew her mind and his parents were very fond of her and delighted when they had got engaged.

He sealed the envelope and placed it on top of a pile of other letters, waiting to be collected. Ever discreet and considerate to their feelings, John always kept the tone of his letters matter of fact and light-hearted.

He looked out at lines of washing pegged to tent guy ropes, drying in the hot midday sun. He watched lizards skittering on the ground around the rear wheels of his truck and listened to the distant rumble of shelling. There were piles of papers on the table, still to be dealt with. Always paperwork.

John was waiting to be transferred as Staff Captain to Arezzo, where the permanent Area 55 Headquarters were being set up after the liberation of the city on 16 July. He did not like hanging around with nothing much to do. There would be plenty to do in his post, fully occupied with the RASC, working with the Allied Control Commission (ACC), which had been established to run the country with the new Italian government in power.

The main objectives of the ACC were to rebuild infrastructure, restore communications, keep law and order, and provide relief to the local population. There was a lot of work to do before they could be effective as the new governors of the district. It had been reported that Arezzo was 'much damaged by [their] own bombing and almost empty of civilians',[3] and there was a lot of work to do in restoring power and communications, including railways and roads, sewers, and water supplies. The transportation of troops and provisions by rail was vital to the success of the war in Italy.

A move to the city meant leaving tents behind and finding proper accommodation in billets in local houses and civic buildings. John would have a proper office again, like the one he occupied at Campobasso (about 160 km east of Naples).[4] After the Germans had abandoned the town and the Canadians had taken over, the Allied troops set up their HQ in some rather fine municipal buildings that had been built by Mussolini. John was put in charge of the postal service, and photos taken of him at the time show him at his desk with an in-tray and nameplate: 'Capt. J.P. Morgan, Administration'. He looked for all the world like a sub-manager at a branch of Lloyds Bank.

John liked order and disliked idleness. There was not much he could do out in the field, waiting for orders and news of deliveries. This temporary inactivity was known as 'resting'. John's unit were waiting particularly impatiently for a mobile field bakery to arrive, as they were short of bread. The 2 August entry for the War Diary records:

> 498 Coy, RASC (Artillery) Admin Instructions: Bread issue will be reduced to 3¾ ozs per man, with biscuits on scale of 6ozs. This is due to the inability of the Fd. Bakery to cope with the increasing numbers of British troops.

They were also waiting for canteen equipment, vehicle parts, petrol cans, latrine paper, flycatchers, razorblades, and underpants. The Italian soldiers particularly suffered from a lack of proper clothing and equipment, including boots, which prevented many from working:

> Maintenance of Italian Troops, 1 Oct 44: The clothing and equipment of Italian Coys is deplorable ... I am quite satisfied that labour and guard duties have suffered very considerably on account of the lack of suitable clothing. There are numerous cases of men who cannot go to work on account of lack of boots.[5]

At least John's men all owned a good pair of boots. However, soap and toothpaste were always in short supply. There had been a report of a *signora* near Caserta who had offered to do the officers' laundry at their farmhouse billet. She had refused payment, asking instead to keep 'only the cake of soap'. The currency was very different in wartime.[6]

Food was a constant problem. There was never enough to go around, and the number of hungry soldiers and civilians continually increased as the Allies moved northwards through the German lines. In parts of Italy there was no shortage of food, but often it was the means of transporting it elsewhere that was the problem. There was a constant worry that trucks would not be able to get through with the supplies, being blown up, lost, or diverted in transit. In the latter cases, the food inside would then end up on the black market.

Tuscany had been badly hit. One only had to look around to see the state of the country and the damage sustained. The local economy was rural, dependent on farming and rearing livestock, growing olives for oil and grapes for wine. That which had not been damaged or destroyed had been stolen, and John had seen plenty of starving peasants foraging in fields and scavenging among the ruins of bombed-out villages. Survivors were living off their wits or dying in isolated and abandoned places.

In the cities, life was different. John had gone through Rome in the last month, travelling in the wake of the US Fifth Army. His company stopped in the city for a short break, and John took a few photographs of Mussolini's headquarters in Palazzo Venezia and the balcony where *Il Duce* had given his impassioned speeches to his adoring public. Just off Piazza Venezia, there were shop window displays of all sorts of food and commodities in addition to *trattorie* with welcome signs (in German and Italian), full of people eating and drinking. Those with money, good positions, and connections could do very well out of the war, but there were many who had nothing and nowhere to turn to for help.

For example, there was a young boy who hung around John's camp; he had recently appeared out of the woodland nearby, and he did not seem intimidated by all the loud-mouthed foreign soldiers. It was young Dino Tiezzi, and he had become used to fending for himself since he had lost his home, his father, and his brother. Dino usually turned up at John's camp when the men were brewing up or cooking on a camp stove. He was willing to do any little job in exchange for something to eat, often offering to polish soldiers' shoes.

John later recalled that his CO, Maj. Donald Birkmyre, said that an officer should always be able to keep himself occupied. Back in Britain, John would often go for a ride in the Brecon Beacons on his motorbike when he was bored, but in Italy, he would have to go for a drive. He had heard reports about German atrocities that had been committed in Tuscany, and he had also heard accounts from Allied troops about what they had found in the aftermath. John wanted to see for himself, so he went to investigate the fortified village on the hilltop in the distance.

John took a jeep and set out along the local road through the valley. A few kilometres along, he came to a steep and almost inaccessible track leading up to the castle, but he pressed on regardless. He eventually reached the top and went into the main square, where he was confronted with the scenes of devastation.

John did not need any official military report to form an opinion on the state of the village he had just entered. He only had to wander the silent streets, look at the blackened remains of houses, and smell the air to know that dreadful things had happened inside those medieval walls. On 20 July, members of the Allied Command Commission had visited the village to inspect the damage. Maj. Walter D. Stump, provincial legal officer for the ACC, stated the following in his report:

> Almost completely destroyed by the Germans on 29 June 1944, the few remaining residents being chiefly women and children. Large areas on the pavement adjacent to the wall are still covered by dried up pools of blood, mute but powerful testimonials to this exhibition of brutality. The village is now a place of utter desolation.'[7]

From the damaged walls of the historic village, John could survey the magnificent Chiana Valley, lavender-blue distant hills girdling the horizon and slopes of thick woodland embracing the village above. All that beauty was now transformed by the butchery of war beneath.

There was quiet – but not Peace,
For Peace is warm as the gay laughter of a child,
Knows colour and hums with the sweet breath of life –

But this quiet was cold,
Like the grave with its mould.
Torn, blackened walls rose out of their shroud
Of grey mist and dripped into twisted earth
That had once been homes.[8]

John was no stranger to death and destruction. After a while, he developed a sort of immunity in order to be able to carry on in his job. He had seen friends blown up before his eyes in the deserts of North Africa, and he had helped injured men at Monte Cassino. He had passed through the remains of many bombed towns and villages in the last twelve months, witnessing lines of families snaking along roads, people and their barefoot children carrying their worldly possessions on their backs. John's journey through Italy had been a continuous slog following in the wake of the German and Allied destruction. Although this was enough to bring tears to the eyes of even the most seasoned soldiers, an officer had to hide his feelings; he always had to be in control and not show any weakness.

Civitella was yet another village that had been almost wiped from existence. In the square outside the church, John found two boys in shorts and grubby shirts. One was barefoot and the other was in badly worn boots that were a size too large for him. They rushed towards John and asked for water, but he had none. As he left, making his way down the steep hill, John passed a woman pushing a small handcart full of kindling and an old mattress with a small child sitting aloft. He then passed another woman, this one bent double, carrying two large jerry cans. Something had to be done.

Two bowsers of water arrived in Civitella later that afternoon.

Amicizia: Friendship

July–September 1944

Drivers Hammond and Simpson uncoiled the rubber pipes and attached them to the outlets on the water tanks, ready to dispense the water into the numerous receptacles brought by the women and children—anything they could find to hold the precious fresh water. John had remembered to bring sweets, and children were following him around.

When the bowsers were empty and the men were getting ready to leave, one of the Sisters came over and thanked them profusely. She asked John whether they would be coming again. They needed food for the children. John promised to return and also bring shoes for the children, many of whom were barefoot or wearing worn-out sandals.

When he got back to camp, John ordered that the tankers were to be refilled from the nearest water station and taken back the next day and every day thereafter until further notice. The paperwork—boxes to be ticked and forms submitted in triplicate—was of no concern; lives depended on immediate action. John asked for contributions from his officer friends (including the CO) and his own men, taking anything they could offer. This included supplies from their own 'compo'—standard-issue field rations. His powers of persuasion must have been great, as tins of meat, packets of instant oatmeal and instant soup, blocks of chocolate, and 'vitamin-fortified' and boiled sweets gradually piled up until there was enough to warrant a journey up to the village. With CO Major Birkmyre's approval (or at least his knowledge), John went to investigate the current situation with supplies and a view to 'trimming off some of the excesses'.

It was not an easy job feeding soldiers in the field and on the front line. Army cooks everywhere did their best with the provisions they received. There were continual shortages, sometimes followed by a glut. Bread rations had been reduced again. Flour was a problem as the war and weather had destroyed much of the wheat harvest. Mutton and potatoes, however, were back on the menu.

For many months, quartermasters had been trying to source extra supplies to feed the constant flow of troops, refugees, and Italian civilians moving around the district.

An entry in the 498 Arty Coy War Diary recorded by Maj. D. M. Birkmyre showed the number of extra mouths they had to feed. On 29 April 1944, the entry read: 'Rations issued to unit BFS 8999: Italian military 400; Italian civilians 1,720; RAF 1,828; SA European 9,612'.

In August, John would start his new job at Area 55 HQ in Arezzo. There, he would be better-placed to help the people of Civitella further. He refused to abandon them. He would be working right at the heart of the supply and transport services. There were other organisations to consult, such as the Red Cross, who knew more about of the conditions and needs of victims of massacres in the region. A Red Cross supervisor had visited Civitella on 27 July and reported to the ACC that women and children were returning, but there were no clothes, blankets, or bedding, no wells, no electricity, and no water supply in the village: 'No milk for babies, no sugar for invalids, no salt. Infirmary intact but pharmacy & contents destroyed. No priest'.

The health of the military and the civilian population was of major concern to the local authorities, the Red Cross, and the Allied Command Commission, as villagers did their best to live in the remains of their homes and whatever buildings remained. Children continued to play among the ruins of the tower; women picked through piles of rubble, looking for wood, pulling at sticks of charred beams and fractured posts. One of the Sisters, possibly on the advice of the Army or the Red Cross, was recorded as having taken a group of children around the village after dressing them in white aprons and arming them with watering cans full of disinfectant. They sprayed the streets and walls of buildings, reaching into every nook and cranny and black and sooty interior. This was a sensible precaution to help protect civilians from the ever-present threat of tuberculosis, typhoid, and dysentery.

John and his men were regular visitors over the next month with water and the supplies John managed to obtain. Each time they arrived in the main square, the number of people increased. Word spread far and wide, to outlying farms and hamlets, that the British Army had come to their aid. It was a bit of a free-for-all when it came to distributing supplies. John had no way of knowing whether the food they brought went to the right people—those most in need. He hoped it was not ending up in the cellar of some local Fascist to sell on the black market, as was suspected of some of the Red Cross supplies sent to the communal rationing office in Badia al Pino for fair distribution to the commune.[1]

John needed more help. It was the children who suffered most in wartime; in Civitella, many had lost fathers, grandfathers, uncles, and brothers. Family life and community spirit had gone, ripped apart on that dreadful day of death and destruction on 29 June. News that the parish priest, Don Alcide Lazzeri, had been one of the first men killed by the Germans meant that the church was without its priest. Sweets were all very well, but the children needed something more sustaining. John decided that he would introduce his friend, the Catholic chaplain. He was used to tending to the sick and comforting those in need in addition to his wartime chaplaincy duties.

Father O'Shea (now called 'Pop' by fellow officers) was forty-two years old, a good bit older than most of the other officers and men. He had not been with the company for very long. John had been posted to the 498 Artillery Company RASC on 13 August 1943, while O'Shea's Army record shows that he was attached to No. 3 District Troops (a pool of chaplains) on 1 June 1944. He moved to Area 55 and John's company on 3 June 1944. He and John are both listed in the Field Return of Officers HQ 55 Arezzo for 1 July 1944 and later editions. In spite of their differing ages and backgrounds, John and O'Shea became friends straight away through a shared experience of the BEF in France and the CMF in North Africa and Italy, in addition to a shared sense of purpose. O'Shea's cheerful manner and mischievous character helped keep things in perspective during these difficult times; he was simply good company.

Allied forces had gradually and painfully broken through the German lines. The long battles for Monte Cassino had preceded the push northwards to Rome and into the Chiana valley region and Arezzo. The servicemen had lost comrades and friends and witnessed civilian population's suffering. They had stopped in Tuscany to strengthen their defences and maintain a hold on the region while waves of fighting forces advanced north to Florence, which the Germans evacuated on 4 August. The Allies then continued to beat a bloody path onwards to the German stronghold at the Gothic Line.

Chaplains became even more important as the fighting intensified, men began to suffer battle fatigue, and lives continued to be lost. Chaplains took their ministry anywhere and everywhere. They might be giving an impromptu communion service from the back of a truck or in a bombed-out chapel, or working at a field dressing station or an evacuation hospital as O'Shea did. They would check on the welfare of the men, whatever denomination, who had been brought in sick or wounded. They could hear confessions if a Catholic padre was not available, give the sacrament, or—as was often the case—administer the last rites. There were letters to write to families about dead sons and funeral arrangements to make. At the end of the day, a chaplain would return to base camp for church parade or private prayers with small groups, or he would go to the mess and try to be bright and cheerful. A kind word or a pat on the shoulder could put things into perspective; a shared joke could make the days, weeks, months, and years spent away from home bearable.

O'Shea had recently been appointed as the Senior Chaplain to No. 3 District, which extended from Rome southwards to Calabria. His office was in Rome, but he regularly visited the chaplains and clerical staff of the Chaplaincy Department HQ, as well as continuing with his duties at camps and in the field. However, O'Shea was finding it increasingly difficult to fit in all the work and fulfil his responsibilities. Just as John was short of supplies, so was O'Shea.

In his letter of introduction to his Catholic chaplains in the Rome district, O'Shea brought up the subject:

Now as regards my situation report: there are twelve chaplains under my command—that is less than when there were 40 and more than before the war. If no replacements come from England and these twelve go on release it means we are six short if my figures are correct.[2]

All the chaplains had more work to do to reach their Catholic flock as the areas increased in size. They often relied on Army transport, which they were not always entitled to use. There was such a high demand for vehicles that this added to their problems. It was difficult trying to visit the more distant and overlooked outposts; even scattered units such as field bakeries and mobile laundries were part of the 'parish', and men working there were entitled to the chaplains' services. O'Shea used to hold meetings at different locations every Monday with his chaplains for a chat and a cup of tea, to review their work and support them in their pastoral duties. This tradition, which he started, continued throughout the campaign; no doubt there was also a lot of laughter accompanying their talks.[3] O'Shea was practical and efficient in his work, but he never could supress his wicked sense of humour. He was renowned as an erudite and witty man, not least due to his introductory letter, which contained advice to the new men under his authority:

I would like to tell those Chaplains who are coming under my command for the first time what I told my Chaplains in No. 2 District 'Do not regard me as your Superior', and they were kind enough to obey me in this and 'this was their finest hour' (Luke xll.3). Together we must hunt in the woods for the flowers of perfection, smelling their sweet smell, and inhaling their sweet inhale. I want to look upon you all as the flowers in my little Italian garden—some of you as my sweet peas—others of you as my pansies—but all of you giving off one smell or another so that we can have something in common. For sustenance and life the flower requires water and manure and so I want you to look upon me as your water and your manure and I am sure you will all do this as soon as you get to know me better. In their trials and difficulties the 'Gentiles went to Dumb Idols' (Paul X7.9)—in like manner you must come to me. I want my Chaplains to be happy—a happy Chaplain 'Covereth a multitude of sins' (Peter or Paul Vl.6).

Should a Chaplain find himself a round hole in a square peg, let him not wait 'till the thorns grow up and choke him' (Matt) but rather let him come to me and I will do it for him.

Great difficulty has been experienced in this Office on account of collections not sent in by Chaplains. When therefore this Office sends out a letter re collections, it is not sufficient to return my letter with a note in the corner saying 'You have had it'. The date and manner of how the Office has had it should be clearly stated.

It has come to my notice that some Chaplains have set up their Billets in Brothels. The argument that this is the most certain place of meeting all your men from time to time does not hold, and when I visit a Brothel in future I hope I will not see any of the Chaplains there.

Unlike John, O'Shea enjoyed being the centre of attention—but not in a proud or arrogant way. He was a serious and devout man beneath the bonhomie and joviality. John enjoyed the company of others, but not all the time. Some men thought him standoffish and rather distant, but he was simply not as outgoing as Pop. O'Shea could tell a story to room full of men and make them weak at the knees with laughing—what people call 'the common touch'. John could only look on and admire this man's style, charisma, and sheer *joie de vivre*. O'Shea had been tutored in the way of Saint Francis and knew that 'it is not fitting, when one is in God's service, to have a gloomy face or a chilling look'.

O'Shea enjoyed a varied social life, as officers often did in their leisure time. This is evident from two large Eighth Army albums stored in the Passionist archives at Douai Abbey. The pages are crammed with souvenirs—postcards of places he visited, stamps, money, receipts for restaurant and hotel meals, drinks at cocktail bars, seats at the opera, and race programmes. There are invitations from ambassadors and bishops to official functions and social events, and there are programmes from school concerts and children's tea parties.

O'Shea could certainly claim to move in high circles now—or at least play on that idea—as he was granted a 'private' audience with His Holiness Pope Pious XII. He recounted the meeting to his chaplains in a letter on 3 August:

> Yesterday I was granted the unique and special privilege of a Private Audience with the Holy Father Pope Pius XII, at which some 6 or seven hundred others were present. After explaining to the Holy Father the work of a Senior Chaplain, His Holiness thanked me for all that I had done, and asked if there was any special privilege that I desired. Before I could ask what I wanted most, the Papal Chamberlain explained that the Holy Father meant only to spiritual privileges, and so I asked for a blessing for the people of Rome, Myself and my Patron Saint. This His Holiness willingly gave in the usual form '*ex urbibus et ossibus*' [the usual Papal blessing or address is called '*Urbi et Orbi*', meaning 'for the City [of Rome] and for the World']. That blessing I now pass on to you.[4]

With his wide circle of friends and acquaintances, he sometimes received gifts from grateful people, just as he enjoyed hospitality and presents from parishioners in Herne Bay. Because he was not acquisitive, he usually gave them away—not just cigarettes and sweets (standard rates of exchange in the Army), but also things like bottles of *Vin Santo* and olive oil slipped to him by kind clergy or local farmers, perhaps. O'Shea never had any money because as soon as he received his pay and had settled any mess or other bills, he gave it all away to deserving people—usually children. As his friend Newman recalled in France in April 1940, O'Shea was like the Pied Piper of Hamelin. He had a line of children following him around:

> The coins he kept in his pocket for the children. They soon got to know him and when it was all gone he would turn the linings inside out, indicating that there was none left.[5]

When John first took O'Shea to visit Civitella, the chaplain was welcomed with open arms. Children rushed up at the sight of a new face and a dog collar, clamouring for attention and sweets.

John recognised Dino as one of the children, remembering him as the boy who had cleaned mess tins in the camp. Today, Dino and Luciano vividly remember O'Shea and his effect on everyone. They were excited to see him, not just for the sweets he brought or the magic tricks he performed, but also for how he made them laugh and forget their sorrows. Dino remembered how pleased the nuns were to discover that Father O'Shea was a Passionist. When they first met him, O'Shea recognised the heart and cross embroidered on the breast of their habits—symbols of his own order. He was invited to say prayers and bless the other members of the community and the sick at the home for the elderly and infirm.

14

Winter

October–November 1944

The office of the new Deputy Assistant Director Supply and Transport (DADSTC) was on the second floor of the central post office in Via Guido Monaco in Arezzo, now Area 55 HQ. The beautiful Art Deco building had escaped damage in an area of the city that had suffered sustained heavy shelling. John took a photo of the view from his window, which looked out over the entrance on to the main street at the front of the building, with a clear view of traffic and military personnel coming and going. The city was coming back to life after suffering heavy damage before its eventual occupation by the Germans. The debris was quickly cleared and the walls rebuilt after the city's liberation and the Allies' consequent occupation, which meant there were many more hands to help.

Like Rome, Arezzo was still a beautiful place, many of the grand buildings and landmarks having survived intact. The Piazza del Duomo, a short walk uphill from John's billet in Corso Italia, was a haven of beauty and tranquillity, and the impressive thirteenth century cathedral, Bishop's Palace, and town hall were all largely untouched. John's office was impressive, with high ceilings, wood-panelled walls, and smart furniture and shelving. It was slowly filling up with files of paperwork that were accumulating as part of the bureaucracy of the very important Supply and Transport Department. Without the Royal Army Service Corps, soldiers would have no ammunition for weapons, drivers would have no fuel for vehicles, bakers would have no flour for bread, and surgeons would have no scalpels for operations.

John's experience in the RASC made him appreciate his father's job back home in Merthyr, organising the transportation of coal from colliery to consumer all around the country. John was well-suited to his new position. During the selection process for RASC officers to work at headquarters, the candidates' personal details and records had undergone rigorous scrutiny before any appointment was made. John kept a copy of his 'Return of RASC Officers Recommended for Promotion or Special Employment' dated 7 August 1944:

These particulars are the main source of information for the posting and promotion of an officer. It is the policy of S & T in this theatre to use every endeavour to put 'square pegs in square holes', and this can only be done if higher formations are in possession of all available information. No matter is too trifling to be inserted.

His reference went on to say:

An officer of above average ability. Shows special aptitude for administration and organisation. Has had experience in the field of petrol; ammunition and supplies with very good results.

John displayed all the qualities necessary to succeed in this important administrative role at HQ. Although he was recommended to the rank of Major, he did not achieve that position until much later.

Arezzo was now a good city to work in. However, a few months earlier, a few hours after the liberation of the city, the war correspondent for *The Times* described the place as 'deserted and ghostlike in the silence that was only broken by the rumble of approaching tanks'.[1] When John arrived, the city was all activity and noise, the Allied military operations breathing life into the area once more. By the end of October 1944, there would be nearly 300 Army units in the city, in addition to the independent Poles.[2]

Electricity and water supplies had been restored in some areas, along with the telephone system. Debris in the main thoroughfares was slowly being cleared and the streets were filling with people emerging from their imposed confinement or places where they had fled or had been evacuated to. Even if some buildings were not fit for use, all kinds of business were being carried out in improvised premises, on street corners, and in squares, where market stalls were appearing every day. Cooperation, support, and law and order would win the war and put the nation back on its feet.

The Allied forces were still in the process of setting up support services such as garages and workshops, transport depots, and storage facilities in disused or empty premises. There were many opportunities for Italian civilians to work for the military. Unskilled men could find labourers' work clearing debris and repairing roads and bridges. Skilled workers were sadly in short supply—there was a need for bakers, mechanics, metal workers, and interpreters, among others. John's department kept a close eye on every aspect of ordering and transporting supplies, storage, and distribution, as well as the movement of troops and refugees.

As with any large, bureaucratic organisation, mountains of paperwork were generated. There were records to keep, returns to complete, and reports to write. Office staff were responsible for dealing with the communications that came into the sections of Supply and Transport. The appointed officers—like John—would go through the messages and deal with them or refer them onto the appropriate person in another unit or section.

Every day, staff typed up 'Telephone and Verbal Decisions Log' sheets, which recorded every message (or 'event', as they were called) by telephone, letter, or in person that came through the office, along with the action that was taken. At the end of the week, the log was passed on to superior officers—in John's case, Lt-Col. C. J. Midmer OBE, Assistant Director Supply and Transport (ADST). He scrutinised the log entries, noting any important issues and including them in his weekly report on the 'general situation in Area 55', which he sent to his boss, Col. Longridge, Deputy Director Supply and Transport (DDST) of No. 1 District. Problems came in and solutions went out.

The majority of the work was handling orders and directives and trying to solve problems that arose from them. The main areas of concern related to fuel supplies, trains (the lack thereof), maintenance of vehicles (a lack of skilled men and workshop facilities), and food provision (which featured heavily—an army marches on its stomach, after all).

A log entry in the ST Branch Area 55 War Diary on 20 August 1944 records a problem with contaminated chocolate in the 'compo' (Army ration pack). The contamination meant the Indian Corps were prevented from eating it:

(1) Will examine Compo to see if contaminated by cigs. Corps had some in which chocolate had melted and cigs damaged commodities so that Indians wouldn't eat it. (2) Have we any without cigs? (3) There is a new pack recommended by Corps. Have we any?

A report dated 15 October states:

Some cabbage and cauliflower have been issued. Issues of fruit have been restricted by inability to reach farm owing to culverts being washed away.

Other notes reveal shortages of custard powder and insect repellent, 'tomato paste' not arriving, and a shortage of macaroni before Christmas, although rice was available. On one occasion, Lt-Col. Midmer informed his superior about a problem with tainted bread:

Samples of tainted bread baked on 29 August have been despatched to 13 CRASC for analysis. Bread has been baked in a civilian bakery from samples of all flour held in the Area is being carefully watched.

Meat was a very important commodity. There could sometimes be problems with livestock; for example, a delivery of Sudanese sheep was disrupted due to the death of some of the sheep from cold during transit in uncovered wagons. A log entry for 21 October 1944 reads:

Will make representation to Base for sheep to be sent in covered trucks. Deaths at 7–9% and remainder in very poor condition. These sheep are Sudanese and cannot stand cold.

As Staff Captain, John had the autonomy to organise his own time, delegate jobs, and respond to emergencies as they arose. Records show the diversity of the problems that came through the office, including inspecting and reporting on field latrines, checking maintenance work on bakery equipment, checking sites for cold storage units for fresh meat, ensuring trucks transporting supplies were not overloaded or returning from a base empty, and, in one case, interrogating Italian soldiers about stolen cases of bacon.

It is certain that Civitella was a priority for John, and he made time to help the villagers. He was lucky to have Driver Hammond and another driver, Paine, transferred with him, so they knew John well. They also knew all the roads, backroads, and shortcuts well, which helped them get to Civitella. If there were supplies to pick up and deliver, they could be trusted to deal with it and use their initiative as required.

War teaches a person to be resourceful—to make the most of what there is and to use one's wits to find what is lacking. Within such a vast organisation, mistakes are made, inefficiencies and wastage occur, and there are opportunities for someone to use the situation to his advantage. John came across the results of human error every day, officers ordering too much or the wrong type of item. Goods were sometimes returned due to damage, and other supplies were misdirected or lost.[3] John used this knowledge to his advantage and thus to the benefit of the women and children of Civitella.

Over time, John accumulated a good deal of knowledge about local affairs; he had a large number of military contacts, connections with Italian authorities, and relationships with local civilians. He knew who was helpful to the military and those who were more interested in personal gain, and he knew who was stockpiling goods and who was dealing on the black market. The theft, looting, and reselling of stolen good was a perennial wartime problem.

Norman Lewis, an intelligence officer in North Africa and Italy, wrote that 'the impudence of the black market takes one's breath away'. It was reported that during May 1944, the equivalent of the cargo of one out of every three Allied ships unloading at the port of Naples was stolen. Norman Lewis described how Italian tailors turned Army uniforms into smart new suits for civilians, and stolen tyres even appeared on the car of the Papal Legate.[4]

Luckily, John had recently made a new friend in Civitella, Gigi, to help with this problem. Luigi Lammioni, the town clerk and secretary of the hospital, wanted to help John to make sure that supplies the Army brought were distributed fairly. Others agreed that it was a good idea for Gigi to occupy his mind and distract him from the depression he was suffering after the deaths of his wife, Marietta, and daughters, Giuliana and Maria Luigia, who had been overcome by fumes from the fire in the loft where they were hiding from the Germans.

His surviving daughter, Vittoria (cousin of Lara Lammioni), was five years old at the time, but she always remembered the kindness Capt. Morgan showed to her father. She met his son, Keith, many years later at Malfiano, the Lammioni family home, where he was staying. She spoke a little English and wanted to tell him how John Morgan got to know her father and how the friendship developed—based, it seemed, on liberal amounts of wine. Wine was readily available, unlike water, which was scarce or had been polluted. Wine and laughter bound them together as well as a mutual interest in the relief of the suffering of others.[5] In addition to Luigi's help, John was also relying on O'Shea, more so now there was a new enterprise in hand.

O'Shea was a frequent visitor to Arezzo for his chaplaincy work and also for the social life with fellow officers and other ranks in the mess. He also put his artistic talents and amusing turn of phrase to good use in contributing to the Area 55 HQ magazine, which was produced by the men to entertain and inform everyone. Father O'Shea kept a copy of the Christmas 1944 edition of the Area 55 magazine; it is of particular interest because he designed the front cover, which depicts a Tuscan landscape with cypress trees in the foreground and a winding road leading to a hilltop village with a tower in the distance. It can only be Civitella.

O'Shea knew a lot of people and had good connections in the military and with civilians. He and John met regularly to talk about Civitella and discuss the progress of the aid. O'Shea visited the village on his own from time to time to see the Sisters and visit the old people in the home. He also helped the children with their catechism (and entertained them with games and magic tricks, no doubt). Although he often brought sweet treats, he knew that this was no substitute for proper meals for the youngsters. He had visited some of the Vatican soup kitchens set up around Rome and knew how effective they were. Food was still the main priority, especially as the weather was changing; hot meals were urgently needed.

Eighty-year-old Dino Tiezzi remembers his ten-year-old self and what he and others owed to the two British officers and the other men.

Captain Morgan and Father O'Shea decided that the only way to provide everybody with a hot meal was to reopen the *asilo* [nursery school], what is now the *Casa Parrocchiale* [church hall]. It had a refectory in the basement and homeless families were camped there sleeping on mattresses on the floor. The British kept bringing up food and other supplies, the only food that the survivors had. The nuns helped to prepare and serve the meals. I think that Captain Morgan must have bent a lot of military rules to supply all this food because the quantity was so large that it could not just have been surplus. I think that he risked a lot to help us. We were happy there not only because we ate but also because there was food that we had never seen in Italy before. For example, there were tins of pork paste (Spam), which were excellent. We used to spread it on bread. For us it was an exceptional thing.

As word spread around the commune about the canteen, more people (and especially children) arrived from surrounding hamlets and villages each time John and his men came to Civitella. John sometimes brought an Army cook to assist while he supervised the food with the nuns, and O'Shea tried to keep order in the queue and entertain the children while they waited. The nuns were busy fetching and carrying, and O'Shea loved bossing the Sisters around, and they would scurry off to do what he ordered. The first meals consisted of soup—which came in blocks to which water was added—accompanied by hardtack biscuits, tins of bully beef, and spam, which were easy to get as they were part of standard-issue rations. Over time, John was able to bring fresh meat, vegetables, and, most importantly, bread.

Bread was an important part of every soldier and civilian's diet, and a lot of the RASC work was related to getting enough supplies of flour and keeping bakeries running efficiently and hygienically. There were many bakeries now in operation in and around Arezzo, but villagers like those in Civitella, in isolated rural communities, still had no access to such provisions nor the currency to purchase goods.

After food, what the people of Civitella most needed were ways of keeping warm as winter approached. After the massacre, there were said to be 1,500 homeless people from the commune; eighty-seven houses (696 rooms) were reported completely destroyed and 1,100 houses damaged. Those who stayed through choice or circumstance sought shelter in barns, huts, basements, and parts of derelict buildings that were just safe enough to be used as refuge. There was still no electricity or running water, and going in or out of the village was dangerous, with roads and fields either destroyed or mined. The relentless autumn rain had caused the banks of the river Arno to burst, bringing misery to the region as well as to the soldiers fighting on the front. Trench foot was soon to be followed by frostbite.

The cruel hand of winter took its grip on the country and across the whole of Europe. It was the worst winter on record in the twentieth century. How would Dino, Luciano, Palombo, and all their friends survive? Dino recalls:

> We did not have any clothes other than the ones we escaped with. Captain Morgan found out that the Arezzo shopkeepers had hidden a lot of merchandise out of fear that it might be taken away by the Germans. He went to the shopkeepers and bought all these civilian supplies from them with A-M lire occupation money [the Allied Military currency].[6] He used to come over with shoes and clothes. He had organised the soldiers under his command so that one would supply underwear, another trousers, another shirts, another shoes and so on.
>
> I remember that my feet were so small that they were not able to give me shoes of the right size and he got angry because he could not find some that fit. In the end he stuffed some paper in the shoes and made them fit. I went around looking like a clown because of my big shoes. It began a daily routine. Captain Morgan was in command of these troops and Father O'Shea came too. Father O'Shea had nothing

of the Englishman in him; he was more like a temperamental Italian. He was very dynamic but he was also very close to us.

John and O'Shea continued to visit and support Civitella for over five months while also carrying out their normal military duties supporting the Allied Military Government and the front line forces in the Allied offensive. It was a long, hard slog for the forces on what was to be called 'the forgotten front'. They worked to break through the German defences of the Gothic Line, which ran from La Spezia, on the west coast, through the Apennines to Pesaro, south of Rimini, on the Adriatic coast in the east; in *Italy's Sorrow*, military historian James Holland described the landscape as 'mountain passes and bloody ridges'. He wrote that 'the battles along the Gothic Line were proving to be among the most brutal and costly of the entire campaign'.

This part of the Italian campaign lasted from 25 August to 17 December and was known as Operation Olive. The hostile conditions, bad weather, and civilian and soldier casualties continued.[7] The time was approaching for them to move on.

December 1944

As Christmas approached, John and his company were preparing to leave Arezzo and move north; it was time to say goodbye to the villagers. John and O'Shea wanted to do something special for the people they had grown to love, so they planned a festive meal and organised presents for all the children. The meal was also attended by around fifty men, including John and O'Shea's CO, Maj. Birkmyre, and other officers who had helped over the past months. As part of the celebrations, the nuns planned an entertainment to be put on by the children. It was going to be a Christmas to remember.

Dino recalls:

We still vividly remember the great party those generous men Captain Morgan, Padre O'Shea, and the others prepared for us ... It was a splendid meal and all sorts of food—not properly Mediterranean—but dishes which were cooked by the best Army cooks. At that time, many of us children and adults were living in the *asilo*— where we would eat at least once a day and avoided danger and bombs everywhere in our village. Before the musical there was a banquet that, for them, must have been the best meal ever, but it wasn't to our taste. To eat a hardboiled egg with a bar of chocolate for us was absurd. They were a little disappointed by our reception of the meal because they had made a great effort to put this on as a goodbye present. In the end we were so hungry that we ate everything that was given to us.

An entertainment was organised by one of the nuns who looked after the children in the *asilo*. I remember this musical very well: there were little children dressed like mice and other animals and also some older girls who were singing songs and dancing. We built a stage in the hall of the nursery school, with makeshift scenery made out of jute bags that worked as wings. Father O'Shea was looking at all these preparations and joined in helping with the scenery and costumes because he was a man out of the ordinary. When the sister did something that he did not like, he used to shout at her: '*Stupida donna!* You stupid woman! You don't understand, come here!' He knew a little Italian but mainly the bad words. We were surprised at this behaviour between a priest and a nun but this was because he had lived among soldiers for so long.

I remember that on the day of the musical, when we were coming into the place, we saw the auditorium full of soldiers and when the older girls came on the stage dressed up and looking very pretty, there were wolf whistles and cat calls. Father O'Shea did not like this and went round the audience hitting the more rowdy soldiers. One of them had a beer bottle in his hand, which he took from him and sprayed all over him and then sent him out for misbehaving. He obviously had authority over the men and must have been an officer.

Eighteen-year-old Alba Bonichi, who had cradled her dying father, Eliseo, in her arms after he was shot by Germans in their house, forgot her sorrows that day as she joined the others in the entertainment.[8] She described the occasion years later:

> It was a theatrical show, with a little ballet and some songs, which I still recollect. I played the leading lady and sang with my friend Malfalda Caldelli, '*...vorrei un bacio solo, o Caterina pietà, pietà*—I would just like a kiss, O Caterina, take pity, take pity.'[9]
> Next to me, dressed up as a little mouse, was ten year old Luciano Giovannetti, who went on to become the Bishop of Fiesole in later life.'[10]

At the end of the show, each child received a parcel with some clothes and a toy inside. Dino said:

> This made us immensely happy ... When you have lost everything, the smallest gesture can be overwhelming. We later learned that all the soldiers who were at the party had given some of their own occupation lire, to buy toys for the children from the few toyshops left in Arezzo. I received a wonderful toy aeroplane. We were very sad when they left. We loved them all for what they had done.
> In the meantime, the front had reached Florence and the Eighth Army had relocated north and the time came for them to move on too. It was a very difficult winter because it snowed a great deal and one day, shortly before Christmas, they came back with two lorries full of blankets, which they gave to the town clerk, Luigi Lammioni to distribute. Because of this nobody died of cold during that winter.
> This was our special Santa Claus who arrived, not in a red suit or riding a sleigh, but dressed in a military uniform, driving an army truck full of aid. So our Christmas

holiday turned out less bitter than we thought. We lost all trace of Captain Morgan from that point but we have found him again with his son, Keith Morgan.

There is only one photo of the Christmas party taken by John; it shows a group of men, including Maj. Birkmyre, posing outside the church among the rubble. They are enjoying a glass of *Asti Spumante*; the bottle—one of many that they brought over to Civitella—can be seen at their feet. The shadow of John holding his camera is just visible in the picture.

The other photo, which is the only one to show John Morgan and Father O'Shea together, was taken after Christmas, in the snow, at another location. At some point, John sent a copy to the villagers; they found it to be important enough to frame and display it in the church, above an eternal flame in the side chapel. It remained there for many years, and it was seen by John and his teenage son, Keith, when the family visited the village briefly in August 1965.

Going Home

HQ Area 55 CMF
Thursday 22 March 1945

My dear Father and Mother

Well, as you have probably realised, I am on now on leave in Florence with three more days of freedom still left!

Yesterday we went to Pisa and had a very interesting afternoon. Amongst other things, the tower was climbed and the church in the same area visited. It's really a most extraordinary tower—13 feet out of vertical!! It's leaning [*sic.*] really makes it most extraordinary to climb. One minute one feels that one is climbing, as you go up the spiral staircase, and the next minute it feels as if you are downhill!! All most weird!!

This evening I'm going out to see my old unit and I shall probably have dinner with them. Really it is most restful to have no work to do for a whole week. Trouble is that I really won't feel like doing any when I have to return on Sunday.

The war news is really grand isn't it? There seems a general feeling of optimism. Everyone can at last see the end of the European war in the not so distant future. Gosh! What a blessing that will be! At one time there seemed no end to the business.

I'm writing this letter in the lounge of the hotel. In peacetime I should say it was probably one of the best hotels in Florence [The Savoia Excelsior Hotel]. It is still run by civilians under the supervision of the military.

I've got another completed film in my camera, so as soon as I get back, I must get it developed and printed. I'm very glad that I took my camera overseas with me. It certainly was a grand idea. This morning I think I shall make a tour on foot around the town and see if there is anything at all worth buying. You really can have no idea of the price of things. A pair of shoes for example for a man—a fairly decent pair would cost the equivalent of approximately £17!!—Nuff said!

Now I must sign off and get ready. I have two officers waiting for me to go out, so no more news for the present.

Cheerio love from John

John Morgan moved northeast with the Eight Army into the Veneto region, supporting the front-line troops pushing forward through the German defences. They liberated Venice on 19 April and on 2 May arrived in Trieste, an important Italian port, now on the border with Yugoslavia. The British forces came face to face with President Tito's Yugoslav partisans, who were planning to take over the town, taking advantage of the instability of the area after Germany's surrender announced on 8 May 1944. The war did not end immediately for the soldiers, sailors, and airmen; they continued with their work, many on the move to new assignments or, like John, remaining to help stabilise the area and keep troops and supplies moving. John's company stayed in Trieste until September 1945.

John photographed some of the places while he was stationed there. His pictures show Naval ships in the dockyard and military vehicles on the quayside, but also off-duty fellow officers having fun, relaxing in and around the outdoor swimming pool amidst the beautiful gardens of their headquarters, a comfortable and commodious villa. There was plenty of hanging around, waiting for things to happen and orders to arrive.

In October 1945, John went home on leave and became formally engaged to Barbara. As he had another six months to serve, he was posted immediately to Greece after his leave. He was part of the British military contingent sent to help restore order during the civil war, which had erupted after the German occupation of the country had ended. The objective was to stop the communists, who threatened to take over the country. Before his release, John, now with the rank of Major, was faced with a big decision—whether to continue his career in the Army or to return to Civvy Street and a career at Lloyds Bank. John decided to return home to Merthyr Tydfil for good.

> HQ 212 Area
> LFG
> Sunday 15 Feb 1946

Thanks for fixing up the calling of the Banns. I feel a married man already!! I bet it causes a spot of chin wagging amongst the locals!! Must have made very amusing reading in the paper....

At the moment we are getting a spot of cold weather here too. The hills to the north are covered in snow and the road to Salonika is blocked. So far, excepting the odd flake or two, no snow has fallen in the city of Athens itself....

No special news again from this part of the world. The last few officers of group 24 are leaving units for a reception camp, ready to sail to Italy next Tuesday so I can't have much longer to wait now.

Bung ho! Love from John

Official notification of his release from the Army came in a letter from the Home Office dated 3 May 1946, which thanked him for 'the valuable services' that he had 'rendered in the service of [his] country at a time of grave national emergency'. The letter also informed him: '... at the end of the emergency you will relinquish your commission, and at that time a notification will appear in the London Gazette (Supplement) granting you also the honorary rank of Captain'. John told his family that he was disappointed not to have kept his rank of Major.

On 23 March 1946, John returned home to No. 9 The Parade, having been granted ninety-five days' leave followed by his formal release from military duties with effect from 26 June. A week later, on 30 March, he married Barbara Jenkins at St Woolas Church, Newport, and went to live at 22 Edward VII Avenue, Newport. Sadly, O'Shea was unable to attend the wedding, but he received a piece of wedding cake as consolation.

HQ
No. 2 District
CMF
9.04.46

Dear Barbara & Johnnie

Congrats! Congrats & Congrats. I am not referring to the niceness of the cake, but to the great event. Not being there saved me a good hangover, and I hope that everything went splendidly. Will go to the pictures tonight and hope to see all the 'Gallant Major from Greece marries beautiful girl'—'Morgan does it again'— no, that sounds as if you were married before!—perhaps 'Ex "6" mess boy goes straight' will sound all right.

You wouldn't have a set of coffee spoons to spare, as I might get married myself one day?

And Johnnie don't take Barbara to see fireworks.

I am off to Rome in a couple of weeks to take up residence there until the end comes and I drop down from 19/- a day to a few crumbs in the weekly collection.

Nothing much doing, but all the very best to you both and lots love to Barbara.

Yours in the Italian elections

Clem/Shea of Milan

Father O'Shea continued his chaplaincy work in the Army, volunteering to extend his service year by year. He resumed the supervision of chaplains still working in No. 1 District, staying in Rome to continue with his pastoral work and enjoying the pleasures of the post-war Vatican life, no doubt. The Church maintained its charitable efforts through the Vatican committee, which had worked hard during the war to alleviate the hunger of local people and refugees. In the period that O'Shea and Morgan were running their own canteen in Civitella, the Church kitchens were serving an average of 250,000 meals per day. An Allied Military Government report stated: 'The work done by this committee was beyond praise, and by its active help in the early days much severe suffering was prevented'.

After a few months' residency in Rome, O'Shea moved to No. 2 District, which covered the western part of North Italy including Lombardy and Piedmont. In January 1947, O'Shea was posted to the Pool of Chaplains, from where he was sent back to Egypt, where the British had set up their headquarters, with the Middle East Land Forces (MELF). It was important for Britain to continue to protect her interests in the Middle East and maintain stability in the region. O'Shea was back on familiar territory in Cairo and Suez and continued to move around extensively in his duties, a mixture of administrative and pastoral work. He was finally discharged from the Royal Army Chaplains' Department on 30 August 1948 and returned to his parish in Herne Bay, Kent.

He had been home on leave to his home at The Retreat a number of times during his long service, and he was lucky not to have become a stranger, as so many returning soldiers were to family and friends. His flock welcomed him back with open arms, eager to hear about his adventures, and he was not shy in recounting his exploits—self-deprecating and droll in the telling.

Nine-year-old Eve Comper was thrilled when O'Shea came home on leave in September 1941:

> All the pupils at St Mary's Catholic School had missed his visits. The reddest Red Letter Days were when Father Clement came home on leave. We loved to see him—he made us laugh, he told us jokes, he showed us tricks. There was a special one with a matchbox that we all remember him doing—but not what he did! We loved him dearly.

Years later, when Eve got married at the church in 1951, Father O'Shea lent her a gold guinea for her 'something borrowed'. 'He made sure I returned it after the ceremony!' she said.

Tony Pozzetti, aged eleven, remembered having his first ice cream after the war: 'Father Clem took a gang of us lads down to Macari's Ice Cream parlour on the sea front. He bought me a Knickerbocker Glory. A wonderful treat.'

O'Shea stepped back into his parish work as vicar. There were services on Sunday, youth group on Thursdays, monthly 'Children of Mary' group for young women, catechism classes at the school, visiting families, and looking after the sick and elderly brothers in the parish. He continued to oversee the temporal needs of the community, which included buying food and taking care of housekeeping. He kept the accounts and paid the bills and was in charge when his superior—the Rector, Father Romuald McConnell—was absent. From 1950 to 1953, O'Shea took over as Rector of the Herne Bay Passionist Community and used his position to ensure that his plan for a special gift to the parish was realised.

A month after the wedding, John returned to Lloyds Bank to the same position he had held at the Dowlais branch before the war. Sadly, two colleagues did not return. Initially, telegrams sent to their families stated that the men were 'missing in action'. Months later, letters arrived: 'It is my painful duty to inform you that a report has this day been received from the War Office notifying the death of...' One of the Morgans' neighbours in The Parade remembered hearing a terrible wailing sound coming from one of the houses nearby, where such a telegram had been delivered.

John was determined to do his best and make up for the years away. He had a young wife to look after, rent to pay, and eventually a mortgage when he bought his first house in 1956, after they moved to West Wickham, Kent. He got his head down, worked hard, and took the appropriate exams and training to progress up the career ladder. He attended the Senior Courses at Lloyds College, Kingswood, in Surrey; the courses included management training. They were military-style, in essence, assessing skills and competencies such as *esprit de corps*, appearance, organisation and management, ability to motivate, and leadership. Much was familiar to John from his own officer training, so he found it easy.

He moved to the Newport branch in December 1947. Following training, he became an assistant on the inspection staff in May 1949, qualifying as an inspector in July. He was sub-manager at Newport from August 1953 until 1956, when he moved to the head office in London as inspector for the organisation and methods department. He commuted by train each day from West Wickham, with his bowler hat, rolled umbrella, and briefcase. In 1960, John was promoted to assistant manager at the High Street branch, Cardiff, where he stayed until his death in 1968.

The family, which now included, Keith, born in 1949, and Alison, born in 1953, moved to 19 Celyn Grove, Cyncoed, Cardiff, which remained the family home until Barbara's death in 2006. Barbara trained as a pharmacist and went back to work after the children started school. Life was comfortable; there were holidays abroad in the summer, a new car every two or three years, a fitted kitchen with all the latest appliances, and a cleaning lady once a week. John and Barbara had a good social life that was mainly centred on the bank—attendance at dances and dinners were a mixture of duty and pleasure, no doubt. It was necessary to be seen at these events in order to get on in the bank. Barbara attended church with the children and was involved with various church activities, including the Mothers' Union. John stopped going to church; he had no time for religion. He preferred his Sunday routines— mowing the lawn and servicing his beloved Morris Oxford.

John spent a lot of his spare time with his head stuck under the bonnet of his car, checking that everything was in order—spark plugs, oil level, radiator water, tyres, wipers, and lights. He always kept the car spotless inside and out, with no fluff, dust, or mud on the upholstery or the mats. He was obsessive about keeping the already clean and shiny car even cleaner and more highly polished. The ritual polishing of a separate quarter of the body each week, working over and over the same small patch, seemed to give John a sense of inner peace when he felt the pressures of family life and work.

He was a perfectionist. His son remembers:

[He was] sometimes almost obsessive compulsive. He had a temper and got very angry over the silliest thing, when something wasn't done correctly. I remember Mum having to hold tools or a light for him when he was working on the car. Hours and hours, she stood, not daring to move in case he got cross. He had a special routine for cutting the grass, in exactly the same way every time. Everything had to be done a particular fashion.

Whatever it was he was trying to suppress, frustration or anger, when the pressure got too much, he erupted, shouting, banging doors, and storming out of the house. He could be a difficult man at home, but he never displayed this more troubled side outside the house. He was much loved and appreciated by his colleagues and customers at Lloyds. John Meredith, who worked at Lloyds High Street, Cardiff, remembers his deputy manager:

John Morgan was a very kind and approachable man, so easy to work for. I remember once I was summoned to his office to be told that I would need to travel to London the next day to be interviewed by the Chief General Manager of Lloyds which meant that I was to receive my first managerial appointment. I was worried because my wife was a teacher and settled in her job and if we were asked to move away to take up my new responsibilities she might have had to leave her post, which would have been financially difficult for us.

In those days it was only the Chief General Manager who could tell you where your management position was going to be even though the local branch manager would know. John Morgan said, 'I am just going to pop out of my room for a moment but if you look at the top right hand corner of the blotting paper on my desk you may find something that will put you at ease.'

He left the office and I walked around his desk to look at the blotter and there was written 'Mumbles, good luck!' In a few moments he returned and said.

'Well done, now I have not told you anything, have I?'

It was such a kind thing to have done, as I was able to tell my wife and talk to her before I travelled to Lombard Street the next day on the train.

There was another time when there was a national postal strike, which was a real issue as it made it impossible to transport the Cheque and Credit Clearings to London. It was decided that Cardiff Branch would be a central collection point for all the South Wales branches and I volunteered to work with several others to sort all the packages to be taken to the Clearing Houses in the early hours of the morning.

It was late at night, around 10 p.m. I think, when there was a knock on the front door of the branch. In walked John and Barbara with dozens of packed sandwiches, beer and other items to keep us going through the night. We all thought what a great thing for them to have done for us mere juniors. When the sacks were full of the post we took them to the railway station for the London train so they would arrive in time to be distributed in the morning to branches.

I also remember a time, towards the end of your John's life when he was so terribly frail as his health had broken. A group of us decided to pool our cash together and take him out to lunch to cheer him up as best we could. It was so sad to see him across the table looking so ill but still cheerful. He never gave up.

We never heard anything about his war service until years later we heard about the BBC television programme *Dead Interesting People* presented by Michael Aspel. A team of experts set to investigate untold personal stories in Wales's most beautiful and historic graveyards, including John Morgan's story. Keith was filmed returning to Civitella and talking to survivors. We were bowled over with surprise and admiration when we learned about John's time in Italy.

John did not talk much about the war at home, but if he did, it tended to be in a light-hearted way. He never commemorated Remembrance Day or wore his service medals. His 1939–1945 Star, Africa Star, Italy Star, Defence Medal, and War Medal 1939–45 remained in their boxes, unopened. However, he must have felt the need to be with those with similar experiences as he joined the Cardiff branch of the RASC Regimental Association and attended meetings regularly. He must have found comfort in the comradeship of fellow veterans, just as O'Shea did with annual reunions of the 12th Casualty Clearing Station.

However, Keith remembers times spent with his father and the stories he told him about his escape from France and how he blew up mines in North Africa. This is what a son wants to hear from a father—tales of adventure and derring-do. John used to show Keith the souvenirs he had brought back from the war. Apart from Army shirts and a leather jerkin, he had billycans—Army mess tins—and his camp bed, which appears in one of his photos of his sleeping quarters in Casa Reale, Italy. As a teenager, Keith took the folding bed to use at Scout camp, unaware of its history or significance.

John also had in his possession a Mauser, a German automatic pistol. It was his pride and joy, and he kept it in a suitcase in the attic along with a quantity of ammunition and other bits and pieces. John enjoyed going to a friend's farm to do a bit of shooting—mainly target practice on tin cans. Sometimes Keith accompanied him, but he was never as good as his father, feeling all the more a failure when he missed and his father shouted, 'Stupid, boy, you're not trying!' Eventually John decided that because he did not use the gun enough and he was not a member of a gun club, he ought to hand it in to the police during one of their weapon amnesties.

War changes a man, and John was a very different person from the youngster who had left Merthyr in January 1940. Returning safely home to family and friends was what every soldier, airman, and sailor dreamed of. Domesticity was something John had craved while he was away, which he reflected on in a letter to his parents dated 27 April 1944:

I'll be rather glad that when it's over, I shall be able to say 'Well, I didn't spend all the war in England.' Damn! I forgot Ireland too!! Really though, life isn't at all bad and I generally manage to see the funny and amusing side of incidents that would annoy most people. In addition to which, I enjoy the most excellent health. I've my own life according to my own principles and don't care a damn for any of those that make up my immediate surroundings. Sounds rather cynical but who cares. I shall enjoy home comforts and a normal life much more when I return than I should have probably have done had I not experienced the other side of life. Sounds rather the words of a sage!!!

John found security in marriage; the love and support of Barbara gave him stability. He needed a comfortable home to come back to after the stresses of his work, which increased as he rose to a senior position at the bank. The Cardiff branch, where he worked from 1960 to 1968, was the corporate centre for Lloyds Banking in Wales. He handled some very large and important accounts of local businessmen and industrialists, lending money to men such as Julian Hodge—later Sir Julian Hodge, the founder the Commercial Bank of Wales and the Hodge Foundation.[1]

Keith remembers the effect on his father:

> He was the one lending these people large sums of money and there were moments when it all looked as if it might all go terribly wrong and my father's career might be in jeopardy. He had reservations, but it all came right in the end and, of course, later on, these people went on to do great things.

Keith was eighteen and Alison fifteen when their father died on 15 February 1968. John had always prided himself on his good health, which he often referred to in letters home, always assuring his parents that he was well:

1 May 1941

> Now don't just worry 'two hoots' about me. I'm quite convinced that I have a charmed life. Once, thank God, with the excellent health that I enjoy, I can face the struggle in front of us with courage. Just let me get a grip at Jerry, that's all. Gosh, what wouldn't I do!!!

27 April 1944

> Please don't worry yourself about my getting malaria, Mother. I'm dosing myself with Mepacrine and with my hardy constitution the poor mosquito just doesn't get a chance!!

And even when he 'developed a slightly yellow colour' from repeated doses of the anti-malaria drug the Army issued to everyone, he joked:

Despite the colour one knows, I can reassure you, that there is no known harmful effect. Keeps the malaria bug away and that is what matters oh yes! I'm developing quite a good tan already.

All this meant that it was a surprise to him and his family when they were told that he had bowel cancer. John had only gone to the doctor about what he thought were haemorrhoids, when he could no longer ignore the blood he found in his stools. As a result, he failed to catch the cancer early. When the surgeon at Cardiff General Hospital opened up John on the operating table and removed the part of his colon where the malignant tumour was growing, he noticed something familiar inside.

'Did you serve in North Africa?' he asked John soon after he had woken from the anaesthetic.

'Yes, I was with Monty's lot. All over the place, Tunisia, Tripoli, Constantine.'

'Thought so. You've still got the desert sand inside you and it hasn't done you any good.'

Professor Jenkins, John's doctor, knew only too well what conditions were like in the desert, having served in the Royal Army Medical Corps himself during the North African Campaign. A few years' later, when he, too, was diagnosed with rectal carcinoma, he knew what lay ahead. He knew, unlike John, that there was no effective treatment after surgery, and that all that lay ahead was a long, lingering decline to his death. He went to Malta—a place he had loved since being stationed there during the war—wrote a farewell letter, and took an overdose of barbiturates with a glass of whisky in his hotel room.

Maybe it was the desert sand that ended John's life prematurely, or perhaps it was the pipe he smoked all those years, combined with the filthy, acrid air of Merthyr's industries that he breathed as a child. Perhaps it was the continuous use of Mepacrine while serving abroad. Could it have been the constant exposure to petrol, the legacy of working with the RASC? They would use empty petrol cans to carry drinking water for brewing tea; a photo of John dated April 1944 shows him and his driver picnicking between Naples and Casa Reale, petrol can and mugs nearby. They even washed clothes and showered in petrol when water was scarce. Jack Barrance, Middlesex Yeomanry, recorded in his diary on 4 July 1941: 'Day off. Did some washing in petrol and some sewing'. Had this contributed to John's ill health?

Whatever it was, having been away for nearly six years, John only enjoyed twenty years of life after the war. He did not live to see retirement, his children married, or his grandchildren born. His 'charmed' life ended, as his father's astrological chart had predicted, in 1968.

John had been spared the truth about his terminal diagnosis, and after several operations he eventually went home when there was no more to be done.

Barbara wanted him to enjoy family life and the children, and she tried to make the most of the time he had left—she did not know whether it would be six months or a year. John, however, insisted on returning to work as soon as possible. Barbara found it hard knowing that he was not going to recover, but she put on a brave face and tried to keep domestic life as normal as possible, supporting him even if she disagreed with what he was doing. He was stubborn and difficult, but she always put his needs first.

John still hated idleness in himself and others. He would get cross with his son when he felt that Keith was slacking or not using his time and brain to do something worthwhile. He would ask Keith if he had homework to do, and if he had finished it, John would tell him to go back and improve it, to try and get a better grade. Even though he was weak and dying, he retained his tough disposition.

What John had witnessed during the war only made him appreciate how lucky he was. He had survived, unlike his fellow officers and friends who had been shot to pieces or blown up by mines. His home had not been burned down, nor had his family been killed in front him. He often thought about the children he had met, who were grateful for a cup of water, a pair of shoes, or a blanket. He thought about the widows rebuilding their lives and their homes, and the orphans who were sent a long way away. He thought about the houses rebuilt, the church restored, and water and electricity in abundance. Nowadays, nobody had to go without. Britain's new welfare state was a wonder; no one need ever be hungry or thirsty again, or go without medical care.

The Grotto

'One night, I heard a man shouting. It was Padre Pio having a fight with the devil,' O'Shea recounted to his audience of eager schoolchildren. 'I was staying in the cell next door to Padre Pio at the monastery of the Capuchins in San Giovanni Rotondo. I was in Italy, on my way to liberate Rome.' For the children, listening to Father Clem talk about his experiences during the war was far better than reciting their Catechism. All the young Catholic people loved and admired their priest, respecting him all the more since his return from military service overseas. Patricia McMahan, one of his flock, recalls: 'He was so kind. He used to visit my sick sister every day during a lengthy illness'.

Father O'Shea had served as an Army chaplain for nearly nine years by the time he returned to Herne Bay in August 1948. He came home to the Passionist Brothers at the Retreat House, Sea Street, and resumed parish duties as vicar of the Church of Our Lady of the Sacred Heart, Clarence Road. He went back to the daily routines of the community—the timetable of faith and devotion—and to his own small room with its single bed, desk, chair, and bookcase, just as he had left it. He had learned to sleep anywhere and to carry few possessions except for what was needed for his work as a chaplain. Simplicity and poverty were the principles of his calling, and the war had not changed that. He did, however, bring back several albums full of photos, postcards, tickets, menus, and other ephemera—the souvenirs of his service and travels.

The parishioners welcomed his return and saw that he looked a bit older and more careworn, but they knew that his spirit remained undiminished. He could become short-tempered and impatient, and saying mass became a race to the end. Tony Pozzetti remembers:

[It was] twenty minutes instead of thirty, he rattled through the words, probably because he was used to that in the Army. He didn't give long sermons. [It was] as though he had so many things he had to get on with and not enough time.

He was a man in a hurry—a man with a mission. He had special plans for the church and a special job for the boys and men of the parish to undertake.

It is every Roman Catholic's wish, at least once in a lifetime, to make a pilgrimage to Our Lady of Lourdes' Grotto in France and stand where Saint Bernadette experienced her visions of the Virgin Mary. O'Shea had visited Lourdes many times as a young seminary and as a parish priest. Few parishioners had travelled abroad or were likely to be able to afford such a trip. He understood the power of the shrine, a place of healing and a place for the renewal of faith. If he could recreate one in Herne Bay, it would not only be a monument to the faithful, but it could also serve as a war memorial. O'Shea wanted to thank his Blessed Mother for his safe return and to remember those who had died in the two world wars. He had lost two brothers in the first conflict; he had been spared in the second.

In early summer 1950, O'Shea started work with a group of volunteers from the church congregation and boys from the youth club. First of all, before any plans had been drawn up, they demolished old greenhouses to clear the site that O'Shea had chosen for the grotto—the garden facing the main entrance to the church. Today, committees would be set up, planning applications made, and campaigns for fundraising started. As Rector now, O'Shea saw no need for any of this bureaucracy. His years of military service had taught him to be self-reliant and to use his own initiative. He was used to cutting through red tape and, by force of character, bend people to his will—or, as he saw it, to 'God's purpose'. He was in charge, used to making do and improvising; he was used to leading men in the Army and exerting authority as a captain and a senior chaplain. He was a man of action with complete faith in a successful outcome. With God and his parishioners behind him, he plunged straight into the work he had commissioned.

O'Shea called a parish meeting in July, over which he presided. Herbert Walker, a local artist from Whitstable, presented a beautiful drawing of the planned grotto based on a photograph of the original given to him by O'Shea.[1] Everyone was impressed by the plans and agreed that it would be a worthwhile project and a fitting contribution to the Festival of Britain, which was being planned across the country. The dark days of war were over, and a new age of peace and prosperity was being heralded. It was just as well that this was the mood, as O'Shea had already ordered two terracotta statues—a 6-foot Virgin Mary and a smaller Saint Bernadette—from France. He had made enquiries to local merchants about supplies of Kentish ragstone for the structure of the grotto, and he had talked to local nurseries and gardeners about suitable rock plants for the area around the stonework.

When asked about the cost of all the work, O'Shea shrugged and stated that God would provide for them—and if not, he would have to sell off some of his family silver. He had a wide circle of friends and acquaintances from all walks of life, including some well-connected older ladies in the parish who had a soft spot for their priest (as well as deep pockets). Many who donated money, goods, and labour were happy to show their appreciation for the work of the Church and their clergy, and Father Clement in particular. His enthusiasm, along with the love and respect of those in his flock, were enough for the vision to become a reality.

Dennis Adams recounted the story of the beginning of the work on the grotto for the church's centenary celebrations in 1989:

> A few of us were gathered at a place where the Grotto is now. Father Clement O'Shea and Father Declan Fallon were there. We were discussing how to go about beginning the work and where to start. Father Declan, a Dublin man, suddenly took hold of a spade and began to dig a hole. Then he threw a couple of bricks into it and to the amazement of all said, 'We have started.' The rueful smile of Father Clement's face said it all. As he looked at Father Declan the message was clear—'You so and so, you have beaten me to it."

Word spread round the parish that O'Shea was recruiting for an ambitious new project and many people offered help, from labour by builders to beer from publicans. Michael Baker remembers he and his friend Tony Pozzetti helping when they were teenagers:

> Tony and I spent a lot of time at the church helping Father Clem. He was a great organiser. I remember that he managed to get 24 ex-army shovels from somewhere for us all to get stuck in. He got a load of bricks and sold them individually to people for signing which were then used to build some of the grotto walls. We were very proud to be part of it.

O'Shea did not inform the Diocese of Southwark about the work on the grotto until it was well under way, only writing to Father Wall, the Bishop's secretary, at the end of July 1950:

> The men of this parish have been working for the past six weeks on erecting a Grotto to our Lady of Lourdes as a War memorial for both wars and also the Dead. It will take about five months as the evenings are getting darker and we want everything done as well as we can—for instance we are laying on running water, and electricity to light the twelve stars in the crown of the Mother of God [made of small pieces of chandelier glass]. Even iron gates are being made by one of the men in his spare time. Would it be in order to write and ask the Bishop if he would send his blessing to the workers? When we get more certain as the date of opening, how much time would His Lordship require for an invitation to open it for us?

Everyone kept a close eye on the building works, and the *Herne Bay Press* reported regularly on its progress:

> Covered with between 500 and 600 alpine plants of many varieties, specially chosen for their colour and different flowering periods, backed by a row of eight cypresses and surmounted by a six-foot statue of the Virgin Mary, it should when completed

be a thing of real beauty. A stream of water is to flow from the base of the statue over the rocks into a little water grotto on one side, an altar will be contained in the larger centre recess and a statue of the kneeling Bernadette will complete the scene. [13 April 1951]

O'Shea liked being in control of everything—directing work, encouraging the workers, and maintaining morale with jokes and silly tricks. However, if something was not quite going to plan, those around him dived for cover as someone shouted, 'Watch out, Father Clem's on the war path!' He wanted everything to be perfect and nothing to be shoddy or unfinished. He was impatient for the grotto to be finished, but he knew it would take years for the rock plants and wall creepers to grow and for it to look its best. He wanted the place to be worthy of the pilgrims he was certain would come. It was his legacy, after all. The *Herne Bay Press* reported:

In fact, nothing has been left undone and will ensure the Grotto is perfect in detail and as lovely as the ingenuity of its creator can devise, a worthy memorial to the dead and a tribute to God.

The ceremony was held on 5 May 1951, and *The Catholic Herald* published a full account under the headline 'Korea Dead Honoured in New Grotto'. The newspaper listed all the guests who attended and the guard of honour provided by sections of the British Legion, Royal Naval Association, Royal Artillery Association, British Red Cross, St John Ambulance Brigade, Sea Cadets, Army Cadet Force, and Air Training Corps:

After an address by Father Laubenque, a steel casket containing the names of the fallen was placed on the altar by Tony Pozzetti and Michael Baker, two of the boys who had helped with the work. Flying Officer Laurie Shilcock R.A.F. and Major Hayden Curry. U.S A.F. placed beside it scrolls containing the names of British, Commonwealth, and American fallen in Korea. The casket containing all the names will he set in the rock beneath the statue.

Later that year, the Garden of Remembrance was opened and the iron gates formally blessed. O'Shea continued with his traditional parish activities and fundraising events, including the annual summer fête in the grounds of the convent and the St Patrick's Day party, which was always an important date in the father's calendar. Patricia McMahan remembers the celebrations:

Father Clem organised these lovely dances at the King's Hall. All the girls dressed up as traditional Irish colleens who gave out shamrocks to guests as they came in. Father O'Shea was the life and soul of the party but also very kind and attentive to everyone. He always arranged taxis at midnight for all the helpers to get home safely.

The goodwill engendered by these activities between the Church and the town continued to strengthen, and years later the Remembrance Sunday service became a regular event at the grotto, with VIPs and ex-servicemen's organisations attending as part of the town's commemorations. O'Shea is also remembered today for his support at a particularly difficult time for the whole town—the Great East Coast Storm, which struck during the early hours of Sunday 1 February 1953, causing widespread flooding and damage to buildings. It was second nature for him to come to the rescue of people in need.

In 1956, Father O'Shea left his home of twenty-two years—and the parish to which he had devoted so many years of his life—to join the Passionist Community at St Joseph's English-speaking Church in Avenue Hoche, Paris.[2] It was known as 'a well-established church playing a vital role in the spiritual life of the city's English-speaking Christian community'.[3] As he was under the authority of the Provincial, O'Shea had no choice in the matter. It is common practice in religious life, and the Passionists are no different, for brothers to be moved fairly regularly.

Father O'Shea's home had been at Herne Bay since 1934, with only the interruption of his service with the Army Chaplaincy Department. He was nearly sixty, and his health was beginning to fail. What particular mission did they see him performing? Why was he sent abroad to a congregation and parish very different from the one that had been his home for so long—why was he sent to a cosmopolitan and peripatetic population in this European capital city? The church dated from 1863, and was situated on the Avenue Hoche, a wide, tree-lined boulevard leading to the Arc de Triomphe at one end and the lush, green Parc Monceau at the other. In the past, the church and its Passionist community had welcomed the fashionable, aristocratic, diplomatic, literary, and financial world of Paris through its doors.[4]

The Passionist community was no doubt under the strain of dealing with the challenges of post-war Paris:

> The early years were hard ones for the residents of Paris, with few material comforts and strict rationing. St. Joseph's was all the more important as a place of spiritual nourishment, both in the sacraments, and in the cups of tea and shared loaves of bread that the priests would bring out for visitors.[5]

Perhaps O'Shea's wealth of experience in France and Italy were thought relevant to supporting the community and its mission, or maybe it was simply a matter of filling a vacancy with any brother whom the Superior felt needed a change of scenery.

O'Shea did not want to leave his home and move to France, even though he knew the country well from pilgrimages to Lourdes and Lisieux, from his time with the BEF, and from visits to his brother Dermot's grave at Newfoundland Park, near Beaumont Hamel. He must have felt that he had done enough travelling during his life, but personal preferences are not compatible with a religious vocation. In fact, there are occasions when priests are moved because they become too attached to their parishes or particular aspects of their work. However, he kept in contact with many of his friends and met up with them when he returned to England on business and for retreats; he also accepted invitations to weddings and christenings from former parishioners.

Tony Pozzetti and Michael Baker remember stopping off in Paris on their student travels one summer to meet their old friend, who showed them around the city: 'Father Clem was really pleased to see us. I got the impression that he was not happy in Paris, that he was bored and did not have enough to do.' However, O'Shea always managed to make the best of whatever situation he found himself in, and he kept himself cheerful and busy in whatever duties he was given.

He continued to write to his good friend Philip Newman. His Christmas letter dated January 1961 is full of humour and self-deprecation as he describes his festivities—although they were somewhat muted that year:

> It's a pity you are not making Paris for Christmas. Our crib could do with a first-class surgeon. Several of the shepherds are three times the size of the ox and the ass, and a couple of them three times smaller. We are short of helpers, so I am called down to assist at the erection of the crib and get the job of holding the drawing pins to fix the 'brown-paper-rocks' into position. The others don't think much of my efforts, but I have pointed out that they had to have a man to hold the 2 million five hundred thousand rivets when they were building the Eiffel Tower.

He must have thought about how different his life was now, far away from his friends. 'I rather spoilt the Christmas dinner for the other three priests I live with, as I drank milk all the time.' He describes the funny looks from the other men and how this continued when he started playing marbles with nuts on the table and then billiards with tangerines and a banana to keep himself amused: 'My boss seemed to take an interest in the game as I saw him remove a glass vase (Venice) from the centre of the table and put it one side.'

Perhaps he was remembering the riotous times he had with his fellow officers in France in March and April 1940 at their mess dinners recorded in Newman's diary— the time everyone dressed up as padres and a live frog was passed round in a dish of potatoes, those jolly occasions before the German blitzkrieg began and the wounded began to arrive at the station.

Richard Newman still treasures O'Shea's hand-drawn menus from the mess at Bethune, which his father kept along with O'Shea's mock 'Wanted' poster: 'A reward of 10 cents will be given for information as to the whereabouts and known abodes of C. O'Shea, 12th C.C.S.' O'Shea lists all his supposed 'crimes', including not putting down the toilet seat, kidnapping their pet hen 'Hetty' and one egg, absconding with the funds from the Purity League, and interfering with the religious beliefs of the goldfish. It is a perfect example of the humour and sense of fun that made the men adore O'Shea so much.

He missed his friends back in England, and the parish work was not as fulfilling. He was getting older and less able to participate in the community's activities, but

O'Shea did not forget his vocation and his own journey to salvation and that of others. After his death in 1965, an appreciation of his life was published in the parish news of Our Lady of the Sacred Heart, Herne Bay:

His visits to the *Chapelle de la Médaille Miraculeuse* [Chapel of the Miraculous Medal] Rue du Bac were very frequent. To everyone who visited the Passionist church he would tell them of the wonderful Sanctuary of Our Lady, and in his own words many went, some, distressed persons to seek consolation, others, to honour Our Lady by their presence.

Father O'Shea retired to St Mary's Retreat, Harborne, Birmingham, in 1961. He was suffering from a number of health problems, including hardening of the arteries and problems with poor circulation. He had to have a leg amputated, and who better to trust to the job than his good friend 'Pip' Newman, who worked at the Middlesex Hospital. Newman was an exceptional man and surgeon whose reputation was further enhanced by being asked to operate on Winston Churchill's fractured leg in 1962.

Before the operation, Philip Newman returned the crucifix that O'Shea had given to him as a parting gift before he was evacuated from Dunkirk. The CO had ordered that one officer and ten men per 100 casualties were to remain behind. O'Shea had been responsible for the draw for the officers' ballot used to decide who would leave and who would remain. His friend Maj. Newman's name was one of those drawn last.

In his memoir, Newman wrote that their 'beloved Roman Catholic padre' said goodbye before he left. O'Shea took his hand and gave him his crucifix, saying, 'This will get you home safely.' Newman was deeply moved by the gesture because of the significance of the cross:

On one occasion I had seen him lay this cross on the chest of a recently departed patient while giving him the last sacrament. I imagined it was of inestimable value to him and I was overwhelmed that he should give it to me especially at a time when it was most needed.

Richard Newman, who was sixteen at the time, remembers visiting his father's friend in hospital. The day before the operation, he found a cheerful O'Shea sitting up in bed;

He had put one of his slippers at the bottom of his bed with a hand written notice attached which read, 'For Sale, no longer required'. That really summed up Cockie's attitude to life. When I visited him I always came away feeling that I had gained far more from the visits than Cockie, and I returned home greatly uplifted by just being in his company.

Even then, Richard knew that O'Shea was a very special man:

> Everyone felt unbelievable faith in him. My father put his own conversion down to Cockie's influence. My father found his faith in Rouen Cathedral while he was on the run from the Germans, having escaped from captivity at Dunkirk. He wrote in his memoir, 'My heart was lifted. I was alone no longer.'
>
> It was a faith my father never lost. Cockie, of all the people I have met, and that includes Father Trevor Huddleston, seemed to exude a complete faith. Not that he was pious, but he had an absolute belief in God and Jesus Christ, which seemed to shine out. He was also a joyous man with a wicked sense of humour and great fun to be with.

Father O'Shea died on 16 July 1965, aged sixty-seven. His death certificate recorded his cause of death as 'ischemia, chronic nephritis and general debility'. The crucifix came back to the Newman family after O'Shea's death, and Richard took over the care of it after his father died. 'We all felt that it was an important symbol.' 'Cockie's Cross', the family treasure, is displayed in a frame alongside the military decorations of Maj. Philip Newman CBE, DSO, MC.

17

'In My Father's Footsteps' Keith Morgan Remembers

My father did not live to see me follow in his footsteps into banking, starting my career as a junior clerk at Lloyds Bank in City Road, Cardiff, or when I was transferred, years later, to the High Street branch where he had been assistant manager. He did not live to see me join the inspection staff, as he did, and become a bank manager. I'm not sure what he would have said about my career path, or my links at one point to the military, as I became Armed Services Liaison Manager at Cox and Kings, bankers to the British Army, from 1971 to '73.[1] I was keen to join when I was young, but my father did not want me to go into the Army. I remained with Lloyds for thirty-two years and retired from my last post as branch director in Bath in 2012.

John was fifty-two when he died at home on 15 February 1968. Mother and I were at his bedside. I had taken the morning off from college in Cardiff, where I was studying Business Studies; my sister, Alison, was away at school. Dad had fought his illness for over two years, and although he must have known deep down that he did not have long to live, he never mentioned his condition and carried on working up to the day before he died. I remember he used to sit in his armchair, and when the pain became too much, he would screw up the corner of a handkerchief tightly and twist and turn it as he repeatedly intoned lines from his favourite poem, 'Invictus': 'I am the master of my fate:I am the captain of my soul'.

It was heartbreaking to see my once strong father so physically weak and helpless at the end, although his spirit was never broken. I knew he was 'undefeated'—'my head is bloody but unbowed.'

I always looked up to my father and thought he was immortal, that he would always be there for us and look after the family. It was terrible losing him; a dreadful chasm opened up. I felt I had been cheated of a father, of getting to know the man properly. I wanted him to see me become an adult and achieve things that would make him proud. I know I was a bit of a disappointment. I know he wanted me to go to university, something he never did, but I was no scholar.

I loved the outdoors, camping, and climbing, and the Brecon Beacons were my second home. I was thrilled by Dad's stories of wartime action and derring-do in escaping from the advancing Germans on a stolen motorcycle in France, defusing, collecting, and blowing up mines in his path across the deserts of North Africa, and getting frostbite in the terrible winter of 1944–45. But when I expressed an interest in joining a junior leaders' course at the Army Apprentices' College in Chepstow, my father didn't want that. 'Not the Army. University, that's what gets you on the ladder to a successful career.'

As an officer, he had always been smart, efficient, and reliable, and he expected his men to obey orders. This continued in his domestic and working life after the war. He had high standards. Everything he did at the bank seemed to mirror exactly what he had done in the Army as Deputy Assistant Director Supply and Transport (DADSTC). For example, when he was promoted to Inspector Organisation and Methods (known as 'O&M') at Head Office in London, he was overseeing how the bank was run, the systems and ways of working and checking activities and personnel. He went to work immaculately turned out in suit, polished shoes, bowler hat, and rolled umbrella on his daily train journey to the City (Saturday mornings included). All he needed were some Army trucks and mountainous terrain to feel completely at home.

I can see now, from all that I now know about my father, that he wanted me to do the best I could in the world. He had seen so much death and destruction during the war, facing numerous obstacles that would have tested any man. All he wanted was for the world to be a better place.

I remember how upset he was when he heard about the Aberfan disaster on 21 October 1966. Everyone was shocked, of course, by the dreadful accident when thousands of tons of mud and colliery waste, 'a black avalanche', slid down Merthyr Mountain, near Aberfan, after a period of very heavy rain, destroying what lay in its path. A farm, several houses, and a school were buried beneath. One hundred and forty-four people died, including five teachers and 116 pupils aged between eight and ten years, from Pantglas Junior School—half of all the pupils there.

The news reports affected the whole nation, with the raw displays of emotion on our screens, bereaved families, and desperate miners digging by floodlight, still hoping to find survivors. John Humphreys, reporting for the *Merthyr Express*, wrote: 'I saw the miners, faces black save for streaks of tears. They dug and prayed and wept. They were digging for their own children'.

The BBC headlines declared: 'A generation of children has been wiped out'. My father was in hospital, undergoing his first operation to remove the cancerous tumour in his bowels. He was vulnerable and helpless, which he found hard to bear. The news must have brought back memories of Civitella, the suffering and loss of the women and children, living among the rubble of the destroyed buildings. Aberfan, with all those young lives lost, children buried under the coal waste, reminded him of the fragility of life and the effect of the terrible loss of innocent lives in such disasters. The failure of the National Coal Board to protect those living near the unstable coal tips was a criminal act.

As soon as I heard the news, I rang home. We lived only a few miles from Aberfan and knew quite a few people there. My father had customers who were miners and ex-miners and their families. Mum told me that there had been a call for volunteers to help find survivors, so I rushed home and went to report for duty with a load of other students. We were organised into gangs, working different shifts during the day and night.

There were lines of us snaking along from ground level areas up the lower sides of the great black coal waste mountain. We were digging into the mud and passing buckets of slurry of wet coal waste down the line. Some filled sandbags with the black mud, which were then banked up to try to prevent the tip collapsing further. We were like robots, doing, not thinking, and closing our minds to what might be beneath this hellish pile. The silence; there was no sound of traffic or voices or laughter. A pall of grief covered the town; no one else was found alive.

I remember when Princess Margaret put out an appeal for toys, for some crazy reason, and the whole world sent them and there were warehouses full of toys in Merthyr Tydfil, but no children to play with them. It was the most awful business. It makes me think how lucky my father was to bring toys to the children of Civitella that Christmas in 1944. He saw their smiling faces; he felt their warm embraces.

There was no escaping the news reports and stories of families who had lost children. Later on, when he insisted on returning to work, my father was going to the bank each day with this collective grief that hung heavy everywhere. My father knew about suffering and understood the effect of such a loss on a community and the feeling of helplessness by those left to deal with the aftermath, not knowing whom to turn to for help and justice. He must have recalled his friend Gigi Lammioni, whose wife and two daughters died in Civitella, and how their friendship, sealed over shared bottles of wine, helped heal his broken mind.

My father was angry when he heard that the Treasury and the National Coal Board, who were found guilty of negligence, demanded that some of the disaster fund, set up to help survivors, should be used to help pay for the removal of the tip. Dad knew how the survivors of the massacre in Civitella had been neglected and left to fend for themselves, and how grateful they had been for the help they received. I know that compensation and justice, of a kind, came much later for them.

Six months after my father's death, I was working at Lloyds Bank, and five years later I moved to my father's branch at High Street, Cardiff, and found myself sitting in the same chair and in the same office that he had occupied. I was handling papers and documents with his signature at the bottom. I was meeting the same businessmen who had received loans from him. They would say, 'I remember JP. Very fair, very considerate man,' or 'He was always there to give you a helping hand.' I felt proud, but also rather intimidated. Could I live up to his reputation? Could I be my own man, or would I always be compared with my father, judged by what he did and said?

It's strange, but I also found myself on the same training course as my father at Lloyds Bank Staff College in Surrey. I have the group photo of him on the 10th

Senior Course, 1951, lined up with all the other hopeful managers, and me, thirty-five years later, on the 175th Senior Course, 1986, among the next generation of young hopefuls.

Life went on for me as I moved up the career ladder from PA to the Chief Inspector to my first branch-manager job at Taunton in 1986. I got married in 1975 and my daughter, Catherine, was born in 1980; we moved house several times as I was promoted, also buying a rundown watermill in Brittany. All was well with the world.

However, things started to change over the next few years. I don't know what it was—perhaps a mixture of unrest and unhappiness. The stress of work and family life maybe took its toll, but I started thinking about my father, who still cast a long shadow over my life. Maybe I was finally growing up and realising what being a man meant. I still missed Dad. What advice would he have given me about responsibility and duty? Why did he die before I got to really know him? I began talking to my mother more about him as compensation. I muddled on for a long time like this.

One particular event that occurred one summer at our holiday home in France really rekindled interest in my father and what he did during the war,

In 1989, I bought a run-down watermill called Moulin De Treusac'h in Guénin, a small village not far from Baud, inland from Lorient in the Morbihan region of Brittany. It was a beautiful place that had been built in around 1890 of granite stone with ashlar and a slate roof. The local community was friendly and helpful, and as my French improved, I was able to communicate better and make friends and feel less an outsider and more part of village life.

One day, my friend and neighbour André Le Gallo, who used to help me with various jobs around the place, was working in the field behind the mill. We were clearing space to put a wood store for logs for my new wood-burning stove. I was at one end of the field, scything long grass, and André was at the other, digging up stones. Suddenly I heard him cry out. I rushed over, thinking he had hurt his back or stuck a fork through his foot. I could see the top half of him sticking out of a hole that had opened up beneath him. It was nearly 3 feet deep, and as he struggled to get out, he dislodged more material within.

I managed to help him out, and when we both looked down the hole to see what was going on underground, we could see bits of metal sticking up—what looked like pieces of aluminium tubes. I went and got a rake and tried to see what on earth it was. We uncovered more bits and pieces and what looked suspiciously like the edge of an old metal ammunition box. We retreated hastily from the scene.

André went off to alert the local brigade of the *sapeurs-pompiers* (fire service), who came immediately and cordoned off the area. They took a close look at what we had uncovered and decided that it was too dangerous for us to stay, so we had to move out while the area was surveyed and all the stuff eventually removed. This was just as well as it turned out to be an ammunition dump. I later learned that the mill had been the headquarters of the local resistance and was used as a store for armaments and ammunition. That area of Brittany had been very important during the Second World War in the struggle against the occupying German forces. What we found were metal canisters that had been dropped by Lysanders for the resistance to use, and they had been hidden there.

After the hole was filled in and everything went back to normal at the Moulin, I got talking to André about the war, my father's escape story, and his being sheltered by locals in Brittany. André put me in touch with a gentleman in his eighties who had been in the Resistance. He came to visit and presented me with a list of names, nationalities, and occupations for over 100 people who had been involved with or received help from the Resistance within a 30-km radius of Moulin De Treusac'h. He told me that the mill had been used by the local *maquisards* (guerrilla fighters) with the French underground, and that during the war, my neighbour Madeline Simon used to empty the millpond to give the impression that the mill no longer worked. She then filled it up again at night so they could mill the wheat into flour.

It is more than likely that my father passed through the area on his way to Brest and was helped to join the rest of the men for their evacuation during Operation Ariel on 16 June 1940. Who knows, maybe Dad stayed at the mill or in a farmhouse nearby, helped by sympathetic locals, as this was before the formation of the Resistance. If the French population had not helped my father to escape from France back to England, then his war might have been very different.

I talked a lot to my mother about this, and one day she brought out his photo album, which I had never seen. However, as I flicked through, one photograph looked familiar—a picture of my father with three other men, standing in the snow. Where had I seen it before?

We usually went abroad for our summer holidays and in 1965 Dad booked an apartment in Fano, just south of Rimini, on the east coast of Italy. I was sixteen and Alison was thirteen, and we were going to drive across France to Italy, stopping overnight, and then stay a couple of weeks in the resort, soaking up the sun, going swimming, and playing tennis, I hoped. My mother decided to plan a little surprise—a visit to Civitella. I did not know anything about the significance of the place, although I had heard my father mention his 'special village' to Mother.

What prompted Mum was the visit to Father O'Shea in Birmingham a couple of months before. The sight of his old friend, legs amputated and helpless in a wheelchair, his voice soft and cracked, shocked and upset John. It was obvious that O'Shea was nearing the end of his life, and the visit revived memories of their time together in Italy. Maybe Mum thought it would help John come to terms with the past.

Any journey of length was a major undertaking for our family; nothing was left to chance, and holidays were organised with military precision. Dad always hired a car in England, deciding that his own was not up to the journey. He made sure that the AA (Automobile Association), gave him spares for everything, including lightbulbs, fan belt, spark plugs, and oil. He mapped out the route, working out petrol consumption and cost.

My mother decided to write to the Italian Tourist Board in advance to find out where Civitella was and how to get there. There was no going on the internet to find the information back then. The tourist board eventually sent her leaflets and maps, which she packed carefully in her suitcase. It took us three days to reach to Italy, stopping overnight on the way, through France to Italy and on to our resort—over 1,000 miles.

A few days after we had settled into the holiday place, Mum suggested the trip to visit Civitella, which was about 100 miles away:

Holiday Diary
10 August 1965

Got up 7.15. Mum packed drinks and biscuits. We drove all the way to Civitella where Dad was during the war. Came back about 7.15, had dinner. Went for a walk, came back, went to bed. Big storm in the night.

We set off on mother's little adventure, driving for about two and a half hours towards Arezzo, deep into the Tuscan countryside, in search of Civitella. Mum was telling us a few salient features about the area that she had picked up from the tourist information. I was not listening, as I was more interested in annoying Alison in the back seat. It was a tight squeeze in the Ford Anglia and a bumpy ride, and my knees kept banging against the back of Dad's seat—much to his annoyance. We passed fields and scrubland, vineyards and olive groves, ramshackle buildings and dilapidated villas as we travelled along tarmacked roads and unmade tracks. There were the usual arguments about which turning to take, what the road sign said, what we had just passed. My father's innate sense of direction took over and the memory of the landscape directed him to the right road.

'Look,' Mother said, pointing to the distant hilltop village, the castle tower silhouetted against the blue sky. We started ascending a steep hill that went up and up, round and round, as the ramparts of the walled village and ruined tower got closer. Suddenly, with the engine labouring and nearly running out of puff, we turned sharply into a tiny village square, where my father drew up and parked. There wasn't a soul around. I opened the car door, I got out and surveyed the scene, screwing my eyes up against the bright sunlight.

I can remember the stillness and the atmosphere of the place even now. There was something about it that even a cynical and bored teenager like myself could feel. Within the medieval walls of this fortified village, it felt as though we were stepping back in time. It was almost as if a figure in armour and a plumed helmet might step out from the shade of the arched portico at any moment to ask our business.

It was midday. Everyone was having lunch and keeping cool indoors. My father went off to look at the Church of Santa Maria Assunta and I followed him through the side entrance in the square. It was cool and dark inside, and my father walked slowly down the aisle, looking around at everything until he came to the altar. As my eyes got used to the gloom, I saw he was looking at something in the tiny side chapel. I went over and stood behind him, leaning over sideways to see what had caught his eye. On the left-hand side of the altar was an everlasting flame flickering on a tiny shelf, above which hung an old black-and- white photograph in a gilt frame. It showed a group of four men—three soldiers in uniform and berets and a man in a trench coat and dog collar, standing in the snow in a forest.

Dad stood there for a while, not saying a word, and then turned and walked out back into the sun and heat of the day. I waited for a moment and then looked more closely at the photo. Yes, there was my father—definitely my father—smiling out from the photo on the wall.

Mum and Alison were waiting in the car. 'Dad's gone to look around the place on his own.' I watched him as he strolled off down the main street, the Via dei Martiri di Civitella, hands behind his back, looking at all the buildings and up at the windows and roofs in turn.

Alison felt unable to speak to him or ask him anything about the place. She remembered:

> Where are the people? Why are there holes all over the walls? I could just sense that this wasn't the time to ask Dad—the person who always explained everything to me. He just walked silently ahead, looking sad in a way I had never seen before and deep in thought. I'm not sure that he wanted to be back there, reliving the horrors of what he had seen during the war.

Half an hour later, we drove off without a word, and the significance of that day did not come to light until nearly fifty years later, when I saw the photo again in 1997, in the same side chapel in the church in Civitella.

As I started to go abroad with my own family, France and Italy were always favourite destinations. I liked following in my father's footsteps, guided by his photos. I visited places such as Rome, Venice, Florence, Siena, and Trieste, where I always kept an eye open for buildings or features that appeared in his pictures. Did he stand exactly here? Was he looking over at that view?

During one holiday in Italy, my wife, daughter, and I stayed at the Abbey of Sant'Anna in Camprena, near Pienza, a former Benedictine Monastery that had opened for tourists near Siena. While I was there, I met the Abbess and told her the story of my father in Italy, and I told her that I wanted to contact the priest in Civitella. She promised to find out and write to me. A few months later, I received a letter of introduction to Don Tommaso Tonioni, the parish priest of Civitella. I wrote to him, telling him about my father and enclosing copies of photographs from my father's album relating to his time in Arezzo area and the photos he took of the ruins of Civitella.

When I eventually visited Civitella in 1997, the whole village knew about me. It was a surprise and a shock to discover that all these people—some of whom had been children at the time—remembered Capt. Morgan and Father O'Shea. That was the beginning of my friendship with the people of Civitella, particularly with Dino Tiezzi, his wife, Gloria, and their family, and Lara Lammioni. Fortunately for me, Dino spoke French and Lara spoke good English, and I learned more about the massacre from them both and the terrible things that had happened to their families.

Sadly, my marriage did not last, ending in 2000. I continued to struggle with life, trying to get things into perspective; I found my visits to Civitella and the friendships there invaluable. My mother was a rock, too, at this time, and she was always excited to hear about Dad's 'special village'. She had done so much work over the years to trace the men who had been with John, to find records of their time in Civitella. She wrote to all the military authorities, regimental associations, and the British Legion, but it came to nothing. She was thrilled to become part of this Italian family, which recognised and celebrated her husband's efforts in 1944 in the road-naming in 2001. Civitella became my second home.

In 2003, my mother and the rest of the family (including Alison and her daughter, Jennifer) were invited to Civitella to receive a commemorative medallion. Jennifer was thrilled to see her grandmother being honoured by the people of this beautiful Italian village. I was later invited to stay with Lara Lammioni's family at Malfiano, where they ran a business with the vineyard and holiday lets. I became very good friends with Lara's son, Giuseppe Lucarelli, who had started working on a website dedicated to his mother, archiving all the family photos and Lara's memoir. After the massacre, Lara had sworn never to return to Civitella; the memories of what happened to her and her family were too painful.

About nine months before Lara died in May 2012, Ida Balò Valli, a survivor of the massacre, invited Lara to meet her and other women in the village. Lara did not want to go back to the place where her family had suffered so much: 'The long shadow of those horrors has often darkened my happiness and conditioned the whole of my existence.' However, she told me that perhaps it was time to make peace with the past.

She asked me to accompany her as she was nervous and apprehensive at the thought of setting foot in the place again, even after nearly seventy years. I drove her to Civitella, and when we got there, I took her hand and we walked together into the village through Porta Senese, the entrance that she had not passed through since fleeing the village in June 1944. All the women were gathered under the portico to welcome and embrace her, and they celebrated their reunion with sparkling wine and cake. Lara was finally able to walk the streets where she had played so happily as a child.

I believe that meeting the son of Capt. Morgan began a process of healing for the village. That it gave the survivors and their families a new focus, something beyond themselves and their dark past—it was a reminder of the good British men who came to their aid in their hour of need. They had suffered decades of division within their own community, in their memories of the massacre, understanding and explaining what had led to the events of 29 June 1944. Who had supported the Partisans? Were they to blame for the massacre—knowing about the threatened reprisals by the German command for any killing of Germans by Italian civilians? What had happened to the Germans who gave the orders and to those who took part? The authorities had been blind and silent for so long, and government help had been slow to come. Reconciliation and forgiveness are hard to achieve when no justice has been meted out to those who were eventually proved guilty.

I have benefited from this journey of discovery in many ways. I love, admire, and understand my father better. I am glad that Father O'Shea has received recognition for the work he did, and how they both touched the lives of so many people, particularly the children.

I feel very humble in the company of those who survived, those who rebuilt their lives and had families of their own. I try to keep my father's story alive in the hope that people will learn from it in order that such things do not happen again. All that is needed for the forces of evil to succeed is for good men to do nothing.

18

Forgiveness

Feast of St Peter and St Paul
Sunday 29 June 2014
Civitella

Pope Francis embraced Monsignor Luciano Giovannetti, retired Bishop of Fiesole, at the end of their audience in Rome. He was deeply moved by the eighty-year-old's account of what he had witnessed as a ten-year-old during the massacre of Civitella. He was touched by what Giovannetti told him about his reason for becoming a priest.

Monsignor Giovannetti returned to Civitella for the seventieth-anniversary commemorative weekend to take part in a service of remembrance at the Church of Santa Maria Assunta on 29 June, the day of the massacre. He brought the Pope's message with him, reading it out from the pulpit, watched by the parish priest Don Tommaso Tonioni and the Bishop of the Diocese of Arezzo, Cortona, and Sansepolcro, Riccardo Fontana, who was also invited to officiate at the service.

The church was full of families, visitors, and local dignitaries packed into the pews and standing in the side aisles on this special occasion to remember the martyrs of Civitella and to give thanks for peace and reconciliation. It was a surprise and a wonder to the congregation that the story of Civitella had reached Rome and that Pope Francis was thinking of them. 'Remember the suffering of little children,' he told them.

Like the other children who survived the massacre, Giovannetti has lived under the shadow of those events. His calling to holy orders must have provided a purpose and direction when the world around him appeared bleak and uncertain. It was better to follow a path that leads out of the darkness and into the light. Grief and suffering had become a part of him, surely giving him the capacity to understand and empathise with those in need of care and comfort. The memories of what he saw and heard that June day were forever imprinted on his mind and soul:

I can never forget the screams of 'Kill me, kill me!' from those expecting to die at the hands of the Germans. They preferred a quick death rather than being burned alive in the houses that the soldiers had set on fire. My family and I could hear the massacre from our hiding place in the dense woods below the village walls. The Germans were killing the men in groups of five on top of the walls. At one point, they began to strafe the wood with machine guns to kill those who might have found refuge there. We were not hit but we could hear the bullets whistling close to us.

Even in those circumstances we did not lose our sense of humour and were thinking, 'How will they be able to find us if we die here?' We were convinced that it was only a matter of time before we would be killed too. Two hours we hid in the woods and then we made our way back into the village not knowing what we would find.

The first people we met were a mother with four children still in their nightshirts and pyjamas, all covered in blood because the Germans had killed their father and her husband in front of them in their home. This was the first scene that I witnessed. Yes, the widows and the children. We did not know that the Germans had been ordered to spare the women and children. My mother and I believed that everybody would be killed.

Monsignor Giovannetti is an imposing figure, a tall and dignified man in his simple black clerical dress, white collar, and crucifix. He looks earnest and slightly severe, but his face breaks easily into a smile whether meeting friends or talking to strangers, stooping slightly to listen to what they have to say. He has recounted memories like these before, but this year he was reminded more forcefully of events seventy years ago, faced with the media interest that this particular anniversary brought and the message from Rome that he carried.

There was a deep sadness just below the surface as he talked about what happened to him and his family when he was small boy, mindful that his suffering was nothing compared to that of others:

My father Oscare was a carpenter and he was one of the few men who survived the massacre. He stayed home while we went to early Mass with mother at 7 a.m. We were planning to go with him to the 11 a.m. Mass as well because it was a special occasion. As soon as my mother Nunziatina realised what was happening with the Germans, she ran home to warn my father, then she came back and took us to the woods. He rushed out of the house and went towards a house next to the village walls that had a small vegetable garden and a large rabbit hutch. My father hid inside the hutch and was not found by the Germans. This is how he survived. Only around ten of the men who were inside the village walls survived. Later, sometimes months later, others came back, some of them had been prisoners of war.

Where was God on that day in June? Why did this particular boy not lose his faith? Why did he embrace hope rather than succumb to despair? There were a number of reasons, but the principal one was his admiration for and loyalty to Don Alcide Lazzeri.

The young of Civtella were well-looked-after by the priest. Lina Rossi, Don Alcide's niece, who lived with him, was proud of her uncle and his achievements:

The presbytery was always full of youngsters, of seminarists and young students and the archpriest had advice, help and sometimes reproach for all. Under his direction, the choir and the youth theatre, enriched the feast days and encouraged the growth of a wonderful group of young people who discovered the values of life under the protection of the church.

Giovannetti was one of the *chierichetti* (altar boys), who spent a good deal of time around the church, which was the centre of the religious and social life of the community. There was plenty to do to help the priest and nuns in the running of the church, particularly helping at services.

They loved the ritual of the mass and the colour and splendour of the vestments. Don Alcide's niece, Lina Rossi, remembered that 'Lucianino' loved dressing up in the eccentric vestments that she cut out for him from newspapers and pinned together for him to wear. The boys felt important if they were chosen to carry the cross or processional candle into church. They loved swinging the censer and watching the incense released, the scented puff of mist wafting across the congregation. Present at weddings, christenings, and funerals, they were privileged to be part of the cycle of life from birth to death. They saw their friends and neighbours coming through the church doors at the happiest and the saddest times of their lives. Don Alcide was always there to guide and encourage the boys in his pastoral and clerical work.

Whatever path a boy followed in later life, something of that feeling of being special, of being chosen to represent the church, stayed with him. He learned early the principles of discipline and self-control serving at the altar; he learned to watch and copy and to concentrate on every little detail so that he did not put a foot wrong, ringing the bell at the right time for the Elevation of the Host, holding the prayer book for Don Alcide, watching the priest's face for little signals to make sure it was the right height and angle for him to read the print. He wanted to please him; he wanted to be like him. Don Alcide was not just the parish priest and teacher, but every boy's friend. Giovannetti recalls:

I remember one day he was talking to us after mass. Perhaps a month before the massacre. 'What will happen after I am gone?' Don Alcide said. 'I wish that one of you would take my place after my death.' I did not pay much attention to these words at the time but something must have happened: a seed lodged somewhere deep inside my mind.

On the morning of 29 June, I was one of the altar boys at the Feast Day Mass and was standing next to Don Alcide as the armed Germans entered the church. They marched down the aisle waving their guns, about to round up the men. Don Alcide stepped forward to meet them half way, opening his arms wide and announcing, 'I am the one who is responsible. Take me and spare the others!' He was not spared. He was the first man to be executed in the square outside.

His words really entered my heart and I thought, 'Perhaps I am one of those who is meant to take his place.' This idea remained with me and matured during my adolescent years until I felt the overwhelming compulsion to enter the priesthood and to take his place.

I told Pope Francis that it was because of Don Alcide I had entered the Church. Don Alcide was awarded the Medal for Civil Valour for offering his life in exchange for members of his flock. What better example to have. Greater love than this no man hath, that a man lay down his life for his friends.

Don Alcide Lazzeri was loved and respected by the community. He was a symbol of certainty, a fixed point for everyone. He felt driven to fight injustice and defend the values that drew man closer to God. He was a man of great faith and intelligence, with a wide experience of the world, having served as a chaplain in the 1911–1912 Italo-Turkish War and the First World War, when he was decorated. He was also deeply cultured, with a passion for literature, and he wrote poetry, publishing volumes under the name of 'Alchi Delio'—one in 1919 called *Inter Alia*, and another in 1926 dedicated to Saint Francis of Assisi, in remembrance of his own first vocation as a Franciscan monk.

Don Alcide's life and his sacrifice are remembered today in the name of the central piazza and in the *Sala della Memoria* (the memory room). A large painted banner depicting the priest hangs on one wall. It is a blaze of gold and orange around the central figure of Don Alcide dressed in the red vestments he wore on the Feast Day of Saint Peter and Paul. He holds a communion wafer, offering it up to the viewer and the shadowy congregation gathered at his feet. A baby is blessed with holy water next to an open book showing lines from Saint Francis, the patron saint of children. In the top right-hand corner, the outline of Civitella is in flames; in the opposite corner, Christ looks down on the scene in a crown of thorns.

Young Giovannetti was also fortunate enough to meet another priest and guiding hand, another friend turn to—and a British one this time. He was a man who wore an Army uniform instead of a cassock and who offered the hand of friendship to the frightened, lonely children without shelter, food, or comfort. It was the kindness of this stranger that Giovannetti remembered most:

When we returned to Civitella on 16 July on our liberation, the British troops arrived and gave us a huge amount of help. They brought food and also company. We had so few men of our own now as they had been killed or had left and not come back. Among those who came to us was Father O'Shea, who was also a Passionist, the same order as the Sisters who taught us and tended to the sick and infirm of our village. He didn't wear an embroidered gold heart on his left breast, as our Sisters did on their habits, just a white collar and three pips on the shoulders of his Army jacket. There was something special about him. I got to know him well and his friend Captain Morgan, who always had a pipe in his mouth. They used to come up in their car, sometimes on their own, sometimes followed by a lorry or two carrying food, water and hard army biscuit.

The children would rush over to Father Clement to see if he had anything for them. He would pat each on the head as he counted, '*Uno, due, tre, quattro,*' and say, 'Sweets?' They all nodded eagerly and as if by magic he made sweets appear from behind their ears or out of thin air. They would chase him around shouting 'More, more,' until there were no more sweets.

He made us laugh and we were able to forget our sorrows. I wrote to him once in Latin much later, but, sadly, I didn't get a reply.

It is strange to think how far Giovannetti has journeyed from the 'little mouse' with cardboard ears and string whiskers, standing on a makeshift stage in the church hall under the direction of Father Clement. The Sisters would rush around, making sure the children were dressed and ready to perform their Christmas show to the British soldiers who had saved them.

The blue Lancia official car made its way from Perugia airport along the autostrada, cutting through the Umbrian countryside, past Lake Trasimeno and into Tuscany, towards Arezzo. Perhaps Frank-Walter Steinmeier, German Minister for Foreign Affairs, pondered on his journey, as the roads got smaller and more winding, and the approach to Civitella steeper, that this was the same route his fellow countrymen had taken on that fateful day seventy years before, driving their armoured vehicles and trucks full of armed soldiers—the harbingers of death.

Had he been briefed sufficiently, or had he researched its history fully, he would know that when he stepped out of his car in Via San Francesco and into the main square, Piazza Don Alcide Lazzeri, he would be standing on exactly the same spot that members of the 1st *Fallschirm Panzer Division Hermann Goering* set up their machine guns and executed the men as they came out of mass on 29 June 1944. He would walk across the Piazza, which had resonated with German voices shouting, '*Raus, raus!*' and '*Feuer!*' followed by the sound of machine gunfire, the flagstones underfoot turning red with the blood of the dead and dying. Steinmeier's day was not going to be easy, even for the most practised and polished politician. He would be meeting the survivors and visiting the museum, with its relics from the massacre. The German Foreign Minister carried a heavy burden of responsibility when representing his country at the seventieth-anniversary commemorations.

It was a blazing hot day—not a day to be buttoned up in a uniform or dressed in a dark, tailored, woollen suit. There were plenty of uniforms on Sunday afternoon — *carabinieri* and *polizia municipale*, and military personnel on duty in and around the centre of the village. Every boot, buckle, belt, and badge was polished, each catching the rays of the sun at the slightest movement. There were plenty of men in dark suits and dark glasses, security men protecting the ministers, mayors, and ambassadors who were about to descend on the village. Residents and guests staying for the weekend were dressed in their Sunday best; tourists were in their shorts and sandals, those who had managed to sneak in early, before the lockdown.

Only authorised personnel and vehicles were allowed access to Civitella. Some residents had been prevented from bringing their cars up into the centre of village and had been instructed to leave them on grass areas down below. Signs attached to lampposts threatened the towing away of unauthorised vehicles, and cones had been placed across driveways and parking bays the night before for use by officials and emergency services. Not everyone welcomed the invasion of all these bigwigs, disrupting their peace and quiet and freedom to move around, but it did have some advantages.

The village looked immaculate. Many house-proud residents were happy to make sure their streets and homes looked their best. Doorknobs were polished, drainpipes were painted, flowers were deadheaded, wonky guttering was straightened, and broken streetlights were repaired. Only a few hours before the first VIP cars arrived, council men were still painting white no-parking lines on the roads and disabled-parking lines by the home for the elderly in Piazza Becattini—not that anyone would take notice of any of the markings.

The Commune of Civitella had invited a number of high-profile guests from Italy, Germany, and Great Britain to the commemorative weekend. An official press release stated:

> The joint presence of the foreign ministers of Italy and Germany is a highly symbolic gesture aimed at honouring and passing down the memory of the victims of Nazi cruelty. It falls within the context of a common commitment to the construction of a shared memory of the Italo-German war past.

In addition to the German Minister for Foreign Affairs, the Mayor of Civitella, Ginetta Menchetti, would be welcoming the Italian Minister for Foreign Affairs, Federica Mogherini, the Italian Defence Under Secretary, Domenico Rossi (who was born in Civitella), and Marco de Paolis, Military Prosecutor for Rome.

Other guests included German Ambassador to Rome, Reinhard Schäfers, British Ambassador to Rome, Christopher Prentice, and Keith Morgan, the son of Capt. John Morgan. Although Prentice had prepared a speech about the liberation of Civitella by the Allies, mentioning the work of Capt. Morgan and Father O'Shea, who brought aid to the village, he was not asked to speak. Keith Morgan, however, was given the opportunity to speak at the conclusion of the earlier celebratory mass. He took over the pulpit from Don Tommaso, who introduced their guest from England. In carefully enunciated Italian, Keith thanked the vilage for honouring his father and Father O'Shea in the naming of *Costa Capitano John Percival Morgan*:

> If my father had lived to be with us today, he would be immensely proud and pleased to see what you, the people of Civitella, have achieved since 1944. The beautiful and peaceful place that it is now.

Keith joined the British Ambassador and other guests and members of the public later that afternoon in Via di Martiri to hear the official speeches and tributes. No one knew what was going to be said, least of all what the German minister had prepared.

Franck-Walter Steinmeier looked up from his papers, which were resting on the lectern set up on the platform in front of the *cisterna* in the square. Brightly coloured *gonfaloni* (town banners) from around the region of Arezzo, ribbons and tails fluttering in the breeze, formed a backcloth to the stage. He looked across the sea of people, hundreds stretching the length of the main street; official guests were seated at the front, with members of the public standing behind barriers as far as the war memorial in Piazza Becattini. Every face lifted and every eye focused on the German Minister; they waited for him to speak.

His face stern and controlled, Steinmeier took a deep breath and began speaking in Italian. They were probably the most difficult words he had ever had to say:

They were celebrating the feast of the Apostle Peter, the one to whom Jesus said, 'Thou art Peter; and upon this rock I will build my church, and the gates of Hell shall not prevail against it.' Instead, on 29 June, the very gates of Hell prevailed.

Even though I was born in 1956, eleven years after the war and the end of Nazism, and have only known another Germany, I do not want to avoid the bitter chalice of that guilt. I cannot even conceive how the Germans, my countrymen, could have carried out such acts. I am moved and I am ashamed.

Steinmeier paused to gather his thoughts before continuing. He looked across at the front rows, where some of the last few survivors of the massacre and the descendants of the victims were seated. Addressing them directly, he continued:

We face our history by learning lessons from it. I bow before those who died and those who survived. Only we know the responsibility we carry with us. I ask forgiveness for the unforgivable. That the gates of Hell will never again be allowed to prevail.

It is important now, to stand together and issue a signal for future generations. At the same time, together we are showing that we are building a common future without wars in this united Europe. We want to ensure that this united Europe does not relapse into economic and political crisis.

As he left the platform to respectful applause, Federica Mogherini, his Italian counterpart, came forward to embrace Steinmeier on her way to the platform to bring the proceedings to a close.

With the official ceremony over, guests moved slowly off towards the *Sala della Memoria*, shaking hands with some remaining survivors, including Monsignor Giovannetti, Enza Marsili, and Ida Balò Valli, custodian of Civitella Remembers and curator of the museum. She has devoted her life to reconstructing and recording the events and keeping the flame of remembrance alight, but above all to understanding the reasons for the massacre. As she guided the German Minister around the recently refurbished rooms, she stopped at the display cabinets to explain the contents.

She struggled to speak at times, pointing to the blood-stained dress Alba Bonichi was wearing when she cradled her dying her father in her arms, the charred remains of identity cards and prayer cards taken from bodies, and a wallet riddled with bullets. Memories of her own family tragedy came to the surface, no doubt, as she spoke—the thoughts of the thirteen-year-old girl, never far away:

> All that happened then is still clear in my mind: the terrified faces of the people, the moaning, the trembling voice of Don Alcide, the soulless eyes of the Germans, their orders, the scared eyes of my Uncle Beppe, my mother's brother, who stared at us until he was pushed far away from us. Torquato shaking and hiding under the altar of the Madonna, the first dead, the houses ablaze, my friend Alba with a bloody breast, Mrs Paggi screaming with a nightshirt covered in blood, the mad rush towards Porta Senese, that lone man in the middle of so many running women and then the dead in a line at the side of the road.

Steinmeier was clearly moved by his tour of the memorial room and said:

> These reminders of the tragedy leave you speechless even now seventy years on. The lesson I take away from this visit is that we have to make every effort to keep alive the memories of what happened and to build up a future in peace.

Civitella today is a beautiful, tranquil place unspoilt by development. The casual visitor, not knowing its history, would enjoy a stroll through the picturesque streets, looking at the ancient buildings, the medieval walls and tower, and floral displays colouring every house and square in spring and summer. The beautiful glazed earthenware *Madonna with Child* by Della Robbia, dated 1522, stands in its glass-fronted tabernacle at the entrance to Porta Senese, demanding attention and reverence, contrasting with the many modern sculptures in stone, concrete, and bronze around the village. Visitors would take in the views from rooftop terraces or castle walls, the sweep of land and swathe of forests towards the magnificent bluish-grey of the Apennines, girdling the vast valley beneath, a patchwork of olive groves, vineyards, and farms, ever-changing with the weather and the light.

Civitella is a place that is no longer defined solely by the events of the Second World War. It has opened its arms and heart to the world beyond its medieval walls, beyond its dark past. It is free now to celebrate its renewal and regeneration through the powers of reconciliation and forgiveness. It has embraced a new cultural life with art, music, and dance from around the country, putting on community activities that bring all ages together. It continues its tradition of festivals and celebrations, encouraging local youngsters to take part and build friendships across the country and across the world.

The *Stanza della Memoria*, refurbished and renamed, opens every day; the place is lovingly dusted and polished, and memorabilia and artefacts are meticulously displayed and cared for by volunteers. A video film of the village's history runs on a loop in the background, the commentary keeping visitors company. Refurbished rooms at the rear are open, now used for art exhibitions and meetings; seventy years earlier, the Partisans had burst in, killing two off-duty German soldiers immediately and mortally wounding a third.

There are no bloodstains on floor or bullet holes on the walls now. There are no ghosts, no dark corners to fear, and no chilly feeling on entering. It is a place of commemoration and celebration, of lives lived and lost, of courage in the face of adversity, and rebirth and regeneration. Opposite the blazing banner of Don Alcide Lazzeri, the smiling face of Capt. John Percival Morgan, ubiquitous pipe in hand, looks out from the pages of the *Merthyr Express*, enlarged and displayed on the wall—a copy of an article from March 2001, given to the museum by Keith Morgan. The headline reads: 'War-torn village remembers a soldier from Merthyr'. The caption under Morgan's picture is: 'Face of Compassion'. If Keith Morgan had not visited Civitella in 1997 in search of his father's wartime activities, this part of Civitella's history would have gone unrecorded and forgotten. The memory of those humane acts by members of the Allied forces who liberated and supported the population would have been lost forever. A son found his father, and a village found its hero.

The visitor's book tells a story all on its own; there are pages recording those who have come from around the world to pay their respects or have discovered Civitella's past for the first time. One short message stands out that best sums up what the people of Civitella have striven for over the last seventy years, and of which Captain John Percival Morgan and Father Clement O'Shea would be proud. It was written by German visitors Jeffe Mangold and Stephanie Spitznepel on 17 July 2005, and it reads:

Forse perdonare, ma non dimenticare mai.

Maybe forgive, but never forget.[1]

'Ricordo' ('I Remember')

A sail of stone
in the green waves of the hills.

Old bell tower,
which watched over us with the great white eye
of the clock
fascinating us with the sombre chimes
of the hours that passed;
with the metal embroidery of the long hands
chasing the precious Roman numerals,
while clouds played between the blue
arches of the bells.

Old bell tower,
when I was a boy in short trousers
you always amazed me as I watched
the complex workings of wooden cogs
moved by expert hands, pulling the heavy stone weights,
drawing in those adventurous enough
to climb to the top of the highest tower
that first so aroused fear in my soul;
when evening came to sound the bells for evening prayer
and no one had the heart to climb the wooden stairs
lost in the darkness of night.

Old bell tower,
whose broken stones became monuments to the fallen
among the graves of Civitella
overwhelmed by the tragedy of us all;
I waited often and in vain in the late evening
for the long slow whistle of your weathervane,
like a lament for a time that will never return.

Dino Tiezzi[1]

EPILOGUE

Justice

A single sunbeam is enough to drive away many shadows

Saint Francis of Assisi

In February 1947, Field Marshal Albert Kesselring, former Commander in Chief of the German Army in Italy, was tried by a British military court in Venice and found guilty of two charges. The first was 'being concerned in the killing as a reprisal of some 335 Italian nationals in the Ardeatine Caves on 24 March 1944', and the second was 'inciting and commanding ... forces ... under his command to kill Italian civilians as reprisals in consequence of which a number of Italian civilians were killed'.

Part of the evidence against Kesselring was that he issued orders to Gen. Von Mackensen, Commander of the 14th Army, to 'Kill 10 Italians for every German. Carry out immediately'. Von Mackensen had been tried separately in October 1946 on the Ardeatine Massacre charge, along with another general, Kurt Mälzer. He was found guilty and sentenced to death in November. Kesselring was also accused of issuing orders on 'new regulations for partisan warfare', which included the following directive: 'The fight against the partisans must be carried out with all means at our disposal and with the utmost severity.'[1]

As part of the prosecution's case for the second charge, one of the prosecutors at the trial, Sir David Maxwell-Fyfe, presented evidence about the massacre at Civitella, asking Kesselring if he remembered what had been done by his forces in Civitella.

Kesselring replied, 'At the moment, no.' Maxwell-Fyfe went on to read the United Nations War Crimes Commission statement on the incident.

'Now, Witness,' asked Maxwell-Fyfe, 'do you really think that military necessity commands the killing of babies of one and people of eighty-four?'

'No,' replied Kesselring.[2]

On 6 May 1947, Kesselring was found guilty and sentenced to death by firing squad. On 4 July 1947, Kesselring and the two other generals, Von Mackensen and Mälzer, had their death sentences commuted to life in prison. On 24 October 1952, as an act of clemency, Kesselring and Von Mackensen, the other remaining general still alive, were released.

Kesselring was returned to Germany in British custody. He worked for the US Army Historical Division and became active in veterans' organisations. He retired to Munich, where he died in July 1960 aged seventy-four.[3]

What happened to those who were identified as responsible for the massacres in Civitella, San Pancrazio, and Cornia from the evidence gathered by the Special Investigation Branch (SIB) during the period of November 1944–March 1945? Did criminal proceedings follow? Did the survivors and their families receive justice?

What we know is that the British handed over the original documentation about the massacres collected by the SIB to the Italian authorities. The files that are stored in the National Archives at Kew are copies. What actually happened to the hundreds of original statements of evidence is not clear. Whether they were just put away somewhere and then overlooked or deliberately buried, they were, to all intents and purposes, lost to the world. Perhaps there was no appetite for lengthy trials after the major trials at Nuremburg from 1945–1949; perhaps building bridges and rehabilitation were more important than pursuing the perpetrators.

Dr Paolo Pezzino is Professor of Contemporary History at the University of Pisa, and he has written about the atrocities in Italy during the war. In an interview for CNN in 2011, he commented:

> There was a growing reluctance to embarrass Germany. International justice took a back seat to realpolitik. The Communists were now the enemy. It was no longer the case to look back at the past but to face the future.[4]

However, fifty years after the massacres, a remarkable thing happened. In June 1994, a forgotten archive of military records was discovered in a basement room at Palazzo Cesi, in Rome, the offices of the Chief Appeal Court Military Prosecutor. Inside the unused room was a locked cupboard full of the evidence of hundreds of wartime atrocities documented by the Allied and Italian investigators. It came to be known as '*l'armadio della vergogna*'—'the cupboard of shame'. When the cupboard was opened, it revealed nearly 700 files consisting of witness statements detailing the massacres carried out in villages and towns in Italy, including Civitella, during the last two years of the Second World War.

The discovery of the files caused public outcry and demands again for justice, however delayed. In 1998, through a Memorandum of Understanding signed by the Mayors of Civitella, Bucine, Cavriglia, and Stia, historian Carlo Gentile was commissioned to undertake research in Germany to help build a case. As a result of his years of work, he was able to formulate a specific request for criminal proceedings that went forward to a lawyer in Rome.[5] With the arrival of Military Prosecutor Dr Marco De Paolis to the Military Prosecutor's office in La Spezia, work began on bringing prosecutions to court.

'I felt I had a moral obligation to provide answers,' Di Paolis said, 'to bring a sense of justice to hundreds of people who had been waiting over fifty years.' Thanks to the determination of De Paolis to get to the truth, and his dedication in gathering all the evidence together, the Italian state succeeded in bringing some of those responsible to court.

In October 2006, the Military Tribunal of La Spezia returned guilty verdicts for the charge of 'aggravated and sustained murder against civilian enemies' against Max Josef Milde, former Sergeant in the Band of the 1st Parachute Division *Hermann Goering*. He was tried *in absentia*. Siegfried Boettcher, commander in the same paratrooper regiment, Armoured Division *Hermann Goering*, was also found guilty; he died before being sentenced. Eighty-two-year-old Milde was sentenced to life in prison. He has always maintained his innocence, and he continues to live in freedom in Germany. The German government has refused to extradite Milde to Italy to serve his sentence.

The court also upheld claims against Germany for compensation, filed by the relatives of the victims, to pay €1 million to the relatives of nine of the victims. In spite of continued requests, the German government has not paid any compensation.

On 28 June 2014, Marco De Paolis, Military Prosecutor of Rome, was invited to a special ceremony at the Council House of Badia al Pino, seat of the Commune of Civitella. Before an audience of councillors, visitors, and guests—including some of the remaining survivors of the massacre and their families—Mayor Ginetta Menchetti awarded De Paolis honorary citizenship of the town as a gesture of gratitude to him for the many years of hard work he had undertaken in prosecuting the perpetrators of the war crimes.

Endnotes

Chapter 1

1. From Dr Keith Strange's article 'The Celestial City: Merthyr Tydfil in the 1840s', www.alangeorge.co.uk/china.htm.
2. England (ed.), *Cyfarthfa School, The First 100 years 1913–2013* (2013).

Chapter 3

1. Event reported in *The Catholic Herald*, 4 August 1939.
2. One of 'The Beads of the Five wounds of Our Lord Jesus Christ', *Companion to The Missions, conducted by the Passionist Fathers* (1937).
3. 'The Army was in his blood. And his father and two brothers could, each of them, say with Othello: "I have done the State some service."' From Father Clement O'Shea's Obituary, 1965, Douai Abbey Library and Archive.
4. Also known as the Congregation of the Discalced (from the Latin for 'without shoes'), Clerks of the Most Holy Cross and Passion of Our Lord Jesus Christ, they followed the teachings of their founder, St Paul of the Cross, who believed that the troubles of the world were a result of forgetting the Passion of Jesus and his suffering on the cross.
5. O'Shea was ordained on 23 December 1922 at Mount Argus, Dublin, by His Grace, the Archbishop of Dublin, Most Rev. Dr Byrne, in the chapel of Holy Cross College, Clonliffe.
6. 'Thou Art a Priest Forever' by Jean-Baptiste Henri Lacordaire OP (*A Catholic Prayer Book*).
7. O'Shea had no worldly goods to leave, having taken vows of poverty, chastity, and obedience. He had already written his last will and testament on 22 August, his Superior at his previous address—St Joseph's, Highgate—acting as executor. It appears that he was already an Army chaplain, probably a reservist.
8. Oliver, *The Chaplain at War* (1986), p. 19.

Chapter 4

1. Details from *Safer than a Known Way* (1983), p. 14, and List of Officers, WO 177/640.
2. O'Shea composed and drew the menu, listing everyone present: Theo Pathe; Bill Underwood; 'Spratt' Yule [Maj. A. P. Yule]; 'Cockie' O'Shea; Claude Herbert 'Erbi'

[Lt L. Herbert]; Sam Heddle; Father Gording; Geo. Stewart; Philip Pank CO [Maj R. E. D. Pank]; 'Pip' Newman [Maj. P. H. Newman]; R. S. M. Longridge [Maj.]; Geo Cram; E. Stone Wigg [E. V. Stone-Wigg, Army Dental Corps]; Lise More [Rev. Capt. F. J. H. 'Lissy' Lisemore]; Tim McCoy [Major D. P. McCoy]; Topper Brown [Lt.-QM T. A. Brown]; and M. N. Wright [Head Waiter]. Full names based on Field of Officers return, 12 CCS War Diary.

3. 'Supper in celebration of Erbi and Tim's daughters' birthdays (Joyce and Michele) Guests: Capt Lambley Ellis, Lieut Jackson, Major Gilchrist, QM 11th CCS, Lieut Murdock. All from AA Battery formerly of the Argyles.' Newman's diary, 29 April 1940.
4. Jackson, *The Fall of France: The Nazi Invasion of 1940* (2004), p. 9.
5. *Op. cit.* Newman, *Safer than a Known Way* (1983), p. 25.
6. 9.05.40, WO 167/420.
7. *The Story of the RASC 1939–1945*, (G. Bell & Sons, 1955), p. 79.
8. 3.06.40, WO 167/420
9. The War Diary records problems with vehicle maintenance—'tendency to be slack on oiling and greasing'. 1.06.40, WO 167/420
10. Twelve days earlier, as part of Operation Dynamo, *Lady of Mann* (owned by the Isle of Man Steam Packet Co. Ltd) helped to evacuate 1,500 casualties from Dunkirk on 1 June and on 4 June, embarking 1,244 troops in an hour from the East Pier. Keith Sutton, Paddle Steamer Picture Gallery.
11. WO 167/420.
12. CAB/65/7/66.

Chapter 5

1. F. D. Goode, an inexperienced twenty-three-year-old adjutant, was transferred in 1940 to the War Office General Staff and suddenly found himself responsible for the nebulous 'General Staff Coordination', a new post with no coherent job description. *Royal United Services Institute for Defence and Security Studies Journal*, March 2008.
2. *The Story of the RASC, 1939-45* (1955), p. 438.
3. 'These motor coach companies played a valuable part while our Army was in its defensive role.' *Ibid.*, p. 419.
4. In his father's effects, Keith Morgan found a cloth badge that depicts the three-barred Irish gate in green on a black background. This belonged to units designated British Troops Ireland (BTI), among which was John Morgan's No. 2 Motor Coach Company RASC and 6 Corps Ammunition Park RASC, raised after Dunkirk but disbanded in early 1941. Its HQ was in Lisburn, Northern Ireland.
5. 'Never before ... was a "service" of troop-carrying companies, 32 in number, formed, equipped and operative in a fortnight.' *The Story of the RASC, 1939-45* (1955), p. 419.
6. *Ibid.* p. 126.
7. From 1939 onwards, NAAFI employees rose from 8,000 to a peak of 110,000 and trading establishments from 1,350 to nearly 10,000, including 800 canteens on seagoing ships and 900 mobile canteens to support the war effort. Sales of tea rocketed to 3.5 million cups per day and cigarettes to 24 million per day. In addition, over 4,000 artists were employed to entertain troops on active service.
8. British Second General Hospital Ward, 11.03.42, *Desert Rat Sketch Book* (1959), p. 58.
9. On another occasion: 'General Montgomery's A.D.C. [Aide de Camp] visited the unit and brought some papers, cigarettes etc. for the patients'. 28.10.43, WO1077/628.
10. O'Shea's albums of photographs at Douai Abbey Library and Archive are an extraordinary record of his time in North Africa and Italy and deserve further study and a book all of their own. Along with the North Africa album is a typed

record with detailed descriptions and erudite commentary on the places of religious significance he visited. These were no doubt shown to community brothers, fellow priests on retreats he ran, and to the young people he taught in his parish.

11. WO1077/628.
12. Probably a variation of the well-known 'river-crossing puzzle' using bottle tops, coins, buttons, or whatever was at hand to work out the problem. A farmer returns from market with a wolf, a goat, and a cabbage; he wants to cross the river, but the boat can only carry himself plus either the wolf, the goat, or the cabbage.
13. WO1077/628.
14. 28.10.43, WO1077/628.
15. Driver Jack Cassidy, RASC, from archives at The Second World War Experience Centre (SWWEC).

Chapter 7

1. The Marsili family shop is still in business in what is now called Piazza Giuseppe Mazzini.
2. Banda Renzino was an Italian partisan group. The leader and founder was Edoardo Succhielli, or, to give him his full title, *Comandante della VII banda del IV Gruppo bande, Raggruppamento Patrioti Monte Amiata*. Renzino is the name of a hamlet near Foiano della Chiana (the population of which was mainly anti-Fascist), where, on 17 April 1921, 'Fascists organised punitive action during which the inhabitants who killed three of them had attacked them. The fascists had come back on the same day to avenge their comrades and killed four communists, one of whom was a woman'. Contini, *La Memoria Divisa* (1997), p. 34.
3. On 4 June, Radio Roma was seized by the Allied troops, who found the station in perfect condition. Twenty-four-hour programming resumed immediately.
4. A small community of Passionist Sisters arrived in Civitella in 1928 from the Order residing in the Provincial House in Signa, Florence. It included a mother superior, a cook, a nurse (who had the task of running the pharmacy and the small hospital), a wardrobe mistress, and two teachers (who had the specific task of running the *Asilo Sacro Cuore*, Nursery School of the Sacred Heart, which had been opened by Don Adriano Basagli). Information from Don Francesco Sensini in 2013, and 1994 memories of Sister Maria Pierina Acitelli from Balò, *Giugno 1944 Civitella Racconta*, p. 65.
5. Janet Kinrade Dethick includes a section in *The Arezzo Massacres: A Tuscan Tragedy, April–September 1944* on the fate of Helga Helmqvist Cau and her husband, Giovanni Cau. Helga was eventually accused of spying for the partisans. She and her husband went voluntarily to speak to the commander at Villa Carletti. They were arrested, held prisoner, and later executed, and their bodies were half-buried in an old foundry at Focardi (p. 39).
6. The other German soldier who died later from his wounds was *Gefreiter* Camillo Haag, aged twenty-two years, born in Luxembourg. *La Memoria Riunita*, Gallorini (2013), pp. 78–79. From online archive Civitella—Carlo Gentile (Oct 1998)—*Namentliche Verlustmeldung* (Roll loss report) *Bundesarchivi-Militararchiv*.
7. *Ibid.* Ida Balò Valli (1994), pp. 204–212. In her November 1944 SIB statement, Lina Rossi stated: '[Don Alcide] told them that he had seen several partisans in the village lately and had asked them to leave quickly and so avoid any trouble. The Germans told my uncle that they had orders to kill fifty civilians for each soldier killed by partisans and they would leave when they were ready'.

Chapter 8

1. Witness statements taken at the Special Investigation Branch (SIB) inquiry identified the German soldiers from their uniforms and badges, seeing the words '*Hermann Goering Division*' on grey bands on cuffs, as well as the gorget (the small brass plate on a chain worn around the neck) of the *Feldgendarmerie* (military police). There were also Fascists, men wearing black shirts who spoke Italian. Witnesses saw and heard soldiers playing the instruments. Licia Carletti was held prisoner by the Germans in her home, Villa Oliveto, and later gave a statement in which she described a soldier who left his name and address in a copy of Goethe's *Faust*. It was traced back to the Music Corps of the *Hermann Goering Division*. (*Giugno 1944 Civitella Racconta*, pp. 308–309).
2. A poem attached to an exhibit in the *Sala della Memoria* (remembrance room) of some of the rescued instruments reads: 'suddenly in the square covered in blood, the dusty trombones started to weep'. Dino Tiezzi recalled one woman's account of seeing and hearing the musicians.

Chapter 9

1. On Saturday 1 July, Luigi Lammioni recovered his wife's body and one child, Giuliana. The floor of the loft beside the store of charcoal, where Maria Luisa had been lying, was burnt right through.

Chapter 10

1. Mentioned by Guido Del Buono (*Giugno 1944 Civitella Racconta*, pp. 54–55) as being present on 20 June when Germans came to round up and check the identity of the civilians after the shooting; also by Domenico Mammini (*Giugno 1944 Civitella Racconta*, pp. 68–72), present as interpreter.
2. Nurse Domenica Dondolini was busy with her patients—nine women, five men, and a new-born baby—when she and another worker were ordered out by eight uniformed men. They refused to go and seized and dragged four elderly residents outside and shot them. She later saw a heap of dead bodies, but she found a man alive underneath them. He was treated and then taken by the Red Cross to hospital in Perugia. (*Giugno 1944 Civitella Racconta*, pp. 24–25).
3. The orphanage at Poggiali was run by Sisters who belonged to the Order of the Daughters of Maria Ausiliatrice and their director, Giovacchino Mazzeschi.
4. The SIB is mentioned in the War Diary of Morgan's company: '498 Coy RASC deployment, May—Aug 1944—Special Investigation Br. Requests for the services of SIB personnel in cases of serious crime will be made to the APM 55 Area without delay' (WO 170/2543).
5. In his SIB statement (*Giugno 1944 Civitella Racconta*, pp. 294-3), Dante Salvadori describes having to fetch a ladder for the German soldiers and watching as the hanging took place. Ferdinando Salvadori's wife identified a photo of her husband on 15 August. She went to the cemetery to exhume the body and recognised him by his hair and clothing—the woollen vest that she had knitted for him. He was reinterred.
6. From SIB statements (*Giugno 1944 Civitella Racconta*, pp. 224-6, 251-2, 223-3).

Chapter 11

1. On 4 July, the Allied Fourth Infantry Division crossed the Siena road 'to push forward to abruptly rising ground about Civitella della Chiana and San Pancrazio'—Linklater, *The Campaign in Italy* (1951), p. 311. The same day, 'The Germans massacred the villagers of Meleto, Castelnuovo della Sabbioni, Massa dei Sabbioni and San Martino, all in the commune of Cavriglia'—Nash, *The Price of Innocence* (2005), p. 150. Cavriglia is 35–40 km north-west of Civitella.
2. Lt-Col. P. G. C. Preston wrote in the 4th Recce Regiment War Diary, 16 July: 'The enemy withdrew during the night and patrols from A & B squadrons went forward at first light to Cornia, Civitella & Badia Agnano. Mines, road blocks and craters made the going very slow for wheels'. Another entry read: 'Civitella itself is a shambles.'
3. *Op. cit.* Belco (2010), p. 95.
4. The Battle of Campobasso, 11–14 October 1943: 'As the Allies drove north from Naples and Foggia, the Canadians found themselves pushing into the central mountain range. Now the enemy resisted with full force. On October 1 at Motta, the Canadians fought their first battle with Germans in Italy, and there followed a series of brief, but bloody actions'. The 1st Canadian Infantry Brigade took Campobasso on 14 October. http://www.canadaatwar.ca/content-24/world-war-ii/the-italian-campaign/.
5. WO 170/2543.
6. 'Soap was in constant deficit, with resultant outbreaks of scabies.' Harris, *Allied Military Administration of Italy* 1943–1945 (1957), p. 193.
7. *Op. cit.* Belco, p. 105, p. 434 f. 5.
8. From 'The Dead Village', Sgt N. A. Brown (Eighth Army in Italy), *Poems from Italy* (1945). To see the reality of the damage, there is film footage of the aftermath of the Civitella massacre taken by the Army Film & Photographic Unit when SIB Investigators visited the Arezzo area to record their findings. They filmed the ruined village and meetings they held with partisans, including Edoardo Succhielli (a.k.a. 'Renzino'). John Morgan, with his trademark pipe, identified by family, appears briefly in a couple of posed shots with a group of officers discussing plans. National Archives.

Chapter 13

1. *Op. cit.* Belco, p. 431 f. 77.
2. O'Shea's letter from the Senior Chaplain's Office, Rome, 3 August 1944, Douai Abbey Library and Archive.
3. Dempsey, *The Priest among the Soldiers*, (1947), p. 102. O'Shea held informal meetings of chaplains every Monday in different locations, reviewing their pastoral work over a cup of tea: 'One chaplain told another of some forgotten pocket of his unit which he found near him. Neglected batteries and gun-sites were looked up, new units that appeared from nowhere were discovered and put under somebody's care' (p. 108).
4. *Op. cit.* O'Shea's letter. Army nurse Jessie Park 'JP' Smith (now Aylett) recalls being on leave in Rome after its liberation (4 June 1944): 'The Pope gave a special service in the Vatican for all the Allied personnel in uniform and we all piled into this beautiful room to await the Pope who was carried on a white throne by four hefty men.' 'WW2 People's War', BBC Article ID: A2090792.
5. *Op. cit.* Newman, *Safer than Known Way* (1983), p. 26.

Chapter 14

1. *The Times*, 17 July 1944.
2. *Op. cit.* Belco, p. 120.
3. Area 55 HQ Weekly Report, Midmer to Longridge, 4 September 1944: 'Frozen meat has provided the week's major problem. On 5 days it appears 13 Corps requirements were duplicated in our pack and in Corps. We sent back 40 tons to your store at BASTIA, made over issues on 4 days and sold 32,000 lbs to AMG [Allied Military Government]'.
4. Lewis, *Naples '44: Journey into the Italian Labyrinth* (2002), pp. 122–123.
5. Luigi's daughter, Vittoria Lammioni Lucci, spoke to Keith Morgan when he visited the Lammionis at Malfiano in 2006. Luigi ('Gigi') never recovered from the loss of his wife, Maria Sandrelli, and two daughters, Giuliana and Maria Luigia, and died, aged fifty-two, in 1952.
6. AM-Lire—the Allied military currency was issued in Italy after the invasion of Sicily in July 1943 by the Allied Military Government for Occupied Territories. The last issue of the currency was April 1945, but it continued to circulate until June 1950, when it ceased to be legal tender.
7. Also known as the Battle of Rimini. 'The Allies suffered 40,000 casualties during the Gothic Line offensive'—C. Peter Chan, WW2 database.
8. Alba Bonichi was eighteen years old when her father, Eliseo Bonichi (fifty-two), was shot by Germans in their house. He died in her arms. Her bloodstained dress is on display in the *Sala della Memoria*, Civitella.
9. The two women sang the song in the BBC television programme *Dead Interesting People* (2006) with Michael Aspel. The programme featured the story of Capt. Morgan and Civitella as told by Keith Morgan.
10. Luciano Giovannetti became a priest in Arezzo in 1957 and was appointed Bishop of Fiesole in 1981, retiring in 2012. His grandfather Egisto Giovanentti, a sixty-eight-year-old woodcutter, died in the massacre. See Chapter 18 for Giovannetti's memories of the massacre and his account of why he became a priest.

Chapter 15

1. 'Sir Julian Hodge, 1904–2004. After the war he bought up local garages and sold cars by hire purchase. Becoming a director of numerous other companies, he acquired a reputation in the 1950s as a combative shareholder and boardroom agitator. His own group went public in 1961 but remained an impenetrable financial maze which was understood completely only by Hodge himself. In the mid-1960s it hit problems of financial control, and had to be urgently restructured.' Obituary, *The Daily Telegraph*, 20 July 2004.

Chapter 16

1. Details from the *Herne Bay Press*, 13 April 1951.
2. The only reference found to O'Shea's position in Paris: 'The provincial chapter opened on 5th May, 1959. Fr. Philip (Hayes) succeeded Fr. Patrick as Provincial—subsequently Fr. Martin (Dougherty) was re-appointed Superior of this Retreat and Fr. Jerome (Boyd) became Vicar in place of Fr. Edmund (O'Farrell)—Fr. Clement (O'Shea) and Fr. Richard (Appleyard) continued as members of the Community'. *The Book of Chronicles 1953-72*, St Joseph's Church, Paris.
3. http://www.objectiftech.fr/st_joe_paris/index.php/st-joseph-groups/history.

4. From the History page of the St Joseph's Church website: www.stjoeparis.org. One notable link with the literary world was Oscar Wilde's conversion to Catholicism after he left Reading Gaol and moved to Paris. The day before his death on 30 November 1900, Oscar Wilde was received into the Catholic Church by one of St Joseph's Passionist priests, Father Cuthbert Dunne CP. He was called to Wilde's bedside at Hotel d'Alsace, Rue des Beaux-Arts, where Dunne baptised Wilde before administering the last rites (*The London Magazine* Vol. 1, No. 2, 1961).
5. http://www.objectiftech.fr/st_joe_paris/index.php/st-joseph-groups/history.

Chapter 17

1. Cox & Kings had been Army agents—bankers to the British Army—since 1758. They had been taken over by Lloyds Bank in 1923.

Chapter 18

1. Gallorini, *Forgive, But Never Forget* (2014), p. 97.

'Ricordo' ('I Remember')

1. Poem translated by Alfred and Dee La Vardera.

Epilogue: Justice

1. Law-Reports of *Trials of War Criminals: The United Nations War Crimes Commission*, Volume VIII, London, HMSO, 1949.
3. Transcript of trial online: http://forum.axishistory.com/viewtopic.php?t=74617.
4. Battistelli, *Kesselring* (2012) pp. 60–61.
5. Amella, 'Hidden Archive Exposes WWII Slaughters', CNN.com, 12 August 2011.
6. Mayor Ginetta Menchetti's speech is available at *Archivio della Memoria Civitella in Val di Chiana*, 2014.

Bibliography

Allport, A., *Coming Home after World War Two* (Yale University Press, 2009)

Balò Valli, I., *Giugno 1944 Civitella Racconta* (*Editrice Grafica L'Etruria Cortona*, 1994)

Battistelli, P. P, *Albert Kesselring* (Osprey, 2012)

Belco, V. C., *War, Massacre and Recovery in Central Italy 1943-1948* (University of Toronto Press, 2010)

Brookes, D. R., *Father Dolly, Guardsman Monk (*Henry Melland, 1983)

Carver, M., *The IWM Book of the War in Italy 1943-1945* (Pan Books, 2001)

Carver, T., *Where the Hell Have you Been? Monty, Italy and One Man's Incredible Escape* (London: Short Books, 2009)

Centenary—Parish of Our Lady of the Sacred Heart, Herne Bay, 1889-1989

Contini, G., *La Memoria Divisa* (Rizzoli, 1997)

Darlington, A. F., *The D-Day Dodger* (Laundry Cottage Books, 2006)

Davies, M. (ed.), 'Brecon Beacons' in *National Park Guide No. 5* (HMSO, 1967)

Dempsey, M. (ed.), *The Priest Among the Soldiers* (Burns Oates, 1947)

England, J. (ed.), *Cyfarthfa School: The First 100 Years 1913-2013* (Cyfarthfa High School, 2013)

Frediksen, J. C., *America's Military Adversaries: From Colonial Times to the Present* (ABC-CLIO, 2001)

Gallorini S., *Forgive but never Forget* (Edizione Effigi, 2014)

Geyer, M., 'Civitela della Chiana on 29 June 1944: Reconstruction of a German "Measure"' in Heer, H., and Naumann, K. (eds), *War of Extermination: The German Military in World War II 1941-1944* (Berghan Books, 2000)

Gentile, C., *Le Stragi del 1944 in Provincia di Arezzo ed I loro Perpetratori* (online Civitella archives, 1998)

Harcourt, M., *Tubby Clayton: The Impudent Dreamer* (OUP, 1953)

Harris, C. R. S., *Allied Military Administration of Italy 1943-45* (HMSO, 1957)

Hayman, R., *Working Iron in Merthyr Tydfil* (Merthyr Tydfil Heritage Trust, 1989)

Holland, J., *A Pair of Silver Wings* (Arrow, 2007); *Italy's Sorrow, A Year of War 1944-45* (Harper Press, 2008)

Kinrade Dethick, J., *The Arezzo Massacres, A Tuscan Tragedy April-September 1944* (*Edizioni Duca della Corgna*, 2005)

Jackson, J., *The Fall of France: The Nazi Invasion of 1940* (OUP, 2004)

Jacob, C., Done, S., and Eckley, S., *Images of Wales: The County Borough of Merthyr Tydfil* (The History Press, 2012)

Jowett, P., and Zognik, D., *The Italian Army at War in Europe 1940-43* (Concord Publications, 2008)

Lewis, N., *Naples '44: An Intelligence Officer in the Italian Labyrinth* (Eland, 2002)

Linklater, E., *The Campaign in Italy* (HMSO, 1977)

Mowat, F., *And No Birds Sang* (Douglas and McIntyre, 2012)

Merthyr Tydfil Libraries, *Merthyr Tydfil, Pocket Images* (The History Press, 2011)

Nash, M., *The Price of Innocence* (CC Publishing, 2005)

Nellands, R., *The Eighth Army: From the Western Desert to the Alps (1939-1945)* (John Murray, 2004)

Newby, E., *Love and War in the Apennines* (Penguin, 1975)

Newman, P., *Safer than a Known Way: An Escape Story of World War II* (William Kimber, 1983; reprinted as *Over the Wire*, Pen and Sword, 2013)

Lammioni Lucarelli, L., *Memorie di un eccidio* (1994)

Mount Argus and Ireland 1856-2006: 150 years Passionist Presence (The Passionists, Dublin, 2006)

The Occasion of the Centenary of the Passionist Church of Our Lady of the Sacred Heart, Herne Bay, (Celebrations 1889-1989, 1989)

Oliver, K., *Chaplain at War* (Angel Press, 1986)

Origo, I., *War in Val d'Orcia: An Italian War Diary, 1943-1944* (Flamingo, 2002)

Pelletier, Y. Y. J., 'Faith on the Battlefield: Canada's Catholic Chaplaincy Service during the Second World War' in *CCH Historical Studies*, Vol. 69, 2003

Perraton, J., *One Musician's War from Egypt to Italy with the RASC, 1941-1945* (Amberley, 2011)

Poems from the Desert (George G. Harrap & Co. Ltd, 1945)

Poems from Italy (George G. Harrap & Co. Ltd, 1945)

Royal United Services Institute for Defence and Security Studies, March 2008

Saber, C. (ed.), Galatti, S., *Desert Rat Sketch Book* (Sketchbook Press, New York, 1959)

Sensini, F., *Civitella 18 Guigno 1944, Eutanasia di una data*, 2013

Snyder, H. E., 'Fifth U.S. Army' in *M.D. Medical Department United States Army in World War II*, Vol. 2, Part II, *Surgical Consultants to Field Armies in Theaters of Operations*

Spencer, P. F., *As a Seal upon Your Heart: The Life of St Paul of the Cross, Founder of the Passionists* (St Paul's UK, 1994)

The Story of the R.A.S.C. 1939-1945 (G. Bell & Sons, 1955)

Strange, K., *The Celestial City: Merthyr Tydfil in the 1840s*

Tiezzi Grabinger, S., *Central Tuscany: Valdichiana Hill Towns—Cortona to Civitella* (2011)

Vellacott, H. D. S., 'Twelve Months' Experience with a Field Surgical Unit in Italy, 1944-1945' in *JR Army Med Corps*, 1973

Whicker, A., *Whicker's War* (HarperCollins, 2005)

Whiteman, C., *Patriot, Padre and Priest: A Life of Henry Whiteman* (Churchman Publishing Worthing, 1985)

Williams, G., *A Life* (University of Wales Press, 2002)

Archives and Libraries

Archivo di Stato di Arezzo

Archivo Generale Comune di Civitella

Army Personnel Centre, Support Division Historical Disclosures, Glasgow

Bundesarchiv, picture database

Cyfarftha Castle Museum and Art Gallery, Merthyr Tydfil

Douai Abbey Library and Archive

The English-speaking Church, Avenue Hoche, Paris

Il Centro di Documentazione e Museo di San Pancrazio, the Commune of Bucine, digital archive

IWM, London

Library of Congress, The International Military Tribunal, Nuremburg Trials
Lloyds Banking Group Archives and Museum
Musée Les Sanglots Longs, Réguiny, Brittany
Museum of Army Chaplaincy
Our Lady of the Sacred Heart, Herne Bay, Kent
Second World War Experience Centre (SWWEC)
Southwark Roman Catholic Diocesan Archives

National Archives

WO 167/373 (1st Arm Div. BEF RASC)
WO 167/420 (2nd Arm. Div Brig)
WO 170/2543 (498 Army Coy RASC)
WO 170/707 (55 Area: Q)
WO 170/708 (55 AREA: ST)
WO 177/640 (12 CCS RAMC)
WO 177/628 (3 CCS RAMC)
WO 204/1170/79/54/55/56 (SIB inquiry into Civitella massacre)
WO 204/11479 (Section 78 SIB statements)
War Cabinet papers: CAB/65/7/66

Websites

Ancestry.uk
BBC History online, WW2 People's War
Canadian Archives: http://www.canadaatwar.ca/content-24/world-war-ii/the-italian-campaign/
http://www.comandosupremo.com/
Old Merthyr – www.alangeorge.co.uk_
http://hernebaymatters.com/hbhrs/
http://www.comandosupremo.com/
www.war-experience.org/research/default.asp
http://thedunkirkproject.wordpress.com/the-dunkirk-project-2/the-dunkirk-project/3rd-june-1940-towards-the-end/ http://passionistcharism.wordpress.com/the-black-scapular-of-the-passion/

Diaries

Maj. Philip Newman (RAMC) CBE, DSO, MC. Courtesy of the Newman family
Capt. John 'Jack' Douglas Barrance MBE, Middlesex Yeomanry, courtesy of Barbara Summerfield

Newspapers

The Catholic Herald
Corriere di Arezzo
The Telegraph
Der Spiegel

East Anglian Daily Times
Herne Bay Press
La Nazione
The Merthyr Express
The London Gazette
The Times

Index